Hollies for Gardeners

5059.
1.
2.
W. Fitch del. et lith.
Vincent Brooks Imp.

Hollies for Gardeners

Christopher Bailes

Susyn Andrews, Botanical Editor

Timber Press

All photographs are by the author unless otherwise noted.

Frontispiece: *Ilex cornuta*, the Chinese holly, an early illustration from *Curtis's Botanical Magazine* (1858). Courtesy of the Lindley Library.

Published in 2006 by
Timber Press, Inc.
The Haseltine Building
133 S.W. Second Avenue, Suite 450
Portland, Oregon 97204-3527, USA
www.timberpress.com
For contact information regarding editorial, marketing, sales,
and distribution in the United Kingdom, see www.timberpress.co.uk.

Design by Dick Malt
Printed in China

Library of Congress Cataloging-in-Publication Data
Bailes, Christopher.
Hollies for gardeners / Christopher Bailes ; Susyn Andrews, botanical editor.
p. cm.
Includes bibliographical references and index.
ISBN-13: 978-0-88192-774-0
ISBN-10: 0-88192-774-0
1. Hollies. I. Andrews, Susyn. II. Title.
SB413.H7B35 2006
635.9'77385--dc22
2006009782

A catalogue record for this book is also available from the British Library.

Contents

Foreword

Hollies have always been around, indeed they are part of our history and folklore. For centuries, they have stood mainly in the background, albeit in shades of green, silver or gold. However, as this book shows, there is much more to the genus *Ilex* than first might be supposed, and Chris Bailes has done a first-rate job of exposing their inherent qualities.

He has approached the genus through the eye of a gardener, introducing a fresh and exciting range of hollies, as well as practical ways of using them in cultivation. There is a holly for everyone, whether evergreen or deciduous, and this publication will help find the one for you!

As one who has been fascinated by *Ilex* for over thirty years, I have been thrilled to see an increasingly large selection of hollies grown by enthusiasts on both sides of the Atlantic, even if they are not all readily available within the nursery trade. This is a book that is long overdue, and it will form a welcome bridge between the gardening communities of Europe and North America.

FLORUIT *ILEX*!

Susyn Andrews
Holder of the Shiu-Ying Award (2004) and the Wolf-Fenton Award (1993) from the Holly Society of America
Honorary Research Associate, Royal Botanic Gardens, Kew

Acknowledgements

First place in this list must go to Lady Anne Berry, for creating the holly collection at Rosemoor that first alerted me to the diversity of the genus. John Lanyon and Jonathan Hutchinson, past and present custodians of Rosemoor's National Collection of hollies, also helped to nurture my growing interest. The assistance and encyclopaedic holly expertise of Susyn Andrews have been invaluable throughout the project. This book also owes much to the hospitality of the garden and nursery owners and managers (in particular Louise Bendall of Highfield Hollies), who have freely allowed access to their collections for study and photography. Many members and officers of the Holly Society of America (HSA) have also shown great hospitality during my visits to the USA. The Librarian and staff of the Royal Horticultural Society's Lindley Library in London and Wisley have been of particular assistance to me in my research, and I am indebted to Jameson and Diana Bates for their help and interest in the project. My gratitude also to the staff of Timber Press, in particular Anna Mumford for her patience as this book has gradually taken shape, and to Franni Bertolino Farrell for taking the pain out of the painstaking process of editing the text. My heartfelt appreciation is also due to my wife Sue, for her constant support and for her toleration of such a prolonged period of 'holly widowhood'.

My thanks also to Charles Anderson (HSA); Barton M. Bauers Sr. (HSA); A. D. Barnes (UK); Hank Bruno (Callaway Gardens, USA); Andrew Bunting (Scott Arboretum, USA); Koen Camelbeke (Wespelaar Arboretum, Belgium); Allen Coombes (Sir Harold Hillier Gardens, UK); Mark Flanagan (Savill and Valley Garden, UK); Gert Fortgens (Trompenburg Arboretum, Holland); Alan Gray and Graham Robeson (East Ruston Old Vicarage

Garden, UK); Eric Hsu (Scott Arboretum, USA); Tony Kirkham (Royal Botanic Gardens, Kew, UK); Bill Kuhl (McLean Nurseries, USA); Y. Kurimoto (RHS Japan); Jef van Meulder (Bokrijk Arboretum, Belgium); Mr Onoue (Onoue Nursery, Japan); Linda Parsons (HSA); Michael R. Pontti (HSA); Abraham Rammeloo (Kalmthout Arboretum, Belgium); Rondalyn Reeser (HSA); Catherine (Kit) Richardson (HSA); Ron Solt (HSA); Mr and Mrs John Southwell (UK); Barbara Taylor (HSA); Kevin W. Tunison (US National Arboretum); Daniel Castle Turner (HSA); Gidy Van Vugt (Dutch Dendrological Society).

Introduction

Of all the trees that are in the wood,
The holly bears the crown ...

This line from the traditional carol 'The holly and the ivy' indicates the high esteem in which the holly has been held for many centuries in Europe. The roots of that esteem lie deep in folklore and religion and are of ancient origin, for few plants have enjoyed as long and close a relationship with mankind. This broader cultural appreciation of hollies echoes around the globe, in Old and New Worlds alike, and is attested to by the great variety of traditional uses found throughout the world for many holly species. Hollies have also enjoyed a long and distinguished history in our gardens, again encompassing East and West. They remain firm favourites with many gardeners, plantsmen, designers and writers. This book aims to celebrate the tremendous diversity of hollies, from well-established species and cultivars, some with centuries of cultivation behind them, to the new introductions that are enriching the remarkable range of plants in the genus *Ilex*.

Hollies are a truly cosmopolitan group, providing gardeners with plants that will thrive throughout most of the temperate regions of the world. But as with other major plant groups, this does not mean that all hollies will grow everywhere. There is a significant divide between climatic conditions on either side of the Atlantic, which is reflected to a degree in the major groups of hollies that may be grown. For example, American holly species are adapted to the intense winter cold and high summer heat of the eastern seaboard of North America: they may fail to thrive in the softer maritime climates of Western Europe. The same situation applies in reverse, with

European hollies unable to survive the rigours of a continental climate. Conditions along much of the West Coast of North America, however, may suit European hollies very well (when the terms East or West Coast are used in the text, they refer specifically to North America). Species or groups that are particularly well suited to certain areas will be covered in detail in the Directory of Plants, but as a broad rule of thumb there are hollies that will grow and thrive throughout most of the temperate regions.

Plant hardiness ratings are important when choosing hollies; where information on the hardiness of specific plants is available it is given in the Directory. The climatic zones for North America and Europe to which the hardiness ratings refer are shown on the maps in the Appendix. Most holly names in the text are expressed following the usual rules of nomenclature, that is to say with the scientific part of the name (genus, species, etc.) in italics, and the cultivar name in normal type, enclosed in single inverted quotes: for example, *Ilex cornuta* 'Bostic'. In recent times many new plants have been given selling names, or trade designations (i.e., cultivar names that are technically superfluous but which are used to market a plant). Plants marketed under these names may have Plant Breeder's Rights assigned to them or may be trademarked. For the purposes of this book, these selling names will be written in small capitals, with the cultivar names with which they are linked indicated by an = sign, for example, *Ilex* RED BEAUTY = 'Rutzan'. If the plant is better known under its true cultivar name, then it will be given first and the trade designation will follow the = sign.

Hollies have held their position among the elite of garden plants for many years. In today's gardens they face ever-increasing competition for our attention. Over-familiarity with a group of plants with such a long horticultural tradition as the hollies may lead to their being overlooked, as we seek to satisfy our thirst for the new and different. But the qualities of hollies have been proved over many years. Their tremendous range of form, foliage and fruit, combined with their remarkable adaptability, should ensure that they remain a first choice for discerning gardeners. I trust that this review of the hollies will inspire gardeners to explore the wealth of plants, old and new, that the genus has to offer our gardens and landscapes.

Overview of the Genus

CHAPTER 1

History and Classification

The genus *Ilex* is a large and complex group of plants. The name *Ilex* was published by Linnaeus in his *Species Plantarum* of 1753, although he had been using it since 1735. He derived the name from the Latin *Ilex*, the classical name of the holm (or holly) oak, *Quercus ilex*, a spiny-leaved evergreen tree superficially similar to the English holly, *I. aquifolium*. Linnaeus originally recognised five holly species; in the intervening two hundred and fifty years that number has grown by around a hundredfold.

Ilex is a member of the plant family Aquifoliaceae, which for many years has been considered to be part of the larger order of plant families known as the Celastrales. This group includes the family Celastraceae (most familiar from the spindle trees of the genus *Euonymus*). Recent research has led to the proposal that the hollies should be split off from the Celastrales and placed into an order of their own, the Aquifoliales, together with the genera *Helwingia* and *Phyllonoma*. While further research will resolve the final status of the holly family to the satisfaction of the botanist, its close relations should remain the same.

Until recently the family Aquifoliaceae was made up of four genera: *Ilex*, *Byronia*, *Nemopanthus* and *Phelline*. More recent treatments reduced this number to two, with *Byronia* incorporated into *Ilex* at subgeneric rank, and *Phelline* hived off into a family of its own, the Phellinaceae. This left *Ilex* and *Nemopanthus* in the Aquifoliaceae, the latter very much the junior partner with a solitary species amongst the tremendous array of hollies. To add its own small note of confusion to this picture, that single species, *Nemopanthus mucronatus*, a

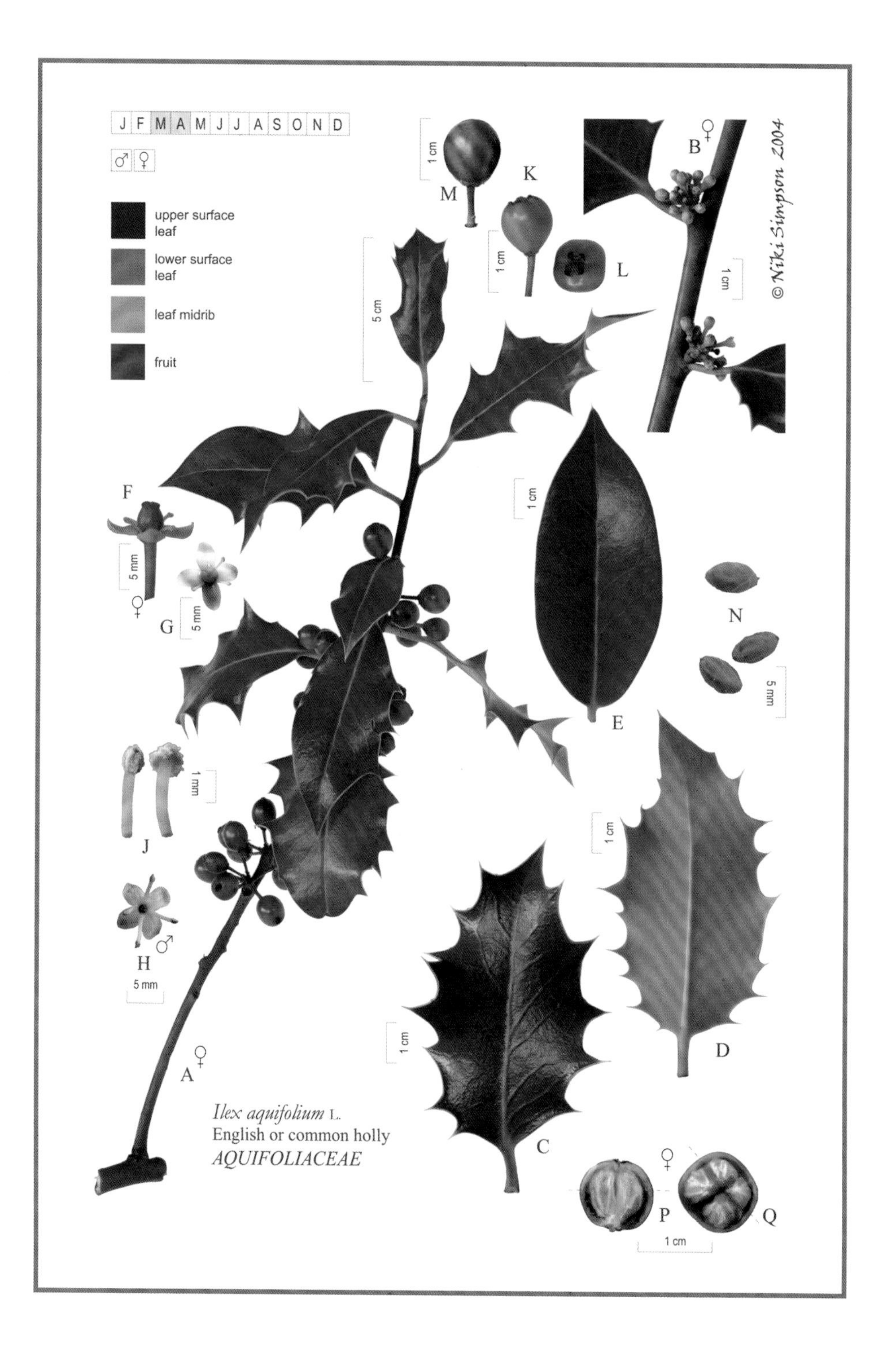
J F M A M J J A S O N D
♂ ♀
upper surface leaf
lower surface leaf
leaf midrib
fruit
© Niki Simpson 2004
A ♀
B ♀
C
D
E
F
G
H ♂
J
K
L
M
N
P
Q ♀
1 cm
5 cm
5 mm
1 mm
Ilex aquifolium L.
English or common holly
AQUIFOLIACEAE

small- to medium-sized deciduous shrub from eastern North America, is commonly known as the mountain holly; however, in 2000 *Nemopanthus* was sunk into *Ilex* and is now known as *I. mucronata*.

In the 18th and 19th centuries the plants we now recognise as deciduous hollies were accorded their own generic ranking as *Prinos*. These were incorporated into *Ilex* at subgeneric rank by Theodor Loesener in 1890. He published a detailed account of the genus in his *Monographia Aquifoliacearum* in two parts, in 1901 and 1908, and continued publishing on the family until the middle of the 20th century. Our understanding of the riches of the hollies of China owes much to the work of Shiu-Ying Hu, who published a multi-part account entitled 'The genus *Ilex* in China' in the *Journal of the Arnold Arboretum* for 1949 and 1950. Much work was done on *Ilex* in tropical South America in the second half of the 20th century. Research on the genus continues with a group from the Conservatoire et Jardin Botaniques in Geneva and the Royal Botanic Gardens, Kew, working to produce an account of the hollies using modern research techniques, entitled *Molecular Systematics in the Genus Ilex*.

While *Ilex* is undoubtedly a large genus, authorities differ greatly in their estimation of the number of species it may contain. Most give a figure of

Opposite: This superb composite photographic image illustrates all the principal botanical characteristics of the common or English holly, *Ilex aquifolium*:

A fruiting twig of a female tree
B inflorescences in bud in leaf axils of a female tree, showing alternate leaf arrangement along stem
C juvenile leaf shape
D underside of leaf (juvenile form)
E adult leaf shape
F side view of female flower
G female flower (one stamen removed)
H male flower
J two views of stamen
K side view of developing fruit
L end view of developing fruit showing remains of stigma
M side view of mature fruit
N views of pyrene (nutlet)
P mature fruit with flesh removed to show arrangements of pyrenes within fruit
Q longitudinal section through mature fruit to show arrangement of pyrenes within fruit.

around five hundred, although some would argue for in excess of seven hundred species. Much of this discrepancy is accounted for by the largely tropical distribution of the genus. The temperate regions of the world, the source of most of the hollies that we grow, are for the most part well botanised; however, much of the range of the genus in the tropics remains relatively unexplored. While further exploration may lead to the discovery of significant numbers of new species, it may also reveal considerable synonymy among those already described.

Our understanding of the hollies, their distribution and relationships will undoubtedly grow as a result of further exploration and the application of new research techniques. It remains a developing field of study and research. Differences of taxonomic opinion may be described, appropriately perhaps, as of 'academic' interest only to the majority of holly aficionados, whose attention is focused almost entirely upon species of horticultural importance.

Distribution

The genus *Ilex* is cosmopolitan in its distribution, with a natural range that incorporates every continent except Australia, and takes in all climatic zones from the humid tropics to cool temperate regions. This widespread distribution points toward an ancient lineage, as does the wide distribution of fossil hollies. Both indicate that the ancestors of the modern hollies were present well before the continents as we now recognise them began their slow drift to their current positions, taking with them the progenitors of the modern species. Hollies have been carried to most corners of the globe, and the genus has responded to the opportunities afforded by this widespread distribution by developing a tremendous number of species throughout its range.

There are three principal centres of diversity and dispersal for the genus *Ilex*. Two are in the Old World. The first of these, the Sino-Japanese phytogeographical region, incorporates China, Japan, Taiwan, Korea, Myanmar (Burma) and Indo-China; many familiar garden hollies hail from this region. The second Old World centre is more tropical in character, taking in Malaya, Borneo, Indonesia, the Philippines and Papua New Guinea, as well as the Pacific Islands. The third major centre of diversity is found in the New World, centred upon tropical South America. By contrast to the hundreds of species found amongst these three major centres, Europe and southwest Asia (Turkey and Iran) together contain merely four species, while North America hosts only twenty-two. These figures further reinforce the fact that *Ilex* is primarily a genus of the tropics and subtropics, with far fewer species to be found in temperate regions.

Alongside the natural distribution of the hollies there is one species that falls within the unfortunate definition of an invasive alien. The English holly, *Ilex aquifolium*, has taken so well to the Pacific Northwest of America that it has spread widely beyond the boundaries of horticulture and has been included by Randall and Marinelli as an example of the threat posed to the environment from exotic introductions by gardeners in their book *Invasive Plants: Weeds of the Global Garden* (1996).

Description

As with all plant genera *Ilex* species have shared characteristics that distinguish the genus and form the basis of the relationships between its various subgroups. Alongside those common characteristics it might be expected (and is indeed the case) that a group of some five hundred different species might encompass a great range of forms. This diversity is one of the key horticultural qualities of the hollies as a group of plants in their own right.

Habit of growth

All hollies are woody plants. Most are shrubby in habit, and come in a great variety of shapes and sizes. The range runs from low-growing plants (*Ilex rugosa*, for example) from the cool climates of northern Japan and Siberia to trees such as *I. latifolia* from Japan and China, which may exceed 20M. Among the giants of the genus the African species *I. mitis* is capable of making a noble tree of over 30M under good conditions. In the tropics a number of species grow as scramblers or climbers, while some have taken up the epiphytic mode of growth, perching upon other plants in order to reach their place in the sun (a strategy they share with another notable ornamental woody plant genus, *Rhododendron*). As shrubby plants many hollies are naturally multi-stemmed in habit, the colour and texture of their bark creating a further feature of value to gardeners.

Hollies can grow into stately trees, as does *Ilex latifolia*.

With age, the grey stems of *Ilex aquifolium* AGM and other larger hollies can develop a fascinating wrinkled bole.

Opposite: Holly leaves do not come much smaller than those of *Ilex crenata* 'Piccolo', scarcely 13mm long.

Foliage

Despite the fact that hollies are celebrated in the popular consciousness more for their fruit than any other characteristic, it is their foliage that is their main feature of garden value. The vast majority of hollies are evergreen, providing year-round foliage effects encompassing a remarkable range of form and texture. Their garden value has been increased tremendously by the activities of gardeners and breeders in selecting and creating a wide range of cultivars and hybrids. The thirty or so deciduous holly species and their hybrids, while lacking the major horticultural advantage of their evergreen cousins, also include a number of plants with good foliage, some bringing the added bonus of distinctive autumn colour.

Holly leaves are almost always alternate on the shoot. The size and shape of the leaves are remarkably variable. This variation is found both between and within species, with some species encompassing a range of leaf forms. Leaves of varying forms may even be found upon a single plant, as in species such as *Ilex aquifolium* and *I. cornuta* (Chinese or horned holly); this characteristic is expressed strongly in the aptly named *I. dimorphophylla* (the epithet meaning 'with leaves of two shapes').

The size range of holly foliage encompasses the tiny leaves of forms of the Japanese *Ilex crenata*, which may scarcely achieve 13MM in length, to the bold and striking *I. kingiana*, which can exceed 20CM, more than fifteen times as long. Leaf shape among the hollies ranges from rounded (orbicular and ovate) to linear and lanceolate (essentially willow-like). Many are elliptic, around twice as long as wide, rounded or tapering at the ends. Amidst this tremendous diversity in leaf shape are many striking examples such as the essentially oblong leaves of *I. cornuta*.

The margins of holly leaves are another variable character. Serrate (toothed) leaves and entire (smooth-margined) leaves are both common. The quality of spininess, while a major feature of many species of importance in cultivation, is surprisingly characteristic of only a minority of the species, a number of which have leaves that may become less spiny or lose their spines altogether as they mature. The spiny leaves of young plants are thought to deter the attentions of browsing animals; older plants of the same species may retain varying degrees of spininess dependent upon the height of the shoots from the ground and their susceptibility to attack from animals.

The leaf blades of many hollies have distinctly wavy (undulate) surfaces, adding to their character in the garden. Their thickness and texture again provides ample opportunity for the expression of the diversity that characterises the genus. Among evergreen species they range from the coriaceous (thick and leathery) texture of species such as *Ilex latifolia*, to the softer and more delicate foliage of *I. cassine* and some forms of *I. crenata*. The high gloss of the shiny, smooth (glabrous) leaves of some of the most important horticultural hollies such as *I. aquifolium* is a feature of great importance in the garden. Another feature shared by many evergreen species is the persistence of their foliage, with a number of species keeping their leaves for two, three and even four years.

A character of holly leaves that is not often remarked upon is their colour upon emergence. The early growth of many species and cultivars may be deep purple, bronze, or attractively flushed with pink. Although these effects are relatively fleeting, they can provide another valuable attribute to be used in the garden, or may simply be enjoyed for their own sake.

The handsome burnished leaves of *Ilex latifolia*.

Flowers

Temperate hollies may flower from early spring (March) to summer (July) in the northern hemisphere. Of the evergreen species *Ilex cornuta* is among the first to flower, with *I. pedunculosa* among the last of the evergreens, only opening its long-stemmed flowers by the end of June or early July in England. Deciduous hollies are generally late blooming; *I. verticillata*, for example, can be seen in full flower in July in southwest England.

Most of the hollies of importance to gardeners flower on stems formed in the previous year. The success of flowering (and therefore fruiting) of a plant in any year is dependent upon two major factors. Weather conditions at flowering time are critical; intense cold can damage or kill flowers, and poor weather will affect the availability of pollinators. Also of great importance are the growing conditions in the previous season, which in most species will determine the amount of growth the plants make and the quantity of flowers available for pollination.

Holly flowers are dioecious (i.e., with male and female flowers borne on separate plants) and are pollinated by insects. The flowers are borne in the leaf axils (between the leaf and stem), typically in a small inflorescence. Male (staminate) flowers are usually borne in larger numbers than female (pistillate). At best, the individual holly flower can only be described as inconspicuous. They are not colourful, with most species of horticultural importance ranging from white through green to pale yellow; *Ilex serrata* has attractive pink flowers, and purple flushing occurs in some *I. aquifolium*. Taken individually most holly flowers are small, around 5MM in diameter. The very largest

achieve a mere 10–13MM across. They may, however, be quite showy en masse, as in male plants of *I. latifolia*, whose greeny yellow staminate flowers, up to 10MM across, are borne in dense masses along the stems, showing up well against the dark green foliage. The white flowers of some male cultivars of *I. aquifolium* and *I.* ×*altaclerensis* are also quite handsome, set off by their dark glossy leaves. In the run-up to flowering, the axillary clusters of purple flower buds of the variegated *I. aquifolium* 'Ingramii' and 'Ferox Argentea' can also be quite showy.

Despite the small size of their flowers, hollies are very attractive to insects, and a plant in full flower may be alive with bees and other pollinators, sometimes much more so than other more showy subjects nearby. Some species, such as *Ilex glabra* (inkberry), are noted as important bee-plants. Apart from pollen and nectar, part of the attraction to insects is the delicate fragrance of many hollies; plants of *I. aquifolium* in full flower may be smelt from a distance, and I have noted a very sweet scent from *I. cornuta*.

Opposite, top: Among the more colourful holly flowers are those of *Ilex serrata*, the Japanese winterberry. Photograph by Susyn Andrews.

Opposite: The male flowers of *Ilex* ×*altaclerensis* cultivars can be very attractive en masse.

Fruit

Although widely celebrated in folklore and horticulture the holly 'berry' of tradition is not truly a berry at all. While the finer points of botanical distinction might understandably be lost on the average gardener or hungry bird, the object of their attention has features in common with the fruit type called a drupe, defined as a fleshy fruit surrounding one or more pyrenes. Each pyrene consists of a hard layer, known as an endocarp, which encloses the all-important seed. Some authorities have proposed the term baccodrupe to describe the particular qualities of the holly fruit, which has some characters in common with true berries. For the purposes of this book, once the botanical niceties are out of the way, the terms fruit and berry will be interchangeable throughout.

Holly fruits are typically small, with many around 7MM in diameter; among the more important horticultural forms a healthy 10MM or more is not uncommon. They are essentially rounded, although they may come in a variety of shapes on the globose theme. The vast majority of hollies whose fruit colour has been recorded have red fruits. This showy characteristic is shared by most of the species of horticultural importance. A minority have black fruits, including some noted garden plants such as *Ilex crenata*. Yellow, white and orange fruits occur as colour variants both in the wild and in cultivation.

Holly fruits may be very persistent upon the plant, another excellent characteristic for gardeners; many species retain their fruit throughout the winter (in the absence of birds or other fruit-eaters). When they are taken by animals, holly fruits are often not eaten until later in the winter; by this time other food sources may have been exhausted and the holly becomes an important resource to overwintering animals. Animal predation is important to holly distribution: many fruit-eating birds swallow the fruits whole, and the tough-skinned holly seeds may survive the journey through the gut of the bird to be excreted away from the parent plant, already 'chitted' and prepared for germination by their exposure to avian stomach acids. Holly fruits are most often taken by fruit-eating birds, but may also form part of the diet of some seed-eaters, whose attacks may begin early in the fruiting season, a predilection that is not good news to holly growers and of little assistance to the plant in reproduction.

Opposite: Generous fruiting characterises many hollies, demonstrated to perfection by *Ilex aquifolium* 'Alaska'.

Ethnobotany

Hollies have a remarkably close and ancient relationship with mankind. Many species throughout the world are recorded as having ethnobotanical uses. This broader cultural relationship predates their horticultural history, possibly by millennia, and written records of mankind's relationship with the hollies go back to before the time of the Romans.

This subject falls under the general heading of ethnobotany, which is the study of the variety of uses, including medicinal, religious and practical, to which plants have been put throughout the world. The ethnobotany of the hollies makes a fascinating area of study in its own right. For more information than there is space to give here, readers are referred to *Holly: A Tree for All Seasons*, by Chris Howkins, which provides a great deal of information upon the rich ethnobotany and history of *Ilex aquifolium*. Richard Mabey devotes a section of his *Flora Britannica* to the common (or English) holly, and in the first chapter of Fred Galle's *Hollies*, Harry William Dengler widens the geographical scope of holly ethnobotany in a brief, fact-packed account, 'Holly folklore and legends'. The brief synopsis given here of the range of non-horticultural uses of hollies concentrates almost entirely upon species of garden importance; for it, I am indebted to these authors.

Religious, spiritual and cultural uses of holly

Hollies have a long history of being used in religious and spiritual practices and rituals. In northern temperate regions it is understandable that broad-leaved evergreen plants would attract attention in an otherwise leafless winter landscape. Bright red fruits would reconfirm to the observer that the plant might be possessed of distinctive attributes. The qualities of many hollies as purgatives, narcotics and stimulants were also of importance in establishing its role in religious rituals and folk medicine.

The use of evergreens to decorate houses around the time of the midwinter solstice is found across much of Europe and Asia; in Japan this custom also includes fruiting branches of deciduous hollies. In historic times evergreens were regarded as symbolic of the continuity of life through the dark days of winter. While the choice of evergreen plants used in winter rituals varies according to what grows locally, wherever hollies occur they are often employed in solstice celebrations and rituals.

In the British Isles mistletoe, ivy and English or common holly (*Ilex aquifolium*) were used in pre-Christian times for winter solstice rituals. As time progressed the symbolic status accorded to the hollies by British and other northern European cultures was taken up by their Christian successors. Whereas the holly may originally have been seen in pagan cultures as a fertility symbol whose spiny leaves might be used as a charm against witchcraft, it was transposed in Christian practice into a representation of Christ's crown of thorns and blood. In this way the holly's role and symbolism in pre-Christian solstice rituals were successfully incorporated into the Christian calendar. While hollies retain a special place in today's celebrations of the turning of the year (which in some countries forms the basis of a significant horticultural industry), much of their symbolic significance, pre- and post-Christian alike, has been lost.

Hollies are also used in China and Japan to decorate houses and temples, especially at New Year celebrations. Dengler reports that *Ilex purpurea* was much used for this purpose in China. Hollies are also to be found growing around temples in the Far East: the American botanist and plant collector Charles Sargent, who travelled widely in Japan, speaks of *I. latifolia* being '*often seen … in temple grounds*', although he does not say whether that was for its horticultural qualities or other cultural significance. Fruiting branches of the deciduous *I. serrata*, according to Sargent, were '*sold in immense quantities in the streets of Tokyo for the decoration of dwelling houses, for which purpose they are admirably suited'*.

Dengler also describes the Native American peoples' uses for hollies. As a hardy, spiny evergreen, the American holly (*Ilex opaca*) symbolised courage and fierceness in battle. Preserved berries were used for decorations that declared the valour of the individual. Sprays of holly would be painted onto shields and jackets, or pinned to clothing prior to going into battle. In an interesting reflection of practices in Europe, hollies would be grown around permanent settlements to ward off evil spirits. Holly's uses in other Native American rituals will be described under the section on medicinal uses.

Over much of the British Isles the ancient superstitious regard for hollies is reflected to this day in modern agricultural practice. Holly trees are often left standing along the line of country hedges, as may be seen in rural North Devon around the Royal Horticultural Society's garden at Rosemoor. This reflects the widespread belief in ancient times that to cut down a whole holly could bring bad luck. Leaving hollies as trees in hedgerows has also been reported as a means of preventing witches from moving around the country-side, given their apparent habit of running along the tops of hedges! This superstition against chopping down hollies remains, even if the reasons behind it have been forgotten. When looked at pragmatically, leaving hollies in hedgerows can now be argued to have a value to the landowner over and above its previous cultural significance, as they may provide useful extra income in good berrying years.

Medicinal uses of holly

Several cultures worldwide have made use of the herbal properties of holly species as gentle but effective tonics or stimulants or fierce purgatives and emetics. Bark, leaves and berries are all used, and the range of species employed is wide, including such garden favourites as *Ilex aquifolium*, *I. cornuta* and *I. vomitoria*.

The most important of the hollies used for their herbal properties is the South American *Ilex paraguayensis*, a tender species of subtropical distribution that does not fall within the remit of this book. A major industry has been founded upon this plant, whose fermented leaves are the source of yerba mate, a tea drunk by many millions of South Americans. Its gentle stimulat-ing properties are generally recognised and accepted and are becoming more

Probably the most important commercial holly in the world, *Ilex paraguayensis* is cultivated to make a refreshing and recuperative tea.
Courtesy of the Lindley Library.

widely appreciated; it is now commonly available in health food stores. Many other hollies are used as teas (Dengler reports over sixty species in all), including *I. latifolia* and *I. yunnanensis*.

Perhaps the most challenging of all the medicinal or ritual uses of the hollies is the use of the strongly emetic *Ilex vomitoria*, or yaupon, whose botanical name is well deserved. With this plant, Native Americans in the southern USA created a brew called cassina or 'black drink'. Tribes would travel for hundreds of miles to the coastal habitats of the yaupon holly to take part in the ceremonies at which the tea was drunk. The gatherings were held in the spring, when holly leaves dried over fires were boiled to create a strong black liquor. The tea was drunk only by the men of the tribe; its powerful effects would apparently throw even the strongest of them into deep sweats and cause many to vomit. The ability to 'hold their drink' was apparently considered a mark of great strength, and the purgative qualities of cassina were thought to be of benefit to the health of the drinker.

Holly was also used as a purgative in other parts of the world. The English writer Gerard, in his *Herbal* (1597), wrote of the use of ripe holly berries, before drying; he counts among their 'virtues' that they were effective '*against the colicke: for ten or twelve being inwardly taken bring away by the stoole thick phlegmatic humors, as we have learned of them who have made triall thereof*'. Culpeper in his *Herbal and English Physician* (1653) repeated much of Gerard's work, writing of dried and powdered berries that '*they bind the body, and stop fluxes, bloody fluxes, and the terms in women*' (fluxes here included dysentery). His description of the overall qualities of hollies is quite fascinating. He dealt with hollies as one of the 'Saturnine' plants, which implied that the humble holly might possess the following qualities (amongst others): '*fortif[ies] the retentive faculty, and memory; makes men sober, solid and staid, fit for study; stays the unbridled joys of lustful blood, stays the wandering thoughts; and returns them home to the centre*'. A most valuable plant, indeed!

Other medicinal uses of parts of our 'garden' hollies from around the world include the Chinese use of *Ilex cornuta* as a tonic and a cure for kidney disease; all parts of the plant were used in Chinese medicine. Culpeper reports the bark and leaves of holly were used to speed the knitting of broken bones and '*such members as are out of joint*'. Many hollies have the reputation of being able to ease fevers; the bark of *I. verticillata* and the leaves and bark of *I. aquifolium* have been put to this purpose.

Practical uses of holly

The wood of holly, hard and close-grained, has been widely used for special purposes. Richard Mabey, in his fascinating account of British holly folklore and uses in *Flora Britannica*, gives some remarkable statistics. As one of its magical qualities holly was thought to have power over horses, and its strong but pliable wood was therefore a favourite source of horsewhips. At the peak of the use of horse-drawn transport throughout the British Isles, this marriage of practicality and superstition led to some 210,000 holly whips being made each year. Another remarkable statistic relates to the manufacture of bobbins for the new cotton mills of the industrial revolution at the turn of the 19th century, when 150,000 trees in one forest were reportedly felled to satisfy the demands of the new industry. Obviously the hard-nosed businessmen of the new industrial era were not in thrall to the old superstitions!

Holly branches also make valuable animal fodder. As Mabey says, '*Holly seems an improbable and unpalatable form of browse. But feeding it to stock (sheep especially) during the winter is an ancient practice that doubtless goes back into prehistory. Its leaves have one of the highest calorific contents of any tree browsed by animals, and are rich in nutrients*'. To overcome the disadvantage of the spiny leaves, grinding machines were sometimes used to make the plants more palatable. This practice was once widespread and continues sporadically to this day. A more prosaic use of holly boughs until fifty or so years ago was for sweeping chimneys, a purpose that possibly carried overtones of ridding the hearth and home of evil spirits.

Hollies also make excellent and practical boundary markers in the wider British landscape. As Mabey says, they are '*capable of outliving changes in ownership and farming practice, and of echoing the contours of ancient estates*'. Their use in estate hedges is dealt with in Chapter 2. Where other evidence is lacking, the British Ordnance Survey will use the presence of hollies as a clue to the line of old boundaries.

Hollies and birdlime

Birdlime is a mucilaginous substance obtained from the bark of hollies, in particular *Ilex aquifolium*. It has been used for centuries in many parts of the world to trap small birds by the simple device of sticking them to the branches where they roost. This served two purposes, for as much as small birds were a feature of the diet in time gone by, flocks of them could also be a major pest.

Birds were also widely caught to become domestic pets. In John Evelyn's *Sylva* (1664), the following poem is quoted regarding the holly's split personality as both beneficiary and bringer of doom to so many small birds:

> *Alas! In vain with warmth and food*
> *You cheer the Songster of the wood*
> *The barbarous boy from you prepares*
> *On treacherous twigs his viscous snares.*
> *Yes! The poor bird you nursed shall find*
> *Destruction in your rifled rind.*

Rodents were also trapped in birdlime. For those who might wish to use this less severe method of trapping mice and rats, Howkins quotes *The Compleat Vermin-Killer* of the early 18th century. The method involved placing a lure ('*rusty fry'd bacon*' was recommended) in the centre of a piece of board, then covering the board with birdlime while leaving narrow channels for the pests to get at the bacon. They would usually get stuck to the birdlime '*and stick, drawing and squeaking, that it will make you Sport*'.

The making of birdlime is a prolonged process. Holly bark is collected in midsummer and then boiled in water for twelve hours. After draining, the inner, green layer of bark is separated and left in a cool place for fourteen days, during which time it turns into the sticky mucilage required. The mucilage is then separated from the rest of the bark or other impurities, washed clean, and then reheated in a mixture of one part fat or oil (goose, capon or walnut were all used) to three parts mucilage, to create a birdlime which will not freeze.

Birdlime was also made in the Far East and is reported as a product of a number of species, including *Ilex latifolia*. The use of birdlime is now illegal in the UK, following the introduction of bird protection legislation. There is also evidence of the use of birdlime for darker purposes, as Gerard reports in his section on holly: '*The Birdlime which is made of the bark thereof … is marvellous clammie, it glueth up all the intrails, it shutteth and draweth together the guts and passages of the excrements, and by this means it bringeth destruction to man*'. How or why anyone would ingest birdlime is a mystery, but the health warning could not be clearer.

I will leave the final comment on holly ethnobotany to Evelyn, who somewhat tersely wraps up his account of the subject thus: '*But to say no more of these superstitious fopperies, which are many, about this tree, we still dress up both our churches and houses, on Christmas and other festival days, with this cheerful green and rutilant berries'.*

In the Garden

CHAPTER 2

As regards the uses of the holly, they are so many in the garden that it is difficult to even generalise them. As shelter in bold groups, dividing lines, hedges, beautiful effects of fruit in autumn, masses of evergreen foliage, bright glistening colour from variegated kinds; elegant groups of most beautiful varieties—every kind of use may be found for them in gardens.

These comments by the great Irish garden writer William Robinson, in *The English Flower Garden* (8th edition, 1900), superbly sum up the garden value of hollies. His words carry even more weight when one considers that they are based upon what was (by modern standards) a relatively small selection of plants. The variety of hollies now available to gardeners far outstrips the largely *Ilex aquifolium*–based selection available to British gardeners at the turn of the 20th century, and the range of uses to which they can be put is correspondingly wider still. This section will discuss the use of hollies as part of the structure of the garden, whether as prominent subjects or as part of the structural underpinning that forms the basis of all successful gardens. Among the wide range of form, texture and colour provided by hollies there is a wealth of plants from which to choose.

The tremendous variety and adaptability of hollies are not sufficiently known to or appreciated by many gardeners. Part of this may be down to over-familiarity: the holly's robust constitution and ability to thrive in a wide range of situations, including polluted urban environments, have led to a long association of hollies with what are essentially utilitarian plantings. Hollies still frequently feature in what the English writer Graham Stuart Thomas described so well as '*lumpy Victorian shrubbery*', where their individuality may be subsumed and lost in a morass of plants of similar habit. The shade tolerance of many hollies is a valuable horticultural quality, but it often results in their being grown in parks and gardens as unkempt understory plants that may have been deliberately planted, or brought in by birds. They may also regularly be found in cemeteries, as part of a typically sombre mixture of conifers and broad-leaved evergreens. This latter use is possibly another reflection of their ancient association with mankind, but, as with the former uses, frequently does no favours to the hollies.

Hollies are also a mainstay of the clipped evergreens which are characteristic of the foundation plantings of so many American gardens—again, a very useful purpose, but often leading to their being rather anonymous elements in the landscape. Of course, hollies are used for all these purposes and more because they are ideal for them. But they also have tremendous potential in the hands of the imaginative. In his article 'A plant for all seasons' in *The Garden* (2000), horticulturist John Glenn makes an eloquent plea to use hollies more widely: '*[Their] sheer diversity of colour, habit and form … has provided the gardener with a fine array of cultivars and hybrids. This extensive planting palette … offers gardeners and designers great opportunities and a choice of plants suitable for the most divergent of tastes and styles*'.

Hollies as Structural Plants

Effective structural planting is the foundation of all gardens, whether formal or naturalistic. In *The Art of Planting* Graham Stuart Thomas discusses the importance of incorporating strong structural elements in the garden: '*If we look at a successful and satisfying piece of planting … perhaps a small garden or portion of a large border—as likely as not we shall find it is dominated by one thing. It may be a tree or a large shrub*'. There are strong arguments for choosing a holly for that all-important dominant shrub, as many combine a strong and effective growth habit with attractive foliage. When considering structural planting, subjects must also be found to act as part of the 'supporting cast', another role in which hollies can be admirable performers.

This discussion will focus on plants grown for their natural growth habit or form. Using plants pruned or trimmed to shape, which is effectively topiary, is dealt with later. The natural form of hollies encompasses a wide range of shapes and sizes, which most will keep throughout their lifetime, making them ideal for structural planting. This is not to say that they may not require occasional formative pruning or trimming to ensure they develop correctly. The advantage with most hollies is that they respond well to pruning and are easy to keep within bounds. If they eventually outgrow their situation they can be cut back severely, should the need arise.

Many hollies are neat and naturally conical in habit, as shown here by *Ilex* BECKY STEVENS = 'Wyebec'.

A broad classification of plant form for gardeners might separate out firstly those plants of naturally upright habit. These typically make a strong impression in the landscape, and may be columnar or conical. Truly columnar plants are rare among hollies (unless they are trimmed). *Ilex* ×*altaclerensis* 'Camelliifolia' may make a broadly columnar specimen when mature, but this cultivar is large-growing, quite rapidly reaching 9M or more. The Japanese holly, *I. crenata*, has a number of truly columnar cultivars including 'Fastigiata' and 'Sky Pencil', both small to medium in height and narrow. *Ilex vomitoria* 'Will Fleming' is also strictly upright in growth; unfortunately, its branch structure seems unable to support its own weight, and it tends to open with age.

The conical habit of growth comes naturally to many hollies, both species and cultivars, and is available in a wide range of heights and widths. Cultivars of *Ilex* ×*koehneana*, *Ilex* ×*altaclerensis* and *I. opaca* in particular may make strong-growing cones, well furnished to the ground and capable of reaching a good height rapidly. There are numerous *I. aquifolium* cultivars of excellent conical habit, typically less vigorous. Smaller-growing selections include some of the new *I.* ×*aquipernyi* cultivars, which combine a naturally upright conical form with superb dense foliage. Conical hollies are featured in the discussion of hollies for screening and hedges. Numerous selections of conical habit can be found in the Directory.

Many hollies have a naturally rounded outline; plants can be found for every size from dwarf buns for the rock garden (*Ilex crenata*), through medium

Ilex cornuta 'Rotunda', a uniquely characterful low dome.

mounds for foundation planting (*I. cornuta* cultivars) to large vigorously spreading cultivars of *Ilex ×altaclerensis* . Weeping plants are always strong elements in any landscape, useful for mounds or when trained into effective specimen or accent plants. While many hollies have a naturally semi-pendent branching habit (for example, *I. serrata*), the truly weeping habit of growth is rare. At present it is essentially restricted to a number of cultivars of *I. aquifolium*, both plain-leaved and variegated, and the weeping yaupons, such as *I. vomitoria* 'Folsom's Weeping'.

Hollies as Shrubs

The vast majority of hollies in cultivation are shrubs. Since their liberation from the Victorian shrubbery, shrubs of all kinds have assumed a more important role in modern gardens: as Graham Stuart Thomas writes in *The Art of Planting*, '*In almost all garden planting, the shrub is the most important ingredient after one has chosen the trees and screened the boundaries. . . . We might compose the picture solely by using shrubs, from giants ... to dwarf creeping shrubs to fill in the foreground and flow around the larger shrubs*'. Such a scene could be composed entirely of hollies, given their wide variety of size, habit, texture and colour, although I would be loath to recommend it to any but the most ardent *Ilexophile*. Thomas too retreats from the extreme possibility of using only shrubs in the garden, stating that '*the most satisfying result is to be had from a judicious mixture of shrubs and low herbaceous plants*'. Hollies provide many possibilities for contributing to the satisfying 'judicious mixture' he describes.

Ilex crenata 'Golden Gem' AGM adds a colourful background accent to this attractive group.

Alongside the traditional mixed garden of trees, shrubs and herbaceous plants, there are also more austere forms of gardening where shrubs may carry the responsibility of providing the interest of a planting without support from other floral displays. The severity of some modern architecture sometimes calls for equally severe or minimalist planting. The requirement for plant architecture to complement the architecture of a building is one that shrubs of very definite habit or outline admirably fulfil, for which again there is great potential among the evergreen hollies.

The abstract modernist approach is one that to a degree echoes the style of classical Japanese gardens. Jiro Hirada, in *Gardens of Japan*, speaks eloquently of the evolution of the Japanese style, in a way which perhaps has resonance for today's minimalist landscape designers: '*The scarcity of flowers and the preponderance of evergreens is very significant in most of the gardens of Nippon. . . . In modern gardens simplicity is sought rather than gaiety, restraint rather than showiness, and constancy rather than too great a variation in different seasons of the year*'. Hollies (in particular *Ilex crenata* topiary) have a long history of making an important contribution to Japanese gardens in which '*monotony is despised, and quiet and pleasing variation is sought. The beauty must not be too apparent: it must be so reserved that the observer may discover it and enjoy the thrill of so doing*'.

The Chinese tradition also values plants with strong structural qualities for the garden. William Chambers (*A Dissertation on Oriental Gardening*) spoke of the various characteristics that the Chinese sought in their plantings: '*The perfection . . . of their size, . . . the beauty and variety of their forms, the colour and smoothness of*

their bark, [and the] shape and rich verdure of their foliage'—all qualities that hollies possess to a marked degree, as is also that of '*making no litter, during the spring and summer, by the fall of blossom*'.

Many hollies are well equipped to fulfil a number of roles in a wide range of garden styles. Almost all hollies also have a long season of display (or more than one distinct season). In stature they offer everything from small- to medium-sized trees to shrubs of all shapes and sizes. In foliage they range from bold, large and glossy-leaved, to tiny and fine-textured, with a wide range of colourful variations among the evergreen cultivars. These desirable qualities are shared by all hollies, males and females alike, and form the backbone of their appeal and value to gardeners. When one adds to them the potential for long-lasting displays of colourful berries, then the icing is applied to the already appetising holly 'cake'.

Many hollies have the character and style to be dominant elements in the garden scene, standing out of the general planting. Likewise, many are well suited to playing a supporting role; but even when used for background structure, if well placed and selected there is nothing anonymous about the great majority of hollies.

Among the smallest of the hollies, *Ilex crenata* 'Ivory Hall' fits perfectly into a raised bed of alpine plants.

Hollies for Winter Interest

Opposite: Winter at Highfield Hollies in England, with *Ilex crenata* 'Green Island' below orange-stemmed dogwoods and golden-variegated hollies in the distance.

Hollies are of tremendous value in the winter garden, whether for their form, foliage and fruit, or bark and stems. Gertrude Jekyll, among the greatest of Britain's garden writers, in her book *Wood and Garden* (1899) wrote of the contribution of *Ilex aquifolium* as winter took its grip: '*Now the splendid richness of the common holly is more than ever impressive, with its solid masses of full, deep colour, and its*

Grey-green *Ilex crenata* 'Shiro-fukurin' in the Winter Garden at Rosemoor.

wholesome look of perfect health. Sombrely cheerful, if one may use such a mixture of terms; sombre by reason of extreme depth of tone, and yet cheerful for the look of glad life'.

Extending the season of display in the garden is of increasing importance. The era when gardens could be 'put to bed' for the winter months and provide little of interest then are behind us. In Britain a number of public winter gardens, dedicated to hardy plants for winter display, have been developed in recent years. These follow the lead of the original winter garden at the University of Cambridge Botanic Garden, and are proving very popular.

Hollies contribute to vibrant winter displays that have made a strong impression upon the gardening public, who flock to see examples such as that at Anglesey Abbey in eastern England. The key elements of these gardens are colourful bark and stems from dogwoods, willows and others; evergreen foliage of trees, shrubs and herbaceous perennials; fruiting plants of all kinds; and an ever-increasing range of winter-flowering subjects. Gardeners in areas where there has been a run of warmer winters in recent years are being tempted out-of-doors during the winter and are demanding more from their plots than a smattering of winter colour, a demand that hollies are well equipped to help to fulfil.

Hollies for Topiary

Among the most malleable of garden plants, hollies respond well to pruning, a fact which has long been recognised and put to good use in both the Western and oriental gardening traditions. Hollies have provided many subjects for garden topiary, the formal clipping and training of hollies and other evergreens into a variety of different shapes.

Early foliage colour is shown off to good effect in this low holly hedge of mixed cultivars, which will mature to green as the season progresses.

A brief history

There is a long history of the use of hollies as hedges, clipped specimens and topiary in a wide variety of styles and forms, with references going back to Lucius Junius Moderatus Columella in the mid 1st century AD, recommending holly for Roman formal gardens. A quotation often repeated, and worth rehearsing here, is John Evelyn's 1664 description of his own holly hedge, obviously his pride and joy: '*Is there under heaven a more glorious and refreshing object … than an impregnable hedge of about 400 feet in length, 9 feet high, and 5 feet in diameter, which I can show in my own ruined garden at Say's Court at any time of year, glittering with its armed and varnished leaves, the taller standards at orderly distances, blushing with their natural coral. It mocks at the rudest assaults of weather, beasts, or hedge breakers*'.

William Paul, in his address to the Royal Horticultural Society's Floral Committee in 1863, describes how '*the Holly hedges at Tynninghame in Scotland, planted about 1705 by Thomas, sixth Earl of Haddington, have obtained world-wide celebrity. They are 2952 yards in length, from 16 to 25 feet in height, and from 14 to 17 feet broad at the base. Mr. Lees, the intelligent gardener there, informs me that they are clipped annually in April*'. (Aside from the tremendous stature of the hedges described, I particularly enjoy the reference to the 'intelligent gardener', Mr Lees!) Decades later William Dallimore, in his standard work on the most important structural garden evergreens of the time (and of today), *Holly, Yew and Box*

'The mark of the scissors on every plant'—deliberately so in the topiary nursery at Highfield Hollies in England.

(1908), maintains this level of appreciation: '*At the present time, really good hedges of holly are held in as high estimation as ever, and the owner of a good one is usually every bit as proud of it as Evelyn was, whilst it excites the envy of all his associates*'. The mental image of neighbours and friends casting admiring and covetous glances at one's holly hedge is certainly one to treasure.

The popularity of the art of topiary has waxed and waned as horticultural fashions have changed over the centuries. Strong positions both pro- and anti-topiary have been taken by many, in a controversy which bubbles on to this day. In 1713 no less an advocate of naturalistic gardening than Alexander Pope wrote in *The Guardian*, '*How contrary … is the modern practice of gardening! We seem to make it our study to recede from nature, not only in the various tonsure of greens into the most regular and formal shape, but even in monstrous attempts beyond the reach of the art itself*'. This comment referred to the craze for topiary men, animals, scenes from nature and other bizarre objects.

In his comments Pope echoed and expanded upon the thoughts of Joseph Addison, who (writing in *The Spectator* the year before) had bemoaned the fact that '*British gardeners … instead of humouring nature, love to deviate from it as much as possible. Our trees rise in cones, globes and pyramids. We see the mark of the scissors on every plant and bush*'. Addison would far rather '*look upon a tree in all its luxuriancy and diffusion and branches, than when it is … cut and trimmed into a mathematical figure*'.

It is remarkable that trends in gardening fashion could be the subject of such controversy and polemics. Perhaps the strength of feeling in the 18th century arose from the diametrical opposition of the naturalistic and formal styles. The decision facing gardeners was either to have formality, with topiary and clipped plants, or to go for the naturalistic option entirely.

Philip Miller (*The Gardener's Dictionary*, 1739) takes a less strident view than his forebears, noting of topiarised hollies: '*These trees were formerly in much greater request than at present, and there was scarcely a small garden of any worth, but was fill'd with these trees, which were clipp'd either into pyramids, balls, or some other figures; but as this was crowding a garden too much with one sort of plant, and the fashion of clipp'd greens going off, so that now they are almost wholly neglected, such are the changes in men's tempers and fancies, that what is one year esteemed is the next despised*'—a wise reflection upon the foibles of gardening fashion then as now.

Although he did not wish to be considered '*an advocate for clipp'd trees*', being '*infinitely more delighted with a tree in all its luxuriancy of branches*', Miller did, however, admit that topiary trees could be of '*great beauty … if rightly dispose'd in a garden … intermixed with other sorts of evergreens to form regular clumps, or placed in quarters of evergreens, or to form columns at the entrances of wilderness quarters, or to plant in the niches of evergreen hedges, in all which places they have an agreeable effect*'. This more measured argument places topiary in what, surely, is its correct place as but one element of the garden's mix. This frees gardeners to either use it in formal situations, effectively as plant architecture, or informally to support or enhance a naturalistic style, as in the Japanese landscape gardening tradition.

The topiary controversy among Western gardeners has ebbed to and fro over the centuries, and does so to this day. In the early 20th century we find that William Dallimore was also an apostle of the freer and more naturalistic gardening style, which was then being expounded strongly by William Robinson and others. He was just as coruscating as Addison about any form of topiary, although, as we have seen, this did not affect his enthusiasm for holly hedges (which he shared with Robinson). He allowed, however, for the desirability of a little formative pruning of specimen plants, to maintain what he described as a 'loose' effect, so that the plant's '*formality of habit is not objectionable*'. However, he continues, '*when as is too often the case, the pruning takes the form of clipping, and trees are made to look like gigantic, green-painted sugar loaves or inflated plum puddings the effect is absurd and positively cruel… . What pleasure people can find in practically planing the head of such a fine tree as the holly passes all comprehension*'.

Topiary hedging, providing an intriguingly different effect.

Dallimore considered that formal gardens with topiary should be relegated to 'the retired list' as museum pieces, with such objectionable practices as '*the hard clipping of beautiful hollies*' as one expression of the gardener's art in dire need of reform. What he might think of today's fusion of formality and topiary combined with sumptuous natural flowing plantings, a dynamic which makes for remarkable effects in many gardens, would be fascinating to discover.

Whatever the subjective feelings of Western gardeners and designers over the centuries, it cannot be denied that trimmed evergreens, whether hedges or topiary, can be a key element in the bone structure of a garden. The style of trimming can be chosen to suit the style of the garden—formal and architectural, flowing and naturalistic, or simply abstract and fun—and among the hollies are many candidates for all these purposes. Today's more inclusive and tolerant climate, where (to paraphrase Mao Tse-tung) we let 'a hundred flowers bloom' in our approaches to garden design and plant use, is well served by the diversity available among the hollies, which provide us with a wealth of plants for screens, hedges and topiary of all kinds. The plants featured in the pages to come are but a selection of the wide variety of hollies in a range of sizes, habits, colours and textures. Between them they will provide material for whatever purpose you might wish to put them to, in the privacy of your own garden.

Common topiary shapes

Given the range of leaf size and texture available with the hollies (and their malleability), hollies can obviously be bent to the creative gardener's will in any number of ways. The 'classical' shapes described here can be seen in many gardens and are available in many nurseries and garden centres. Achieving some of the more complex shapes may take some time if starting from scratch, but a great sense of achievement can be obtained from the creation of a piece of living garden architecture.

The simplest form (and one for which the natural habit of many hollies equips them well) is the cone. Its sides can be flattened to give a pyramid, which may taper to a tip or be flat-topped. Many hollies also clip well into cubes of all sizes. The flat-topped pillar has great architectural presence; when grown on a stem it creates an elegant 'tulip' shape. Rounded forms include the simple hemispherical dome, usually grown directly on the ground; when placed on a stem it becomes an umbrella. A topiary ball on a stem makes the highly effective 'lollipop'. Several lollipops may be strung out along a single stem, as used to good effect at East Ruston Old Vicarage in England.

Among the more eccentric classical shapes are the spiral and, perhaps strangest of all, the 'cake-stand', effectively a multi-layered plant where a number of discs are cut, the width of the discs gradually tapering toward the top, which may be flat or rounded. Shapes can be combined, as, for example, a ball on top of a pyramid. The range of topiary forms is limited only by the imagination (and some may also say the taste) of the gardener.

Imaginative topiary with *Ilex* ×*altaclerensis* 'Golden King' at East Ruston in England.

Trimmed hollies are widely used in the Eastern gardening tradition, particularly in Japan, where *Ilex crenata* lends itself wonderfully to the topiary styles known as *tamatsukuri* and *marumona* (broadly translated as 'making round'), whether as balls and discs at the end of branches, or as mounds. The

simple but effective contrast between mounded forms of clipped evergreens and other 'natural' shapes and forms (whether of plants or rocks) is one of the defining characteristics of Japanese gardens. Mounded forms may represent hills in the distance. Rounded forms at the ends of branches are often referred to as 'cloud-pruning'. Plants may be single or multi-stemmed, with each branch bearing a tightly clipped hemisphere at the end, creating a fascinatingly abstract effect to the Western observer. I have seen this style used in more free-form creations with a range of other plants, and undoubtedly there is much room for experimentation.

Those who wish to see the art of topiary taken to its eccentric extreme are referred to the garden at Levens Hall in Westmorland, England. Although principally wrought in yew and box, it will provide tremendous inspiration for the novice topiarist, as some of the classical shapes have grown over time into what can only be described as Dali-esque living sculptures. While many find it tremendous fun, it was rather sniffily dismissed by the writer of Veitch's *Manual of Coniferae* in 1900 as a garden where '*the topiary foible of our horticultural predecessors is still maintained in all its quaint antagonism to Nature*'. Each to their own …

This assembly of *Ilex crenata* topiary at a Japanese nursery shows that it is capable of any shape that might be formed from box (*Buxus* species and cultivars) in traditional topiary.

Subjects for topiary

Traditional subjects for general topiary work have tended to be relatively fine-textured and slow-growing, chosen to create objects of definite mass that require trimming only once or twice a year. The great diversity of hollies provides us with many plants that are suitable for topiary work. Species or cultivars with a densely shrubby or free-branching habit are particularly appropriate. Plants with small leaves are understandably most favoured, especially for smaller topiary pieces, although leaves of medium size (up to

Creating *tamatsukuri* in a Japanese nursery: free-growing plants of *Ilex crenata* are cut back hard (**above**) to a few stems, which are then tied into position. Plants rapidly grow away from what at first glance seems a very severe 'mistreatment' to form handsome specimens, shown dramatically in the final 'after' photo (**left**).

7.5CM long) may be chosen for larger pieces or for the added attraction of leaf colour or variegation.

The species with the longest history in topiary work are *Ilex aquifolium* in Western Europe (particularly Britain) and *I. crenata* in Japan, both reflecting the long horticultural tradition in those areas. More recently cultivars of *Ilex ×altaclerensis* have been used in Britain (particularly the brilliantly variegated 'Golden King'), bringing vibrant colour to modern planting schemes. The drawback with both the English and Japanese hollies is their inability to thrive in more extreme climates. Gardeners in America had early recourse to their own native species. The American holly, *I. opaca*, brought greater cold hardiness and the ability to withstand high summer temperatures. The yaupon, *I. vomitoria*, proved the perfect candidate for the summer heat of the southeastern USA, ideal in texture with its small glossy leaves and responding superbly well to clipping. It demonstrates its remarkable qualities in the gardens at Colonial Williamsburg and in many public and private gardens, where its robust nature and ability to respond to regular shearing are highly valued.

The range of hollies that can be used for topiary has grown tremendously over the past century. Among the traditional subjects the character of *Ilex aquifolium* can be obtained in more northern areas by using cultivars of *I. ×meserveae*. Hardy cultivars of Japanese holly, including *I. crenata* 'Beehive', 'Compacta' and 'Glory', have been developed, bringing the hardiness of this useful plant to Zone 6. Continuing with the hardiness theme, for the simplest topiary shapes such as low domes in very cold areas (down to Zone 4), compact forms of *I. glabra* such as 'Chamzin' = NORDIC may be used.

The list of other hollies that may be used in topiary is long, as is that of hollies that may be used for hedges. The qualities that make so many hollies highly suitable for hedges also fit many of them well for topiary.

Hollies for Bonsai

A number of hollies, deciduous and evergreen, make good candidates for *bonsai*—the traditional Japanese discipline of growing naturalistic dwarf specimen plants, trained to give the appearance of wizened specimens in miniature (developed from and similar to the Chinese system, *penjing*). Constraints of space make it impossible to deal in detail here with the specialised techniques required by the traditional system of bonsai growing. They are best mastered through recourse to one of the many specialist publications on the subject, or to a bonsai club or society.

True bonsai culture is typically practised upon full-sized plants (rather than dwarf forms or those of restricted growth). Small-leaved species such as *Ilex pernyi* and *I. dimorphophylla* may fit the bill well, but many hollies are simply too large in leaf to lend themselves to bonsai. Many gardeners seek to achieve this 'bonsai effect' while avoiding the demanding cultivation regime required for true bonsai plants. The hollies can provide numerous candidates for this treatment, for example small *I. crenata* cultivars such as 'Dwarf Pagoda' and 'Green Dragon', both characterful plants. Other dwarf cultivars such as *I.* 'Rock Garden' and *I.* 'Jermyns Dwarf' are also highly suited to training in the manner of bonsai.

Deciduous hollies may also make very striking bonsai specimens; *Ilex serrata* is used for bonsai in Japan. Hybrids between *I. serrata* and *I. verticillata* may also lend themselves to the dwarfing process; when well berried, their bare stems make for vivid winter display, as may the smaller cultivars of *I. verticillata* itself.

Hollies for Hedges and Screens

Many gardeners may be put off from choosing hollies for hedges because of the widespread misconception that they are slow-growing. The desire for instant gardening gratification has led to the proliferation of hedges of fast-growing subjects in a variety of broadleaved and coniferous genera, and the range of trimmable evergreens grows ever wider. But among the hollies the sheer diversity of plant form is sufficient to provide candidates for most hedging purposes, from dwarf shrubs to fast-growing small trees. One of the other advantages of hollies over many other evergreens is that most mature holly hedges usually require trimming only once a year, although this characteristic will depend upon the subject and the type of hedge.

With reasonable preparation and good aftercare there are many holly species and cultivars that may put on 20–30cm of growth a year. Even where hollies may be slightly slower off the blocks initially, they will often provide superior, longer-lived results than other subjects. If (for whatever reason) the

Ilex 'Hohman', one of a number of hybrids with *I. latifolia* in their background that can be used for informal screens where space permits.

time is not available to wait for a holly hedge to grow naturally, large plants of many cultivars suitable for hedging are available to reduce the time needed to achieve the desired effect. Gardeners who are in a real hurry will find ready-grown holly hedges available from specialist suppliers of landscape plants, although the range to choose from will not be as wide.

Many hollies will grow well in the shade. This natural attribute makes them highly adaptable as hedging and screening subjects in more crowded urban landscapes, where shade from neighbouring trees, buildings or fences is an ever-increasing problem. Many hollies positively thrive in light to moderate shade, and some may still be effective in darker conditions.

An important consideration when choosing which holly to use in a hedge is the amount (and prickliness) of its spines. Species and cultivars with sharp, hard spines certainly create more effective barriers. There are also distinctly different textural qualities to be obtained from spiny and spineless cultivars. On a very practical note, however, whoever is cutting the hedge, living with it, or weeding around it, should be allowed their say upon how well armed the chosen subject should be. Expense may also be a consideration, as seed-raised hedging plants are invariably cheaper, but this makes itself felt only where large quantities of plants may be required.

The final seal of approval upon the holly's qualities and suitability for hedges, screens and topiary is surely to be found in the long history of its use in Europe, Asia, and in North America, where it continues to rank among the most important plants used by the landscape industry. A reference from a Roman writer demonstrates the long appreciation of holly for hedges. Evelyn (in his *Sylva*) quotes Couleii thus: '*A hedge of Holly, Thieve that would invade, / Repulses like a growing palisade*'.

A screen of plants provides many of the benefits of a hedge, but in a less formal manner. Screens are equally effective for boundary demarcation, creating privacy and seclusion, or separating discrete areas of the garden. Screens may be made up of plants in rows, or in informal groups. Hollies provide us with numerous candidates for screening, in a range of heights. Many conical or narrowly pyramidal cultivars are eminently suitable for screens where height is required without excessive width, with the bonus of needing only occasional formative pruning.

A screen can provide a superior and more practical solution than a hedge for marking the boundary of the garden. Hedges require regular clipping, and space on the external face to allow access for trimming, neither of which are needed by a screen. A screen is also less formal when viewed from within the garden. But the choice is not solely between the formality of a hedge and the informal habit of free-growing plants. Hollies whose habit of growth is almost but not quite what is needed may be maintained in a 'hybrid' condition, between a hedge and a screen, where plants are pruned to a semi-natural habit that enhances their natural character in the way described by Dallimore a century ago. This light pruning regime also serves to keep plants within bounds where necessary and may be required only every second or third year.

Among the deciduous hollies are several candidates for less formal screens of varying heights. They provide a neutral green summer background, which bursts into often brilliant colour with the arrival of autumn, with fruits that in many areas will persist through much of the winter, and attractive silvery grey bark. Some deciduous hollies will create effective screens in poorly drained situations, adding further to the adaptability of this remarkable group of plants.

Foliage colour and texture

Hollies come in many colourful forms. If a garden hedge or screen is intended solely as a boundary to a property, then plain green foliage is best. Relative anonymity is usually desirable in the distance, so that the eye is not tempted away from decorative plantings close to the house, although a burst of seasonal colour is perfectly acceptable and may be desirable. Bold foliage subjects such as large *Ilex ×altaclerensis*, *I. ×koehneana* and *I. cornuta* forms should be avoided for hedging. They will not provide that most important characteristic of a good hedge, which is denseness. This is achieved more successfully with smaller-leaved cultivars, and to clip such large and handsome leaves is almost horticultural vandalism. They can, however, make superb informal screens, for which they may be ideally suited.

Plants for hedges may be seed-raised (with the potential for some variation from plant to plant, a character common in hollies), or they may be of one vegetatively propagated clone, to give a uniform result. The decision upon which to use rests in part upon the effect desired. Uniformity is better suited to more formal situations, particularly where the hedge is in great part exposed to view and its purpose is to act as a neutral backdrop or simply to enclose a space. But a boundary hedge at the rear of a wide shrub border where less formality is demanded could well benefit from the greater diversity of seed-raised plants (or even a variety of cultivars with different foliage or fruit).

Once away from boundaries and formal borders, great opportunities to use foliage colour open up to the adventurous gardener, which hollies can support admirably. The wide range of colours and textures available, let alone the variety of fruit, can be used to good effect to contrast with or support different styles of planting. Yellow-variegated cultivars such as *Ilex ×altaclerensis* 'Golden King' will make a brilliant background for a hot colour planting rich in red, orange and purple. This large-leaved cultivar is a vigorous grower, but may also form a very effective low hedge.

Finer-textured colourful hedges of low to medium height can be obtained using smaller-leaved cultivars such as *Ilex aquifolium* 'Myrtifolia Aurea Maculata'; less showy cultivars such as the gold-edged 'Rubricaulis Aurea' can also be highly effective. The brilliant yellow growths of *I. ×attenuata* 'Sunny Foster', a fine-textured plant with linear leaves, can be very dramatic in good light, while for low hedges, *I. crenata* 'Golden Gem' provides another bright-leaved candidate. The young foliage of many green-leaved hollies, for example the deep red-purple of some *I. ×meserveae* cultivars, may also be put to use as part of the garden's seasonal effects. Free-fruiting cultivars in red, orange and yellow may also spice up the palette for colourful plantings.

White-variegated cultivars will provide a cooler backdrop for more subtle plantings with pastel flower colours or grey and silver foliage. *Ilex aquifolium* 'Elegantissima', with spiny leaves generously edged in pale cream, forms an effective neutral background as a hedge. As the plant is male, the cool effect isn't compromised by berries. A truly grey effect can be obtained for a hedge up to 2.1M tall by using the Japanese *I. crenata* 'Shiro-fukurin' (syn. 'Snowflake') which clips well into a wall of fine textured grey-green leaves with white edges. For dwarf hedges the cultivar 'Weismoor Silber', a sport from 'Convexa', is a compact grower, with leaves that are a mixture of grey, green and palest cream. More ideas for colourful hedges can be obtained from the Directory.

Mixed and tapestry hedges

Hollies have been used in mixed hedges for many years. In earlier times large estates in Britain would plant long boundary hedges of a mixture of hawthorn (*Crataegus*) and holly, at a ratio of as many as six hawthorn plants to one holly. This was intended partly to save money (holly being more expensive than hawthorn) and partly to provide quick and effective, early growth, as the hawthorn outpaced the holly in the early years. In true hare and tortoise fashion, the holly would gradually outgrow the hawthorn, eventually creating what would effectively be a pure holly hedge.

'Tapestry' hedges use hollies with a number of other subjects to provide a hedge of varied texture and colour. The plants chosen must require management similar to the holly. One of the most-quoted examples is the Fuchsia Garden at Hidcote in England, where a mixture of green and purple beech, green and variegated holly, and green and variegated box was used to create a very distinctive hedge. The mixture of russet-brown winter foliage and grey stems of the beech with the deep green of common holly is also particularly satisfying. Another option is to use holly cultivars alone to create a tapestry hedge with a range of different foliage and fruit colours, as has been done at the National Botanic Gardens, Glasnevin, Dublin, Ireland.

Recommended hollies by height

The plants discussed here represent a selection of the many hollies available for hedges and screens at a variety of heights. An important consideration in their choice has been the time taken to reach their effective working height. Slow-growing plants are generally not recommended for tall and mid-height hedges, although they will usually be equally effective in time; for low hedges slow-growing subjects that are easier to keep within bounds and require less frequent clipping may well be preferable to more vigorous subjects. If a screen is used rather than a hedge, it should be borne in mind that the 'footprint' of a screen requires more space than a hedge.

Tallest growers (7.5M and above)

Hollies can create splendid evergreen screens of 11M and more. For screening purposes the narrow conical-columnar cultivars of *Ilex* ×*altaclerensis* such as 'Camelliifolia' and 'James G. Esson', both with glossy, almost spineless green leaves and abundant red berries, are among the quickest growers in warmer areas (Zones 7 to 9, 6b with protection). Cultivars of *I.* ×*koehneana* (*latifolia* × *aquifolium*) are shaping up to be equally if not more effective in Zones 6b to 9. They combine a strongly conical habit with superb foliage, remaining well furnished to the ground. Female cultivars bear generous quantities of highly visible red berries. These cultivars may reach their working height rapidly: Michael Dirr (2002) reports 45–60CM of growth a year for the cultivars 'Ajax' (male) and 'Agena' (female), and 9M of growth in thirty years. 'Wirt L. Winn' (female) is a cultivar of proven standing in the USA. At Rosemoor in south-west England, young plants of 'Chestnut Leaf', a female selection widely grown in Europe, typically put on over 30CM a year. *Ilex* 'Hohman' shares many of the ×*koehneana* qualities. Numerous cultivars of *I. aquifolium* will achieve this height. Among the best are 'Pyramidalis' and 'Pyramidalis Fructu Luteo', both narrowly conical in habit and fast-growing, bearing heavy crops of red and yellow berries, respectively.

Ilex opaca, the American holly, is rather slower in growth but an excellent and dependable candidate for the landscape, with practical benefits of hardiness to Zones 5 and 6 and proven longevity. Faster-growing cultivars of the right shape include 'Bountiful', with a dense habit to 15M and dark red berries; 'Carnival', a rapid grower to 15M, with vivid red fruit; 'Vera', very upright and compact, with red-orange fruits; and 'Merry Christmas', fast-growing to 12M, with bright red fruit. Yellow-fruited cultivars of good shape include 'Boyce Thompson Xanthocarpa', to 12M. To pollinate these, 'Jersey Knight' is a popular male, to 10.5M with fine dark green leaves, and 'Santa Claus' grows to 10.5M; both are hardy to Zone 6. For colder regions to Zone 5 'David G. Leach' is a fast-growing male, hardy to −35C.

Mid-height growers (3–7.5M)

At this lower level many more hollies come into play. Erect-growing green-leaved cultivars of *Ilex aquifolium* (all red-fruited females for Zones 7 to 9 except where stated) include 'Alaska', 'Amber' (orange fruit), 'Balkans' (Zone 6), 'J. C. van Tol', 'Lewis' (Zone 6), SIBERIA = 'Limsi' (Zone 6), 'Pyramidalis' and

Even though it is a vigorous grower, *Ilex ×altaclerensis* 'Golden King' AGM will clip into excellent mid-height hedges and topiary of all kinds.

'Pyramidalis Fructu Luteo' (again). Some of these will probably exceed 7.5M over time, but for practical purposes most are not as certain to achieve as great a height as the previous selections across all regions where hollies are grown.

Some *Ilex ×altaclerensis* cultivars are used in Britain for hedges in this height range, especially 'Golden King' with its vividly colourful foliage. There are numerous cultivars of *I. opaca* for mid-height hedges and screens; these include 'Cardinal', which is narrow, compact, red-fruited, hardy to Zone 5, and 'Morgan Gold', which has vivid yellow fruit. 'Hedgeholly' does exactly as its name implies, combining a dense habit with the bonus of carmine-red fruit, an ideal candidate for a tall hedge as well as a screen.

Another excellent group of cultivars for screens and hedges at this height range is derived from the species *Ilex pernyi.* This has been crossed with *I. aquifolium* to create the *I. ×aquipernyi* cultivars, plants of good hardiness

Opposite: *Ilex crenata* 'Golden Gem' AGM and 'Green Hedger', here used to provide close-textured hedging and topiary.

(Zones 6b to 9a), excellent small dark glossy foliage and neat pyramidal habit; DRAGON LADY = 'Meschick' is a free-fruiting cultivar, as is 'San Jose', a popular plant in the southwest USA. 'Brilliant' (*aquifolium* × *ciliospinosa*), a hybrid of similar character, again is neat in habit, berrying freely. Two hybrids between *I. pernyi* and *I. cornuta* are worthy of note; both are vigorous growers, with rather larger foliage—'Lydia Morris' is a female, with vivid fruit, and has a male consort, 'John T. Morris', which may outgrow her in height over time. Another excellent *cornuta* hybrid (× *aquifolium*) is 'Nellie R. Stevens', again female, with a more broadly conical habit, making a fine screen of glossy mid-green leaves.

The taller cultivars of the hybrid *Ilex* ×*attenuata* (*cassine* × *opaca*) are also very valuable. 'Foster No. 2' (Zone 6b) is particularly useful as a screen plant for restricted spaces, with a good habit of growth and abundant red berries. Dirr (1997) sings its praises: '*Good in groupings, against walls in narrow planting areas where other hollies would grow too wide*'. 'Savannah' is another upright-growing female selection, used more widely in the southeastern USA. *Ilex vomitoria* is a remarkably adaptable plant for screens and hedges in the warmer parts of the southeastern USA; a number of its cultivars, such as 'Pride of Houston', are upright in habit and may be fitted into a narrow space, especially with a little judicious formative pruning when young. This very obliging species may also take very well to training along walls as a form of espalier.

The Red Hollies are a group of comparatively recent introduction with good potential for hedges and screens of 3M plus. These selections from open-pollinated seedlings of *Ilex* 'Mary Nell' are typically upright in growth and dense in texture, with glossy foliage that may be red as the new leaves emerge. Further details are given in the Directory.

Low to mid-height growers (1–3M)

The range of evergreen hollies that can be maintained as low to mid-height hedges is very wide, and subjects can be found for all climates from Zone 4b and upward. Subjects for screens are fewer, as many that grow to the height required with any speed will eventually outgrow it. With the caveat that some pruning to size may be required in time, the following are recommended. Finer-leaved cultivars of *Ilex aquifolium*, such as 'Angustifolia', 'Harpune' and 'Myrtifolia Aurea', form shapely upright conical shrubs, while 'Larry Peters' is slow but broader. *Ilex pernyi* has again been involved in the parentage of several small,

slow-growing cultivars in this size range, including 'Coronet', 'Joe McDaniel' and 'Miniature', although some training to shape may be required for these.

For hedges, many *Ilex aquifolium* and *I.* ×*aquipernyi* cultivars will fit into the upper part of this size range, say 1.8–3M, as will the smaller cultivars of *I. opaca*, *I. cornuta* and the Red Hollies. *Ilex* ×*altaclerensis* 'Golden King' is successfully used in Britain for hedges of around 1.5M and upward. Cultivars of the hybrid *I.* ×*meserveae* also fall within this range (although they may be slower and shorter in growth in colder regions). A distinctive group in their own right, their glossy aquifolium-style foliage with its distinctive colour cast may be used to provide the English-holly foliage effect in colder regions to Zone 5b. BLUE PRINCESS = 'Conapry' and BLUE MAID = 'Mesid' are both free-fruiting, while BLUE PRINCE = 'Conablu' and BLUE STALLION = 'Mesan' are males, the latter more vigorous in growth and suitable for a higher hedge.

The climatic extremes in the USA are catered for by two native species. In cold areas close-textured cultivars of *Ilex glabra*, the inkberry, can make an acceptable substitute for low mounded hedges of box or *I. crenata*. For warmer areas the yaupon (*I. vomitoria*) demonstrates further its remarkable adaptability for hedges and topiary of all kinds, with dense-textured dwarf cultivars such as BORDEAUX = 'Condeaux' and 'Stokes Dwarf' being ideal for low hedges. Its suitability for hedges and topiary is demonstrated to good effect in the formal gardens at Colonial Williamsburg, and it makes a very effective substitute for *I. crenata* in the hotter parts of the southeastern USA, where that species may not thrive.

Japanese holly (*Ilex crenata*) cultivars are ideally suited to clipping and are therefore ideal for low hedges and screens: the Japanese hollies have centuries of history of being bent to the will of the gardener. If a hedge that will remain dense from the ground up is desired, cultivars with a very erect branch habit should be avoided. Some side growth is essential on even the narrowest hedge to keep it well furnished. Low hedges are typically quite wide in proportion to their height; the habit of naturally mound-forming cultivars may be best suited to this purpose, and some will require minimal trimming. The hardiness of Japanese hollies varies from Zone 5b for the toughest, with most being at home in Zones 6 to 9.

There are many Japanese hollies from which to choose: this selection is based upon plants with a proven track record. The sex of the cultivars is not usually of great moment, as the small black (rarely pale creamy yellow) berries are not particularly showy, although with heavy croppers the strain of bearing fruit may possibly affect winter leaf colour. Among taller cultivars 'Highlander' is a male plant which is hardy (Zone 6), with dark green leaves, capable of reaching 2.4M plus. 'Northern Beauty' is another vigorous male of upright habit, with leaves over 1.8CM long, large for a *crenata* cultivar. 'Convexa' is a female cultivar, hardy to Zone 6b, that will steadily grow to 2.4M, with leaves whose convex shape has led to it being used as a substitute for box in formal situations; 'Hetzii' (female, an offspring of 'Convexa') is similar in habit, more vigorous, and equally tough. For a screen or very narrow hedge 'Sentinel' (female) is narrowly conical, achieving 2M after eight years. 'Ivory Tower' is a pale-fruited cultivar of quite vigorous broadly erect growth.

Immature plants of *Ilex dimorphophylla*, seen here in Japan, will provide a bright light green hedge.

Dwarf growers (to 0.9M)

At this level we are no longer considering using plants as informal screens; however, low and dwarf hedges are still well catered for among the many smaller hollies. While, as to be expected, *Ilex crenata* provides the largest input to this group, there are others that can form very effective low hedges. Among the many smaller selections of Japanese holly that are suitable are 'Convexa', 'Dwarf Cone', 'Green Lustre', 'Helleri' and 'Stokes'. A very effective low golden hedge can also be made with the cultivar 'Golden Gem'.

Small-leaved and dense-growing cultivars of *Ilex aquifolium* such as 'Larry Peters' may also be used, and for a variegated hedge, 'Myrtifolia Aurea Maculata'. The slow-growing dwarf cultivar *I.* 'Rock Garden' (×*aquipernyi* × 'Accent') will form a low hedge over time; the juvenile form of *I. dimorphophylla* is faster-growing, forming a densely spiny low hedge. *Ilex vomitoria* in its smallest cultivars is another excellent choice, and the most compact forms of *I. glabra* may be clipped to a low mounded hedge.

Clipping and cultivation

Robust and adaptable as hollies are, like all plants they will benefit from good ground preparation before planting, especially when used for topiary, hedges and screens, which may have a restricted root-run. The distance apart for planting depends upon the purpose to which they are being put. Plants for screens need to be far enough apart that they will be able to achieve something of their mature character as individual plants; the largest-growing species and cultivars may need as much as 3M or more between them.

Plants in hedges will be much closer together. For example *Ilex opaca* and *I. aquifolium* and their cultivars may be planted as seedlings or cuttings, 60CM tall, at 60–75CM apart. Smaller hollies for low hedges should have their planting distances reduced accordingly; cultivars of *I. crenata* being used for dwarf hedges in a way similar to dwarf box may be planted as little as 10–15CM apart. Hedging plants that have been grown in the open ground should have been transplanted or specially treated to encourage a fibrous root system. Of course, if quicker results are required, the nursery industry will supply everything from large plants that have been specially grown to be virtually ready-made hedges, up to and including complete stretches of mature hedging.

Bare-rooted hollies are typically planted in early spring; containerised stock may be planted at any time conditions allow (more on this in the next chapter). Ensure that the area is well drained and incorporate well-rotted organic matter into the soil prior to planting, with a general fertiliser. Aftercare is straightforward: irrigate well, particularly in the first two years from planting; feed young hedges well for optimum growth—the same applies for older hedges, which have to replace a significant proportion of their growth each year. Do not allow the base of hedges young or old to become overgrown by weeds or nearby plants. If lower branches are lost by being shaded out they will regenerate slowly, if at all. Where shading out has occurred with a neglected holly hedge there are two remedies. The first (or nuclear) option is to cut the hedge back to the ground and start again. A gentler option is to buy young plants (or to propagate them from the existing hedge), and plant them along the bare stretches. Good preparation and aftercare are essential for successful establishment.

In common with all hedging subjects, hollies require regular trimming to keep them tidy and within bounds. Clipping usually takes place in late summer (August in the northern hemisphere). Hollies may be close-trimmed, either mechanically with hedge trimmers or manually with shears. This will take no account of the berries on female plants and would probably remove much of the wood on which the flowers for next year's fruit will develop; but close-trimmed hollies are not usually grown for berry effect. Hedge trimmers and shears are perfectly appropriate where sharp edges and close-textured walls of foliage are desired. Where berries are an important part of the show, and a less formal, looser appearance is acceptable, hedges may be pruned more lightly with shears or, for preference, with secateurs, cutting back growths individually; although this may be a long job, it can create very striking effects.

Most hedges should be slightly wider at the base than at the top. This is called the 'batter' of the hedge and helps to create a more robust branch structure. It is particularly important to have this batter on higher hedges with straight sides, especially in areas where the weight of snow and ice that may accumulate on the top of the hedge might cause it to splay.

Cultivation

CHAPTER 3

One of the defining characteristics of the hollies is that they are easy to grow. Their robust and adaptable nature accounts for their success as a genus, with around five hundred *Ilex* species distributed widely throughout temperate and tropical regions. It also lies at the root of the success of the temperate species grown in our gardens for many years. However, there is a major cultural division between the two principal groups of hollies of horticultural importance.

The first group, derived from *Ilex aquifolium*, which evolved in the cool temperate maritime climates of the western fringes of the European continent, is largely intolerant of extremes of both cold and heat. This group includes the *I.* ×*altaclerensis* hybrids. The second major group is centred upon species from the continental climates of North America and the Far East, for example *I. opaca*, *I. verticillata* and *I. cornuta*. They are typically more tolerant of the extremes of heat or cold that are experienced across regions such as the eastern USA. The most adaptable of them are capable of thriving in the sticky subtropical heat and humidity of the southeastern USA.

Under less rigorous conditions, while they might survive perfectly well, some of these 'continental' species may fail to achieve their full potential. This occurs in the softer maritime climates of Great Britain and Ireland and in adjacent areas of Western Europe. As one moves east and south in Europe the climate becomes more continental, with hotter summers and cooler winters. This is more to the taste of many hollies, and I have seen evidence of this in (for example) numerous plants of a range of *Ilex opaca* cultivars thriving and fruiting freely in the arboretum at Bokrijk in eastern Belgium.

A number of species and hybrids are capable of bridging this gap, bringing the potential to perform well under a wide range of maritime and continental conditions. A good example is the Chinese *Ilex pernyi* and its hybrid with

Opposite: A fine hardy specimen holly for many situations, *Ilex opaca* 'Satyr Hill'.

Opposite: A fine colourful plant, even more remarkable in that it will survive periodic flooding, *Ilex verticillata* 'Winter Red'.

I. aquifolium, *I.* ×*aquipernyi*. The Japanese species *I. latifolia* and its hybrids with *I. aquifolium* (the *I.* ×*koehneana* cultivars) are also demonstrating a greater ability to thrive on either side of the climatic divide. The principal lesson to take from the range of climates and temperatures where hollies succeed in the wild is that there are species, hybrids and cultivars available for most conditions experienced by the gardeners in temperate regions.

Choice of site

Finding a holly to suit a particular site is relatively straightforward, as there are plants for almost every garden situation. The difficulties begin if one wishes to grow plants at the edge of their 'comfort zone' (and which gardener doesn't fall into that particular trap?). Judicious use of garden microclimates will help: for example, planting close to buildings or walls that soak up sunshine by day will provide a heat source to raise the average temperature experienced by a plant, reducing the likelihood of cold damage and helping to ripen growth. Cold hardiness can also be greatly assisted by planting in sheltered situations, particularly in areas where extreme low temperatures are accompanied by the desiccating effects of high winds and winter sunshine. Heat tolerance will be assisted by providing or planting in the shade, tempering the effect of direct sunlight on the plants and reducing stress to the root systems from high soil temperatures.

Whatever might be done to assist your plants, it is important to match the subjects to the area where they are to be grown. There is little point in deciding to grow a collection of *Ilex opaca* cultivars in the cool, moist climate of the British Isles; likewise *I. aquifolium* is unlikely to thrive in the steamy heat of the far southeastern USA. If the right plant is selected for the right place there is a wealth of hollies that can be depended upon to thrive in Zones 4 to 9b, in sun or shade, sheltered or exposed situations, and in wet or dry soils.

Soils and drainage

Alongside their requirement for (and tolerance of) different climatic regimes, there is one other major cultural difference between European hollies and those from elsewhere. North American holly species (and many from the Far East) occur mainly in areas with acid soils. The major European species *Ilex aquifolium*, however, is more adaptable as to soil and can take an alkalinity of pH 8.0 in its stride, particularly if there is a good depth of soil. As a general

rule a soil pH of between 5.5 and 7.0 will suit all the holly species and cultivars we grow, with slightly acid conditions of 6.0 to 6.5 being ideal across the board. Very acid soils (pH 5.0 and below) may result in poor growth due to deficiencies of calcium and magnesium, which can be rectified with top dressings of dolomite limestone. Excessive alkalinity (which may manifest itself at around pH 7.0) may also result in poor growth and may be treated with dressings of ground sulphur. Home-testing kits are available for self-diagnosis of soil pH and major nutrients, but if a significant problem with the soil is suspected it may be advisable to seek professional advice. Government agencies, soil specialists and organisations such as the Royal Horticultural Society (RHS) will be able to advise further.

Soil type and structure are not of great importance to the highly adaptable holly. Two of the most important species we grow are prime examples of this wide tolerance of different soils: the American and English hollies, *Ilex opaca* and *I. aquifolium*, can both survive and thrive in the wild in thin sands, organic woodland conditions, on stony soils or in heavy clays. A number of hollies are also very tolerant of wet conditions, the most striking examples being the North American deciduous species *I. decidua* and *I. verticillata*, which can tolerate regular and prolonged inundation in their waterside habitats. Other species such as *I. cassine* are typically found in wet or swampy conditions, and many species are associated with rivers and streams. This is not to say that the association is obligatory in cultivation, although gardeners can, of course, put it to good use. Broadly speaking, all holly species will perform well under 'normal' garden conditions, with some species doing best if attention is paid to the preference that they naturally show for moist habitats.

The gardener's mantra that most plants perform to the optimum in well-structured, well-drained open soils holds as true for hollies as it does for the great majority of garden plants. As a general rule ensuring good and effective drainage is important whatever the soil type in your garden. Soils that remain waterlogged for long periods may be low in oxygen (perhaps anaerobic), leading to poor conditions for rooting and low availability of nutrients, which may result in poor establishment and growth. Heavy soils with a high clay fraction are particularly prone to waterlogging, although even thin sands can be affected, especially if they overlie poorly drained subsoils. Many hollies will survive occasional short-term flooding if the water drains away rapidly, but constant poor drainage leading to a 'gleyed' soil, with its characteristic rusty streaks and bad sulphurous smell (from anaerobic decomposition), will need to be corrected with extra drainage. If you are in doubt about the drainage status of your soil, seek professional advice.

Hollies do very well in moderately fertile soils, although they will tolerate a wide range of nutritional conditions. They are not gross feeders, and typically do not suffer from nutrient deficiencies under normal cultivation. The exception to this general rule is plants that fruit heavily, particularly in the more stressful climatic conditions found in warmer regions of the USA. Under these circumstances it may prove necessary to give a supplementary nitrogenous feed during the summer; this will help to maintain the plant in good health. Stressful conditions can otherwise lead to loss of leaf colour, thinning of the canopy and biennial bearing, as the plants may take alternate years to regather their strength for fruiting.

Improving the structure of the soil prior to planting will invariably pay dividends in the form of better growth and establishment of young or recently transplanted hollies. Incorporating well-rotted organic matter into the top 15–20CM will improve both heavy and light soils. Incorporating a 3.75–5CM layer of sharp gritty sand (or similar material) up to 6MM in size will help to open up heavy, poorly drained clay-based soils. A general purpose slow-release tree and shrub fertiliser should be incorporated at the manufacturer's recommended rate, together with any other soil treatment that may be required following soil analysis.

Today's smaller gardens often feature paved areas surrounded by narrow borders or raised beds and planters, with a relatively restricted root zone. For the best results, soil in planters and small or narrow beds should include some clay loam. Clay is an excellent long-term soil constituent that holds nutrients well. Soils with a high proportion of organic matter may shrink considerably as they decay. The traditional British John Innes compost ratio of 7 parts loamy soil to 3 parts of organic matter and 2 parts of sharp gritty sand is an excellent basis for small beds and large planters. John Innes–type composts are a good choice for hollies in all kinds of pots and containers; if they are not available, adding around 20 percent sterilised clay loam to a potting mix will be of value for plants grown in containers for a long period.

Planting and aftercare

Most hollies (evergreen and deciduous) for garden or landscape use are sold in containers. Large field-grown specimen plants may be sold with their rootballs wrapped in material (rootballed or ball-in-burlap). Bare-root plants are rarely offered and are used mainly for specialist applications—hedging and semi-natural situations, such as woodland or landscape restoration. Great care must be taken to ensure that their roots are not allowed to dry out, or they may fail to establish. They will need to be protected from animals, either by fencing the entire area or individual guards. A 5–7.5CM deep layer of organic mulch or a proprietary mulch mat will help to conserve water and will suppress the competition from the growth of weeds; water well after planting, if possible.

Again, container-grown plants can in theory be planted at any time conditions allow. Planting should not take place when the soil is frozen, and is inadvisable in very hot periods. The traditional time to plant evergreens (container-grown and bare-root) is the autumn, between September and November in the northern hemisphere. Planting at this time takes advantage of reduced stress on the plants from excessive heat or cold, while the residual warmth in the soil assists the root system to establish and repair any damage from planting. Planting in early spring is sometimes advised in areas that experience intense winter cold (which places more stress upon evergreen plants). Where intense cold is a regular occurrence, planting should not take place from around a month before the cold typically arrives. Rootballed or ball-in-burlap hollies are usually lifted from the field as they become dormant (i.e., from the end of the growing season). They are typically available from autumn onward and should be treated much as container-grown hollies.

Gardeners in areas that enjoy a mild maritime climate have the luxury of being able to plant containerised hollies all year round, certainly up to May in Great Britain and Ireland. Extra care is needed if planting in late spring and early summer; hollies planted in full growth may experience a check to growth due to the root disturbance involved, and there is a greater need to water in hot weather.

The soil in the planting pit should be thoroughly cultivated and broken down, incorporating well-rotted organic matter or other soil conditioners as required. If planting in an isolated situation, for example a lawn specimen, avoid the temptation to largely or completely replace the existing soil. On heavy soils an over-prepared planting hole may effectively turn into a sump, with water draining into it from the surrounding area. For long-term success it is important that new plants should establish under conditions which are representative of the general area. In isolated situations a good-sized planting hole of around 0.9M across is recommended, larger if the size of the container or rootball demands. On heavy soils the final level of planting should be slightly above the surrounding soil, a mound of around 50MM above existing soil level. This helps to ensure good drainage and aeration of the root zone while the plant establishes itself, and will gradually subside as the soil settles over time.

Prior to planting it is essential to ensure that plants are watered well, particularly with containerised plants in organic composts which may prove difficult to rewet once in the ground. Following thorough preparation of the planting hole (or area if a group of plants or a hedge is to be planted), container plants should be carefully checked to ensure that the roots are not circling around the container, or they may 'girdle' the plant as it grows. In order to be securely anchored, a plant requires its roots to grow away from the main stem in all directions. To ensure this, any circling roots should be teased out from the rootball so that they will grow away from the plant. Ensure that the backfill soil is in good contact with some of the main root system, as roots may be reluctant to leave the comfort and security of their original planting medium without some encouragement, especially when container-grown.

Hollies should always be planted with the 'neck' of the plant (the point where it emerges from the soil) at the same level as it was in the original container or rootball (not below). When backfilling, the soil should be well compacted so that the plant and its newly developing root system are firmly held; this will also help to ensure that the original planting level is maintained. Otherwise the soil level may sink and the plant end up below the surrounding soil level, leading to water collecting in the planting pit. Newly planted hollies must be firmly staked or they may suffer wind rock, which will be detrimental to rooting and establishment. Large transplants may require specialist staking techniques. Finally, water well and mulch with a layer of organic matter 5–10CM deep, the depth depending upon the size of the plant. This will help to retain moisture, control extremes of soil temperature, and suppress weeds.

Aftercare consists principally of ensuring that the plant is well watered when conditions demand, particularly in the first year after planting. Young and newly planted hollies will benefit from a yearly feed in spring with a high-nitrogen fertiliser mix (say at a ratio of 2:1:1 of nitrogen to phosphorous to potassium). Plants which are showing signs of yellowing foliage or are fruiting very heavily will benefit from a summer application of nitrogenous fertiliser at around half strength. Staked plants should be checked at least twice a year to ensure that the ties are not constricting growth.

Transplanting large or established hollies

Many gardeners may wish to move large or established plants in their gardens. Care must be taken to ensure that a good root system is moved with the plant, particularly with evergreens. The plant should be prepared around a year before moving by using a spade to trim the root system at the edge of the intended rootball, which will encourage branching of the roots close to the plant. Handling a heavy rootball and plant (particularly a spiny holly) can be challenging and is typically a specialist task that may need to be undertaken by a contractor with the correct equipment.

Transplanting is best done in autumn or early spring. Most plants will benefit from reducing the amount of foliage to restore the balance between the roots and shoots. Hollies can be cut back very hard (sometimes called hatracking; see the section on pruning, later in this chapter). A reduction of 30 to 50 percent in the leafy growth, while it seems severe, will assist in reestablishment. Using an anti-transpirant spray as sold for transplanted evergreens may also assist in reducing stress on the plants, as will wrapping autumn transplants against the desiccating effect of wind during frosty weather.

Hollies in containers

Many of the smaller hollies are ideal for growing in containers, and among the larger types there are a number that can be kept within bounds by pruning or trimming. They make excellent formal and informal specimens; smaller-growing cultivars of *Ilex crenata*, for example, can be used as a substitute for box, for any of its uses in containers. Hollies will thrive in all types and shapes of container: clay, stone, plastic and wood are all ideal, although the care of the plant will vary according to the type of container. Water requirement is the key variable: porous clay containers will usually dry out more rapidly than plastic, with stone and wood also being more moisture-retentive than clay.

The choice of growing medium for containers has been discussed earlier in this chapter, under soils and drainage. While loam-based composts are recommended for long-term cultivation in containers, loam-less organic composts are perfectly capable of growing good plants for a shorter period (certainly a year or two). They should contain sand to provide some weight in the container, especially if it is of lightweight plastic; large evergreen hollies in containers can be quite top-heavy and will tend to blow over.

Container-grown hollies require particular attention to feeding. There are numerous products on the market which are appropriate for hollies, and the choice will depend to a great degree upon the gardener's own preference. Slow-release formulations are particularly useful and will provide a steady supply of nutrients over the growing season. If a mid to late-season boost is required, soluble fertilisers or foliar feeds will be effective. A formulation with a high proportion of potash is appropriate for late-season feeds as it will assist in ripening growth and developing fruit and next year's fruiting wood.

One of the chief drawbacks of containers in cold regions is that they might freeze. Apart from the mechanical damage this might cause to the roots of the plant and the container, there is a danger that the plant will not be able to obtain the water it needs from its frozen root system to replace that lost to the cold, dry air; the foliage may then 'burn' or shrivel due to drought. If possible, containers should be moved into shelter, or the container and plant may be wrapped to protect them from the extremes of cold and the desiccating effects of wind.

Pruning and training

Pruning and training may be required for a number of reasons. The principal reason is to ensure a healthy, soundly structured and well-shaped plant. Health and sound structure are relatively easy to define: whether a plant is well shaped and pleasing to the eye is more subjective, and brings other considerations into play. These include the design of the garden, whether it is broadly formal or informal in style. The formal garden calls for neatly shaped or symmetrical plants, with clean well-trimmed lines, making an essentially architectural contribution to the scene. Trimming plants for hedging is discussed in Chapter 2. The informal or naturalistic style of gardening allows plants to grow more in accordance with their natural habit, although they may still require shaping. To make life more interesting, it is also possible to neatly trim plants into informal shapes.

Ilex ×aquipernyi 'Gable's Male', a plant of natural conical habit which has been enhanced by formative pruning every two years.

The other major consideration when pruning is the size of the garden; today's smaller plots often place limits upon the size of plants, making regular attention a necessity. Among the hollies there is a great range of natural plant habit and size that sees them fitted for all sizes and styles of gardening. When deciding which plants to use in the garden, the wisest course is to ensure that their natural habit of growth is as close as possible to the required shape and size. But this may be unrealistic; if a plant of a particular texture, leaf colour or fruiting habit is ideal but grows too large then the natural recourse of the gardener is to cut it to the desired shape and size. The most dramatic form of this is the technique known as hat-racking, where side branches are drastically reduced in early spring to the desired size and shape. Healthy plants will regrow surprisingly quickly.

Formative pruning is usually intended to assist the plant in developing according to its natural habit. Most hollies have a distinct and strong natural habit of growth, which (as long as the correct subject has been chosen for the shape required) should require only occasional attention to ensure the right result. Subjects with upright growth should possess a definite leading shoot when purchased. If they do not, or if the leader is lost for any reason, a strong shoot may be selected and trained (attached to a stake if necessary) to take over. If over-vigorous side shoots are produced, pinching out their growing tips or cutting them back into the plant will ensure that they do not unbalance the plant.

Weeping hollies will make height more rapidly if a strong shoot is trained up a stake; this will also lead to a more shapely plant developing over time. Low-growing mounded forms may occasionally revert to their ancestral type and throw a strong upright shoot, which should be cut out. Variegated forms may also throw occasional green shoots, which should be removed immediately to a point just below where they arose. Some variegated plants are unstable in that they will reverse their variegation, or throw 'ghost' shoots without any chlorophyll. The former might give rise to a new cultivar, and may be tolerated; the latter will typically 'brown off' at some stage, and should be removed.

If a plant requires a relatively minor reduction in size, say in order to fit into a particular area, this can often be achieved with minimal damage to the overall effect by regularly reducing the crown of the plant. This is achieved by cutting into the bush, reducing the longest growths while leaving the shorter shoots. The pruned branches will in due course reshoot and over time will take over from the shoots left behind as they grow out of scale. Judicious pruning into the plant can avoid the unfortunate appearance of a sheared area on an otherwise naturally shaped specimen.

If all else fails ... hat-racking a mature plant will bring it back within bounds.

Propagation

Most hollies are straightforward to propagate using the standard techniques available to all gardeners. The methods chosen will vary according to the species, hybrid or cultivar, particularly if the distinctive characteristics of a particular plant are to be retained in the progeny. The two principal categories of propagation used for hollies are sexual (from seed) and vegetative (from cuttings, grafting, budding, division and layering). Raising hollies from seed is relatively simple, but it must be noted that where cultivars or selections of garden origin are being propagated they are very unlikely to breed true from seed. The same may apply to open-pollinated species, which may have been fertilised by pollen brought by foraging bees from other hollies in the same garden or nearby (and with hollies that may mean within quite a wide range).

Seed propagation

As discussed in Chapter 1, the holly berry of tradition is more accurately described as a drupe, effectively a fleshy fruit which surrounds one or more pyrenes, consisting of a seed enclosed by a hard layer (or endocarp) which may be stony, woody or leathery, dependent upon the species. For our purposes many hollies may be regarded effectively as a scaled-down peach or cherry, i.e., something of a hard nut to crack, requiring patience of the propagator and taking up to two years or more to germinate. This delayed-action germination in the wild confers benefits in that there is a spread of emergence of seedlings, and thus any year's seed production will not all be prey to any of the vicissitudes of nature that may await them, such as late frosts or drought. Hard endocarps and correspondingly slow germination over a period of twelve to twenty-four months are found in evergreen and deciduous species alike, including the horticulturally important *Ilex aquifolium*, *I. cornuta*, *I. opaca*, *I. decidua*, *I. verticillata* and *I. serrata*. Softer endocarps result in typically swifter germination (around six months), and are characteristic of *I. cassine*, *I. crenata* and *I. glabra*.

Successful propagation from seed requires proper handling of the fruits. They should be collected in the autumn as soon as they ripen, and not allowed to dry out (as that may reinforce any natural dormancy and delay germination). The fleshy pulp should immediately be removed. This is most easily achieved by macerating, crushing or abrading the fruits and then soaking them in water for a number of days, after which the pulp should wash off quite easily in a sieve. Living holly seeds should sink in water; any that float are not viable and should be discarded.

Once the cleaned seed has been prepared it should be dealt with immediately, either sown straight away or, in the case of those hard endocarp species which take longer to germinate, it may be stratified prior to sowing. Stratification is a useful procedure, a method of pre-preparing seed to break its natural dormancy by storing it for a period under cold or warm conditions. A method of stratification that has been used commercially for *Ilex opaca*, *I. aquifolium* and *I. cornuta* is to collect and clean the seed as soon as it ripens. It is then stored in a closed container at a temperature of 4C until spring, in a mixture of equal parts of moist sand and peat, before sowing in its final situation. While this process may assist with the more recalcitrant species, all holly seed can be sown immediately after harvesting, with the caveat that the germination of some species may be slow or patchy.

Most gardeners will wish to raise only a small number of plants from seed. The simplest method for small-scale production is to sow in a container, either a pot or seed tray, using commercial seed compost or a free-draining mixture such as two parts peat to one part of sand or perlite. The seed should be thinly distributed over the surface of the container, lightly covered and watered in. With seed that may take a season or more to germinate a thin layer of sharp gritty sand on the top of the compost is useful for reducing the growth of liverworts and mosses, which may choke young seedlings.

The finished container should be labelled and placed in a sheltered, shady place to await germination. It is important that the seed be kept in even, cool conditions; ideal situations may include a shaded area in an unheated greenhouse, or a shaded cold frame or cool spot by a building. It will be necessary to protect the containers from animals; fine-mesh chicken wire is the most useful material, particularly for keeping out rodents.

Containers will need to be checked occasionally to ensure that they have not dried out, especially as spring approaches and germination gets under way. Seed can also be sown outdoors in prepared seedbeds, either broadcast or in shallow drills, and should be lightly covered. This method is particularly appropriate where larger quantities of plants are required: apart from the scale of the operation the same rules apply as when sowing in containers.

Containers need to be checked more regularly when warmer conditions get the process of germination under way. If sown reasonably thinly, seedlings may be left in the container for their first season of growth, or they may be carefully transplanted when large enough to handle. This also applies to seedlings sown in the open ground.

Vegetative propagation

The most important method of vegetative propagation for most holly growers is cuttings. Layering (partially cutting through a stem while it is still attached to the mother plant) is a useful procedure where plants are difficult from cuttings, or only the odd plant is required. Division is used for a very small number of species such as *Ilex glabra*. Grafting and budding, i.e., attaching a stem or bud (the scion) of the plant to be propagated to another plant (the rootstock), were used widely in Britain a century or more ago for propagating variegated forms of English holly cultivars, or to bulk up rare new varieties. While not generally used now, these techniques still have their place for multiplying rare cultivars or for the initial propagation of bud sports, such as the variegated *I. opaca* 'Steward's Silver Crown'.

Classically, grafting or budding usually involved the union of cultivars of a species onto rootstocks of the same species. This can confer some of the characteristics of the rootstock onto the scion, and is used for giving both increased vigour and for dwarfing of many fruit tree crops. In the USA grafting has also been used to confer a degree of climate tolerance by taking advantage of the characteristics of the rootstock species, for example by using *Ilex cornuta* rootstocks to impart tolerance of high soil temperatures to *I. aquifolium* cultivars in hot areas. Although most gardeners will not need to resort to grafting or budding to propagate their plants, a commonly used method of grafting appropriate for hollies is described later in this chapter.

Propagation by cuttings

This is the best and most widely used method of propagation for a wide range of holly species, hybrids and cultivars. While hollies are broadly very amenable to this method of propagation, not all will root easily; the shy-rooters may be cultivars or forms of otherwise more readily propagated species. Sometimes entire species may be difficult to root; *Ilex decidua*, for example, is not that easy, and its cultivar 'Byers Golden' stands out as being particularly difficult. Other examples include the highly desirable *I. purpurea* and *I. rotunda*, a circumstance that goes some way to explaining why these superb plants remain rare in cultivation. However, given that a prerequisite for commercial success for most plants (to which hollies are no exception) is that they should be reasonably easy to propagate, then it should come as no surprise that the ever-obliging holly largely fulfils this important criterion.

Evergreen hollies

Evergreen hollies are most commonly propagated by cuttings taken from the current season's growth as they begin to become firm and woody. These semi-ripe (or semi-hardwood) tip cuttings are available from mid to late summer, depending upon the plant and where it is being grown (with growth starting later in cooler climates). If that opportunity is missed it is well worth trying ripewood cuttings taken later into the autumn and early winter. However, cuttings that are taken during the summer stand the best chance of being well established and therefore well prepared for their next season's growth.

Cuttings should always be taken from healthy new growth that is typical of the plant, using sharp and clean tools, with the cut made just below a node on the stem (the point from where a leaf or bud arises). For semi-ripe cuttings, the tip of the shoot will be soft, while the base will have become firm and woody. The length of the cutting will vary widely according to the plant being propagated. The diminutive growths of miniature *Ilex crenata* cultivars are at one extreme, and it may prove necessary with the smallest of these to cut into two-year-old growth to obtain a cutting that can be easily handled. This problem is unlikely when taking cuttings of the husky young shoots of *I.* ×*koehneana* cultivars, at the other extreme of size and vigour. Where good upright growth is immediately required of the young plant, it may be best to propagate from this type of growth rather than a horizontal side shoot, although most holly propagations quite rapidly sort themselves out to produce growth typical of the parent.

Cuttings are best taken in the morning so that they are fully charged with water, and should be kept in a humid enclosed space (a plastic bag is ideal) while awaiting preparation. If they have wilted they will rapidly firm up if some water is shaken around in the bag to raise the humidity inside; if they cannot be prepared for some time they can be safely stored in a domestic refrigerator in a container that seals in moisture. Holly cuttings are prepared by stripping the leaves from the bottom third to half of their length. An optional (but worthwhile) procedure with large-leaved species and forms, such as the largest *Ilex* ×*altaclerensis* cultivars or *I. latifolia* and its hybrids, is to reduce their leaves by a third to a half in length, cutting down on stress through water loss (and handily providing more space in the propagation area).

Roots are usually produced at the point where the cambium of the cutting (a thin layer of tissue immediately below the bark) is exposed. Rooting occurs as the cambium produces callus tissue to heal the cuts from propagation. This typically occurs at the cutting's base and the points from where the leaves have been stripped. For best rooting response, this area of exposed cambium (and thus the area of callus production) should be increased by deliberately 'wounding' the base of the cutting, using a knife to remove a small sliver of bark to expose the white wood within. This wounding cut can be made once or twice, and although its length will be constrained by the length of the cutting, it usually should not exceed 25MM.

Before inserting the cuttings into their rooting medium, they should be dipped in a hormone rooting compound. These products are commercially available (either as a powder or solution) and consist of IBA (indolebutyric acid), sometimes in combination with NAA (naphthalene acetic acid); choose a product which says that it has been formulated for semi-ripe or ripewood cuttings, as appropriate. After dipping, the cuttings should be inserted into free-draining open-textured compost to the level of the lowest leaves. The makeup of these propagating composts varies from grower to grower, but typically is no more than two-thirds organic matter, such as peat, and around one-third of sharp gritty sand or perlite, although for the purposes of putting roots on cuttings, a mix of 1:1 peat and sand or perlite is very effective. Seed trays or pots are perfectly appropriate containers for cuttings. Relatively shallow containers are best; this ensures there is not a large volume of unused compost to hold excessive moisture, which may lead to rots or disease. After insertion, water lightly to settle the compost around the base of the cuttings.

Humidity is very important to evergreen cuttings; if the leaves are losing water through transpiration that cannot be replaced due to their temporary lack of roots, then the cuttings will fail. Many commercial growers use sophisticated mist bench systems to provide constant high humidity around the cuttings. A closed-case system is equally effective, using a home propagator with a plastic lid, or closed and shaded outdoor frames. Closed systems require regular attention; check to pick off dead leaves and remove failed cuttings so that fungal rots do not set in. Bottom heat can be very useful in encouraging rooting with semi-ripe and hardwood cuttings. Various products are available to provide a temperature of 21–24C at the base of the cutting.

Depending upon the species, cultivar and time of year, evergreen hollies may take from around four to twelve weeks to root. Once they are well rooted, young cuttings can be moved on into a more nutritious growing medium in small individual containers, or they may be spaced out in seed trays or planted in rows in the greenhouse or outside frames. They should be carefully hardened-off from the conditions under which they have been propagated to the conditions of the outside world. Protection from extreme conditions, particularly hard frost, is essential until the year after propagation.

Deciduous hollies

The three principal species of deciduous holly break down into two distinct groups. *Ilex verticillata* and *I. serrata* (and their hybrids) are relatively straightforward to grow from cuttings; *I. decidua*, however, may prove to be more challenging.

The general rule for most deciduous hollies is to propagate from softwood cuttings, typically taken in early summer (usually June and July). The typical softwood cutting consists of the tip of a shoot and the first three to five pairs of leaves (six to ten leaves in all, with the alternate-leaved growths of hollies). The new shoots of vigorous deciduous hollies may be up to 60CM long and may, if desired, be cut into sections to yield two or more cuttings per shoot. The sections should be around 15CM long, cut just below a leaf-node, with the lower leaves removed (exactly as with evergreen cuttings). The cutting should then be wounded, dipped in hormone rooting compound, and inserted into cutting compost before being placed under mist or in closed-case conditions.

Rooting will take around six weeks, and plants can be moved on into beds, trays or individual containers for the rest of the season. Winter protection is advised for young plants, which may be potted on or lined out and grown normally the following season.

The treatment just described, while generally successful, may not prove to be so for some *Ilex decidua* forms, in particular the cultivar 'Byers Golden'. Fred Galle reports a method devised by Bon Hartline of Illinois, using ripewood cuttings taken after the first frost of autumn. New growths 20–25CM long are taken, stripped of their leaves and wounded before being treated with hardwood hormone rooting compound and inserted into peat and perlite compost in plastic-covered beds in a greenhouse, with bottom heat of 20–24C. Rooted plants are moved on into containers in spring.

Propagation by layering

Layering is an ancient and very simple method of propagating hollies. The usual method is to select young, pliable shoots that are close to the ground (up to three- or four-year-old growths are perfectly appropriate). They are wounded by cutting part way through in spring or early summer; hormone rooting compound may be applied before they are pegged down securely and shallowly into the soil or into a container with cutting compost, and then left to develop roots. The plant's rooting response is exactly the same as that from cuttings: the exposed cambium develops callus to heal the wound, from which roots emerge.

If stems cannot be bent down to the soil, air layering may be used. This is essentially the same technique, best carried out in late spring or early summer. The 'tongue' produced by the cut is packed with and surrounded by a moist inert material (for example sphagnum moss), into which the wounded stem will root. It is then enclosed in a waterproof sleeve (for example, polythene), 15–20CM long, which is securely tied at both ends. It may take up to twelve weeks or more to root before the layer is ready to remove and grow on. Layering can produce substantial young plants of 35CM or more.

Propagation by division

Division is used only rarely with hollies, but may be appropriate for spreading species such as *Ilex glabra* and for some others that occasionally develop growths from their root systems. Division is best carried out in autumn or early spring. With *I. glabra*, division will be most successful with young plants, which are small enough for the entire plant and its root system to be split into a number of well-rooted pieces. Small pieces can also be removed from mature plants with as much of their root system as can be readily taken. Divisions will need to have their stems cut back by around 50 percent to keep them in balance with their diminished roots. Aftercare may consist of direct planting into well-prepared ground for divisions of young plants, or they may be placed in containers of an open well-drained compost to encourage rooting, either in a greenhouse or frame.

Spontaneous shoots, often called suckers, may arise from around the main stems of a number of species, sometimes as a means of colonising new ground; one such is *Ilex decidua*. These shoots may be dug up while the plant is dormant, with as long a section of root as possible attached. The stems should then be cut back by half, after which they may be planted or potted to await the growth of new shoots and leaves in due course.

Propagation by grafting

Propagating woody plants by grafting is a highly skilled operation. Before trying this on hollies, or any other plants, those who wish to use these methods are advised to refer to specialist practical propagation manuals for detailed information, and to be prepared to practice for some time to refine their technique (before trying it out on important plants!).

Hollies (in common with most other plants) are usually grafted onto rootstocks of the same species. However, there is a marked degree of compatibility between some of the most important evergreen species and cultivars. For example *Ilex aquifolium* and *I.* ×*altaclerensis* can be propagated by grafting onto rootstocks of the cultivar *I.* 'Nellie R. Stevens' (primarily to provide a degree of heat tolerance to English hollies). Other species that have been used for grafting English hollies include *I. cornuta* and *I. opaca*. *Ilex cornuta* (in this instance 'Burfordii') has also been successfully used as a commercial rootstock for *I. opaca*.

Grafting and budding are usually carried out in autumn and winter in a greenhouse. There are numerous techniques for different plants and situations. A commonly used method for broad-leaved evergreens such as hollies is the side graft. For ease of handling use container-grown young stock plants, seedlings or cuttings, 6–9MM in diameter; the closer the rootstock is in size to the width of the scion the better. A shallow cut around 2.5CM long is made into the side of the stem near to the base of the rootstock, to a depth of about a quarter of its thickness, exposing the wood and the cambium layer, and the sliver of cut tissue is removed with a second cut at its base. A cut of a similar size is made on the scion to expose the cambium over a similar area. A refinement of this method is to make a small secondary cut into both the stock and the scion, which will create a small 'tongue' in each, allowing a greater area of cambium to be exposed and joined when the two are brought together. The stock and scion are then fitted together, with the 'tongues' interlocking and the exposed cambium layers matching as closely as possible, at least along one side of the union. The area of the graft union is then bound with waxed string or rubber strip to hold the two pieces together and to protect the union.

Aftercare of newly grafted plants consists of placing them in close and humid conditions while the union heals. This may be a covered section of greenhouse bench, or an individual graft may be contained in a plastic bag. The plants cannot be hardened off until the scion is in growth; the top section of the stock should not be removed until the graft union has healed and the scion has started into growth.

Pests, Diseases and Disorders

Hollies are generally of robust constitution, with relatively few major pest and disease problems when well grown. For the most part their pests and diseases are 'the usual suspects', common problems which they share with many other widely cultivated plants; the number of pathogens and ailments specific to hollies is relatively small. Most holly problems are unlikely to be fatal; they may often be of nuisance value only, doing aesthetic damage rather than threatening the life of the plant. Gardeners in North America face a greater number of potential problems than those in Britain and Europe; this reflects the wider range of pests and diseases (and more extreme weather conditions) that may occur there. Pests are more likely to present problems than diseases.

Disorders of hollies are often the manifestation of something lacking in their cultivation. Poor or incorrect soil conditions, unbalanced feeding regimes, drought, heat, excess light or shade—all have their own characteristic symptoms which should be considered as potential causes of poor growth along with pathogens.

Diagnosis and control

Most pests and diseases of hollies can be fairly easily diagnosed from their symptoms. Sometimes the causal organism may still be there, but with some being very small, careful checking with a hand lens and a reference book may be required to unmask the culprit. If the problem cannot readily be identified there are a number of advisory bodies, for example, government agencies in the USA, the Royal Horticultural Society in the UK, specialist pest control companies, or the friendly local nursery or garden centre, whose expertise may be called upon.

Having identified the problem the next question will be how and whether to control it. Before recourse to the chemical store, several questions need to be asked. Is the problem sufficiently bad that control is required? It may be that no control is needed. The problem may cause only sporadic damage, or may be a one-off—a chance occurrence where a combination of circumstances or conditions gives a pathogen an opportunity to thrive, but which are unlikely to occur again.

The vexed question of whether to use pesticides or other chemical control measures will also arise. The accepted wisdom is to look at all the options and select that which will have the least environmental impact. The modern approach to pest and disease control (integrated pest management) attempts to blend a number of methods. Initially ensure that the plant is growing well, remembering that plants at the edge of their range or under stress will be more susceptible to pests and diseases. Then check whether barrier or mechanical methods of control may be appropriate, or choosing pathogenic organisms rather than pesticides. Where chemicals must be used it is imperative to choose those that are as benign as possible, targeted specifically at the problem. This has replaced the broad-brush 'shoot-'em-up' approach that characterised the early days of horticultural chemicals, when their side effects were not well understood.

It is not possible to give specific recommendations for chemical control of pests and diseases. The substances and formulations allowed vary from country to country and even from state to state, and regulations are in constant flux. Up-to-date advice should be sought from a local agency or organisation.

Pests

The animal pests of hollies range greatly in size, with deer at one extreme through rabbits and voles and on to a variety of insects, including beetles, aphids, scale insects; at the smallest end of the range are the microscopic mites, whose eight legs place them in the same group as the spiders. A small number of insect and mites are specific to hollies; their damage is usually easy to recognise and diagnose. Most of the pests of hollies are shared with many other ornamental plants.

Deer and larger animals

Much as we may enjoy a garden environment rich in wildlife of all kinds, some of these uninvited guests can have a devastating effect on our cherished plants. Despite many millennia of evolution, the spines and leathery leaves of many hollies may present little deterrent to many herbivorous pests, especially in winter when greenery is at a premium.

Deer are a problem across much of the range of cultivated hollies. Populations of native and introduced species have tended to rise, especially on the fringes of cities, where the mixture of large gardens, parks, nature reserves and other open spaces provide ideal habitat. Deer damage is easy to diagnose as they often leave a characteristic browse-line, denuding the plant of the foliage they can reach at lower levels, and leaving the bare twigs and stems. Older plants will usually recover from a single attack, although their growth may be seriously affected; young plants may be killed outright.

Complete control of deer can only be achieved by barriers, which need to be at least 2.4M high to keep out the majority of deer. This is more difficult to achieve in countries where traditionally gardens are not rigorously separated from one another, as in much of the USA, whereas in the UK gardeners usually enclose their plots. There are many different ways to create effective barriers; the choice will be made on aesthetic or cost grounds. In some cases electric fences may be appropriate, but these have other health and safety considerations to bear in mind, especially where the public or children have access. Fences should create an effective barrier to ground level, or smaller deer may squeeze underneath them. In the UK the introduced muntjac deer from China, which is the size of a small dog, can make its way through very small gaps, and has the potential to be a difficult pest to control.

Deer repellents may be effective, but the product to use depends to some degree upon the conditions in the area (contact repellents may be washed off of the leaves in areas of high rainfall, for example). It is a good idea to seek advice upon what works locally from other gardeners or suppliers. Reducing the deer population by shooting may be an effective measure, especially in the short-term. There are companies that specialise in vermin control, or local government agencies may be able to advise further.

Rodents

Rodent damage is mainly caused by rabbits, hares, voles, and in some parts of North America woodchucks, gophers and others. They may eat leaves and young stems, or more damagingly they may attack the bark of young stems, sometimes completely girdling them, gravely disfiguring or killing the plant. Barrier guards of wire or plastic mesh will keep most rodents out, although in North America they need to be buried 10–15CM deep to stop voles from burrowing beneath. Stems may be protected by a number of proprietary products, usually plastic, although Hessian or cloth wrapping will also provide a good barrier.

There are numerous ways of reducing the numbers of rodents—how effective they are in the long term is graphically demonstrated by how common a pest they remain! Hunting, trapping, and (for voles) toxic baits may be used. Further advice should be sought on the best legal methods available in any area.

Leaf miners

These are the most recognisable pests of hollies, both deciduous and evergreen, with species in both the Old and New Worlds. The characteristic damage of blotches and tunnels (the 'mines') immediately beneath the leaf surface is caused by the small legless maggot-like larvae eating the green tissue while remaining snugly protected beneath the typically thick external layer of the leaf. The damage is typically sporadic where hollies are grown in a mixed garden, but can be sufficiently severe to cause major disfigurement and premature leaf fall, particularly where many hollies are grown together.

The original species of nuisance to holly growers is the European (or English) holly leaf miner, *Phytomyza ilicis*, which is usually found on its historic host, *Ilex aquifolium*, over much of the natural range of its host. Like so many pests and diseases of garden plants it has hitchhiked on the common holly to many of the places where it is grown as an ornamental plant, and in North America is found in the cool, moist Pacific Northwest as far north as British Columbia.

Phytomyza ilicis has a transatlantic cousin, *P. ilicicol*, the American holly leaf miner, whose taste, as might be expected, usually runs only to the American holly, *Ilex opaca*, where it has the potential to be quite damaging through the creation of large and unsightly mines and blotches. Another American species, *P. opacae*, creates only narrow linear mines. It may be found on both *I. aquifolium* and *I. opaca*, anywhere from New Jersey south to Florida, but is not as severe in its damage. The inkberry, *I. glabra*, has a leaf miner all to itself, *P. glabricola*, seemingly found only toward the north of its host's distribution from New Jersey northward and west into Ohio. Another obligate relationship is found between the yaupon (*I. vomitoria*) and its own leaf miner, *P. vomitoria*, reported from Georgia, Florida and California.

Deciduous hollies have their own suite of leaf miners, although they are of more local distribution. *Phytomyza verticillatae*, as its name indicates, is a pest of the winterberry, *Ilex verticillata*. It makes blotchy linear mines on both sides of the leaf, and is found in Maryland, District of Columbia and Florida. The deciduous holly leaf miner, *P. ditmani*, affects *I. decidua* and *I. serrata*, with the irregular blotches on the upper side of the leaf; it is very restricted in distribution, to the District of Columbia only.

Holly berry midge

This is a potentially disfiguring pest of *Ilex opaca* and its cultivars on the East Coast of the USA from North Carolina to Connecticut. As its name would suggest, the problem it causes is restricted to female plants. The midge's life cycle revolves around the fruits, female midges laying their eggs in them while they are very young (while flowers are still present). The larvae then feed upon the developing fruit, which does not turn red, staying green throughout the season. Young midges emerge from the green fruits at flowering time to continue the cycle. In very severe infestations the majority of the fruits on a plant will be affected.

Control on smaller plants which are not severely affected can be by picking and destroying affected fruits in the autumn. Advice should be sought as to the correct pesticide which is cleared to use for this pest. Sprays are applied as the flowering period comes to an end. Spraying may also affect benign insects such as bees, and should be timed to avoid periods when they are active around the flowers.

Scale insects

There are many species of scale insect that attack a wide range of ornamental plants. Some are very catholic in their taste, and have become major horticultural pests, occurring on many different plants; others may be more specific in their hosts. All share an essential characteristic in that they have a mobile young stage (the 'crawler'), which typically emerges from beneath the shell of the female scale in the spring, and soon settles down to develop into the hard- or soft-bodied adult scale in a wide range of shapes, colours and sizes. Sometimes the first overt symptom of scale insect attack is the appearance of black 'sooty mould', a fungus which grows on the sweet honeydew secreted by the adult scales. This may be very disfiguring, but represents no particular threat to the health of the plant.

Control of scale insects is quite straightforward, especially if they are dealt with at the 'crawler' stage. Regular weekly sprays with a pesticide for a period of a month or so at this stage will be very effective. The major problem with scale insects occurs on very large plants, where access to the pest may be difficult. Professional pest control companies may be called to deal with larger plants.

Other insects

Aphids (blackfly or greenfly) feed on the young shoots of many plants, and may be found on hollies. In the USA they are reported on a range of species including *Ilex verticillata*, *I. cornuta*, *I. opaca*, and *I. aquifolium*. They are typically not a major pest, but can affect young growths by their feeding and if present in great numbers should be controlled.

A number of caterpillars feed on hollies in North America. The larvae of the holly bud moth feed communally in web 'tents' on young stems of *Ilex verticillata* and is a pest of *I. aquifolium* in the Pacific Northwest. The holly looper feeds on the leaves of *I. opaca* in the Southeast, but will also attack *I. aquifolium* and *I. cornuta*. Tortrix moth larvae may also be found on hollies, with their characteristic rolled-leaf chambers at the ends of shoots in which the larvae feed on young leaves. In light infestations on smaller plants these pests can be controlled by picking off and destroying the affected shoots.

Weevils are another widespread pest of ornamental plants that include hollies in their diet. The black vine weevil is a common pest in Europe and in both the Northwest and Northeast of the USA. In nurseries the legless larvae can kill plants in containers by feeding on their roots. The nocturnal adults, which are around 10MM long, give themselves away with their feeding damage, a characteristic notching of the edges of mature leaves, often at low level. This pest may be successfully controlled by nematodes (eelworm), which attack the larvae. Other weevils include the two-banded Japanese weevil, which attacks both *Ilex crenata* and *I. aquifolium* in the eastern USA. The larvae again feed on roots, while the adults attack new stems and leaves. A number of other weevil species may also attack holly.

Mites

Mite attack upon hollies in gardens is a particular problem in areas with warmer summers. It is scarcely known in the British Isles, although the red spider mite could potentially attack plants grown against hot sunny walls or in greenhouses. In the USA the southern red mite, *Oligonychus ilicis*, as its name would imply, is a particular pest of hollies in the eastern states, and is also reported from California. These mites feed by sucking the plant sap from the underside of the leaves. In severe attacks the population of mites may become so large that their feeding may cause the leaves to become pale and discoloured, eventually grey-brown, and to be shed prematurely. Many hollies may be attacked by this mite, with severe damage reported upon *Ilex crenata* 'Convexa'. A careful watch should be kept for mite damage from this species in spring and autumn.

A number of other mite species may attack hollies. They are typically widespread pests of ornamental plants, causing broadly similar damage. Control of mites may require a regular spraying programme, although some relief may come from avoiding species or cultivars that are particularly susceptible in the locality. If in doubt as to the cause of the damage that looks like the work of mites or how to control them, contact the local advisory service.

Diseases

Holly diseases are for the most part of less importance than pests. Their occurrence and severity often go hand-in-hand with disorders caused by poor growing conditions. They may also occur far more under certain climatic conditions. Fungi, for example, often thrive in humid and wet seasons. Many fungal diseases overwinter on dead leaves or twigs, and good hygiene can greatly reduce their incidence by removing the source of new infections. As with diseases of people, the susceptibility of hollies to disease can be worsened by other causes, and may be controlled by alleviating those. Selection of resistant species and cultivars may also be an effective method of avoiding a number of diseases.

Leaf and twig diseases

These conditions take the form of leaf spots and blights which may affect leaves and twigs. There are several holly leaf spot diseases. Among the most important are the tar spot conditions (mainly *Phacidium* species) which affect a range of deciduous and evergreen American holly species. They give rise to small yellow leaf spots early in the summer, which may turn to reddish brown. Small tar-like spots then occur in the infected areas. Good hygiene is important to reducing the incidence of tar spot disease. Another common leaf spot disease, particularly in the Gulf States, is *Phyllosticta ilicis*. Yellow-white spots with red borders appear on the upper side of the leaf, and may grow together to cover the entire leaf blade. It is reported on the horticulturally important species *Ilex aquifolium*, *I. opaca*, *I. crenata*, *I. cornuta* and *I. verticillata*. Plants under stress are more susceptible, so good nutrition and adequate water, together with good hygiene, are important aspects of control; fungicide sprays may also provide some control. Other leaf spots that affect hollies may be controlled by using similar techniques.

Of the blights which might affect hollies the fungal phytophthora blight of holly (*Phytophthora ilicis*) is a potentially serious condition that has become of more importance in recent years. The Royal Horticultural Society (2004) has been undertaking research into *P. ilicis* (see Bibliography). It was reported in the Pacific Northwest from the 1930s (although the cause was unknown) and more recently from Holland and Britain. It has occurred mainly on *Ilex aquifolium*, *I. ×altaclerensis* and *I. crenata*, but has been found in the USA to occur on *I. bioritsensis* (syn. *I. pernyi* var. *veitchii*), *I. colchica* and clones of *I. opaca*. The main symptom is leaf blotching, which can lead to defoliation; it can also kill the bark of twigs and young stems.

The leaf blotches develop in autumn and winter; infected leaves eventually fall and turn black. The defoliation spreads from the lowest leaves upward over the winter; on hedges it creates a characteristic wedge-shaped leafless area. Black patches then develop on twigs and young stems, often girdling them. Fruits may also be affected. It is thought to spread from spores carried in water splash from infected leaves or lesions, and may be found in the top layer of the soil. Unsurprisingly, outbreaks of the disease often follow cool, moist conditions.

The first rule of control is not to introduce the disease in the first place, so care must be taken to ensure that only healthy stock is bought into the garden. If the disease strikes, control depends on good hygiene, clearing away fallen leaves and cutting back stems to uninfected tissue to remove potential sources of infection. Removal of mulch and topsoil local to the infected plant may reduce reinfection from spores. Preventative fungicidal sprays that give good control are available to professional growers, but not necessarily to amateur gardeners under local pesticide use regulations. Research in the USA has indicated that the following hollies demonstrate resistance to the disease: *Ilex cassine*, *I. ciliospinosa*, *I. crenata* 'Convexa', 'Hetzii' and var. *paludosa*, *I. glabra*, *I. latifolia*, *I. perado*, *I. pernyi*, *I. sugerokii* and *I. vomitoria*.

Various other twig and leaf blights and cankers are reported in the literature, often as conditions of cultivated plants under stress, sometimes in nursery conditions. A bacterial leaf and twig blight, *Corynebacterium ilicis*, affects some cultivars of *I. opaca*, killing twigs, which take on a scorched appearance. Heavy use of fertiliser is implicated in this condition.

Root diseases

Root diseases may be caused by pathogens, mainly fungi, taking advantage of poor conditions in the garden or in containers. They may be introduced into the garden with plants purchased in nurseries, but typically are more damaging in propagation units and in container cultivation. They mainly occur in poorly drained and aerated growing media, and will affect all hollies as they can occur on a wide range of ornamental woody plants. Control is through providing the correct conditions around the plant and in growing media, and good hygiene practices.

Disorders

Disorders of many ornamental plants may mimic diseases, and arise from a wide range of causes including poor nutrition, drought, excessive wet, severe cold and heat, sun scorch, mechanical damage to the plant, or just general lack of vigour. It follows that to control them one should simply grow the right plant in the right place under perfect growing conditions, a counsel of perfection if ever there was one. Until that horticultural state of grace is arrived at, the following descriptions of the more common disorders may help. Gardeners should also bear in mind that there is no such thing as a normal growing season. Nature's little surprises such as the early arrival of intense heat or cold when plants are unprepared can cause significant damage to plants which are otherwise perfectly hardy, and should be viewed as a one-off.

Most disorders manifest themselves through the foliage. Scorching or browning on the upper surface or at the margins can be caused by excessive sun or cold, typically on the part of the plant exposed to the most extreme weather conditions. The combination of severe cold, drying winds and winter sunshine can be too much for a number of otherwise hardy hollies. The damage is usually merely aesthetic, although under the most extreme winter conditions parts of the plant, or even the whole plant, may be defoliated. This is far more of a problem in areas with cold continental winters. If in doubt as to the hardiness of a particular plant it should be planted in a sheltered position. Smaller plants may be protected from intense cold by wrapping. Hollies grown near to the sea may show some salt-burn on the foliage, particularly if exposed to salt-laden gales when the foliage is soft and young.

Drought can cause leaf browning and premature leaf drop; this typically affects the whole plant, and may begin with the plant losing its older leaves prematurely. It is a particular problem with newly planted hollies. The converse of drought damage is oedema, the development of small warty spots on the lower leaf surface, a rare condition in gardens but symptomatic of excessive wet, found more often on container-grown plants. No control other than adjusting the watering regime is necessary. Prolonged periods of excess water at the roots can lead to defoliation and the death of susceptible plants, although many hollies naturally occur in wet habitats and exhibit a high tolerance of waterlogging.

Nutritional deficiencies, in particular of nitrogen, may be manifested in summer, especially on plants which are bearing a heavy crop of fruit. This will typically lead to a yellowing of the leaves. If plants are not doing well generally, a soil test to determine its nutritional status is called for.

Sudden die-back or steady decline can affect many plants, sometimes with no readily identifiable cause. It is particularly prevalent where plants are being grown at the edge of their comfortable range, as in the southern USA, where the Japanese holly (*Ilex crenata*) is affected; according to Patricia Joseph (1995), '*Japanese holly die-back … occurs especially if you have a row of large, beautiful plants, and losing one ruins everything*'. Her solution was to substitute the tough and resilient yaupon where appropriate.

Directory of Plants

A large group of plants such as the hollies presents a formidable challenge to the compiler of a representative selection, such is the wealth of species, hybrids and cultivars that may be grown in our gardens. Hollies have been well served by a number of gifted growers and hybridisers, many of whom have made the development of this valuable genus an important part of their life's work. An idea of the scale of the challenge involved in arriving at the final list of plants presented here can be obtained from the fact that there are well over two thousand named holly cultivars. Alongside this wealth of existing plants new hybrids and cultivars are regularly being introduced.

Such a large number of names in any major plant group reflects the interest and enthusiasm of generations of gardeners, nurserymen and hybridisers, all applying names to plants which they consider worthy of recognition. It may be argued that the interest of growers over the years has led to there being a greater number of names than there are truly distinctive plants, particularly in the largest cultivar groups. This hypothesis is difficult to check, however, as many named cultivars have been lost from cultivation, or can no longer be found as plants with a recorded history and definite provenance; we cannot compare them with new introductions.

Bringing order to the previously anarchic naming of cultivars is the job of the International Cultivar Registration Authorities (ICRAs) for various plant groups. The Holly Society of America (HSA), an organisation of amateur and professional holly enthusiasts begun in 1947, has carried out this role for the genus *Ilex* since 1958 (for ten years prior to that, a committee of the American Association of Nurserymen registered cultivated holly names). The registration authority exists to ensure that when a name is assigned to a cultivated plant it is in the correct format and has not previously been used for another plant, and that a description of the plant is lodged at the time of registration. This ensures that cultivar names are valid and protected, and over time creates a valuable record of holly introductions.

The selection of plants featured here is founded upon a mixture of personal experience combined with that of holly experts past and present. A wealth of information is available to help guide the process of choosing which plants to include. Major British and European sources used in compiling this Directory include the writings of holly specialists of the 19th and early 20th centuries, such as Thomas Moore in *The Gardeners' Chronicle* (1874–76) and William Dallimore, author of *Holly, Yew and Box* (1908). To these may be added the observations in major reference works on woody plants, including Bean's *Trees and Shrubs Hardy in the British Isles*, one of the most comprehensive accounts of woody plants for temperate regions, and *The Hillier Manual of Trees and Shrubs*, produced originally by Hillier Nurseries; a wide-ranging European perspective on the genus can be found in Krüssmann's *Manual of Cultivated Broad-leaved Trees and Shrubs*. See the Bibliography for more details.

American holly experts have created a formidable body of holly literature. The 1950s saw the publication of two major works, with H. Harold Hume's *Hollies* (1953) followed by the collaborative effort, the 'Handbook of hollies' (1957). The latter boasted a remarkable cast of authors, including Harry William Dengler, Shiu-Ying Hu (botanist and expert on hollies of the Far East), John Creech, William Kosar and Fred C. Galle. Galle made a monumental contribution to holly literature in his work *Hollies: The Genus Ilex* (1997). Other prolific holly writers include Dr. Theodore R. Dudley and Gene K. Eisenbeiss of the US National Arboretum. Research upon both species and hybrid hollies continues with major contributions from experts such as Susyn Andrews, one of the world's premier holly taxonomists.

Among other major American references the *Holly Society Journal*, published quarterly by the HSA stands out as an invaluable record, including horticultural and historical information and reports upon the latest holly research. The HSA has also supported and published a series of publications on hollies and their cultivation, and were associated with the publication of Fred Galle's magnum opus. All these and numerous other publications distil many years of experience and knowledge of hollies across much of the temperate world. As well as holly aficionados the views of Michael Dirr and other noted plantsmen have also been consulted, including such recent works of great practical value as *Dirr's Hardy Trees and Shrubs* (1997) and *Dirr's Trees and Shrubs for Warm Climates* (2002).

While they are not the ultimate arbiters of the quality and desirability of any plant, availability in the trade and longevity in cultivation are valuable indicators. The selection of plants featured here has taken these into account. A number of references on plants grown in nurseries and garden centres in Europe, North America and Australasia have also been consulted to ensure that most of the plants listed here can be obtained by gardeners. They include the excellent *RHS Plant Finder*, published annually in Britain by the Royal Horticultural Society, and similar listings where available from Europe and North America, including the HSA's invaluable *Sources for Unusual Hollies*. Nursery lists from many countries have also been consulted to confirm that plants are available in the trade. Of course, most nurseries and garden centres can hold only a small proportion of the range of hollies described here; many of them may have to be sought out from specialist suppliers, a number of which are listed in the Appendix.

The Directory discusses the hollies under their two major groupings, deciduous and evergreen. Species and hybrid groups of particular importance are treated in greater depth with further details of their botany, introduction, history, role in hybridising (if appropriate) and cultivation. Although they may not have any strictly botanical status, a number of distinct groups of related plants (for example, the Red Holly Group) are dealt with together to assist the gardener using this book. They are cross-referenced in the alphabetical listings.

Deciduous Holly Species, Hybrids and Cultivars

For sheer brilliance in the winter landscape, deciduous hollies can scarcely be bettered. In areas where they grow well, their combination of generous fruiting habit, vivid colour and length of display are the equal of most other deciduous shrubs. It is remarkable that they have taken so long to enter the gardening public's imagination, for they have remained surprisingly little-known to many gardeners until comparatively recently. In 1988 Michael Dirr, in an article entitled 'To know them is to love them', pointed out to the nursery trade that there was tremendous unrealised potential in this group: '*If TV dinners can be marketed, deciduous hollies will sell like hotcakes, with a lot less advertising*'.

Many successful plant groups require an enthusiastic promoter to achieve their deserved recognition, and the deciduous hollies benefited greatly from the work of Robert (Bob) Simpson of the Simpson Nursery Company, Vincennes, Indiana. Galle (1997) says, '*In the 1940s it was difficult to sell a deciduous holly [, but] with Simpson's dedication and persistence, there is now a constant demand for the named selections of deciduous hollies*'. Other early proponents of deciduous hollies include Bon Hartline, Polly Hill and R. K. Peters.

Also in *Hollies*, Galle wrote that deciduous hollies '*are now being recognized for their contribution to late fall and winter beauty. . . . Once seen in winter, their branches laden with abundant, brilliant red fruit and the ground covered with a fresh layer of snow, these hollies cannot be forgotten*'. Their autumn and winter value in the landscape and garden is certainly among the highest. The return for the space they take up is considerable; compared to many shrubs grown for spring and summer effect, where we are quite satisfied with perhaps a month's floral display, plants such as deciduous hollies that can provide several months of vivid colour at the darkest time of the year (birds and squirrels permitting) have to represent a good deal.

In the summer landscape their neat habit and dark green foliage provide a good background for showy summer performers, fulfilling an important seasonal role as members of the garden's 'supporting cast'; a task for which many hollies, deciduous and evergreen, are ideally suited, before they make their own contribution in the front rank as the season progresses. Attractive autumn leaf tints and winter stem effects are further attributes of members of this valuable group.

For the purposes of most gardeners three deciduous holly species are of horticultural significance: the North American species *Ilex decidua* (possumhaw) and *I. verticillata* (winterberry, black alder), with the Asiatic *I. serrata* (Japanese winterberry) completing the set. Hybrids between *I. verticillata* and *I. serrata* are also of commercial importance. Over thirty other species exist, some of high quality; most are not in cultivation, or only rarely to be seen in specialist collections.

A valuable ability shared by the cultivated deciduous hollies is that they come naturally equipped to thrive in poorly drained conditions, so often the bane of gardeners. Many occur in the wild in damp and boggy habitats, tolerating wet feet and even temporary inundation with equanimity, although neither is necessary for successful cultivation. Best growth and fruiting is obtained in moist, retentive soils and full sun, although light shade is tolerated well. Deciduous hollies are, unsurprisingly, excellent candidates for planting by water, taking both practical and aesthetic advantage of their natural affinities and adaptations, and allowing their reflected glories to further increase their effectiveness in the winter landscape.

In common with most North American *Ilex* species and hybrids, deciduous hollies as a group do best in acidic conditions. However, *I. decidua* usefully extends the range of soils where they may be grown (Dirr ranked it the most tolerant of high pH soils of the deciduous species, as well as of drought). Ecker and Larson (from the Dawes Arboretum in Ohio), writing on hollies for the Midwest in the *Holly Society Journal* in 1996 report the cultivar 'Warren's Red' thriving in the Chicago Botanic Garden, on alkaline soil.

Winter hardiness is another priceless quality that these plants bring; the wide geographical range of the key North American species encompasses Zones 4 to 9a (Nova Scotia to Florida), increasing the range of hollies from which gardeners in cold regions can choose. The hardiness of specific deciduous holly cultivars depends to a degree upon the provenance of their forebears. This has led to the development of regional cultivar groups with varying degrees of hardiness of both plant and fruit (the persistence and colour of fruits can be affected by cold weather that may not be severe enough to harm plants). If you are uncertain as to which to choose for your conditions, seek advice from local or specialist nurseries.

To ensure pollination of deciduous hollies male plants should be incorporated into any planting. This need not adversely affect the potential display:

Opposite: *Ilex decidua* in its typical, red-berried form.

Galle recommends a ratio of one male to every ten to twenty female plants, which would be scarcely visible in a mass planting. To make matters easier still, or if the planting is smaller and there is no space for a male within it, there may be a separation of as much as 15M between the females and their consorts, which can quietly carry out their task of fertilization from a distance.

The choice of pollinator for *Ilex verticillata* and its cultivars is slightly complicated by the wide geographical range of the species, which results in plants from different areas having a different habit and, more importantly, flowering at slightly different times. This has led to the development of two major groups or races of cultivars, usually referred to as 'northern' and 'southern'. For pollination purposes, plants of the northern race flower around two weeks earlier than their southern cousins, and each group requires a male of its own race for fertilization. (This is rather counter-intuitive, as one would typically expect the internal time-clock of southern races to be set to flower in advance of northern forms.) Achieving synchronicity in flowering is relatively simple to ensure in practice; details of appropriate pollinators are given below, and further advice on plants for your region should be available from specialist nurseries and garden centres.

Deciduous hollies provide an excellent example of the transatlantic divide in the experience of holly growers. Sadly, and despite being in cultivation in Britain since the mid 1700s, they have yet to be generally accepted as dependable for British gardens. Although their qualities and potential are recognised and appreciated, they are neither widely planted, nor widely available. Their case in British gardens is not assisted by the fact that birds often start to eat their fruit before leaf-fall. It may be that the mild and moist maritime climate does not suit them, as is the case with a number of woody plants from continental climates. More experimentation with different cultivars (particularly *serrata* × *verticillata* hybrids, which may take more readily to British conditions) will establish how successful these desirable plants can be in the British Isles.

In continental Europe, however, there are examples of deciduous hollies doing well. In Holland an *Ilex verticillata* cultivar, 'Oosterwijk', has been developed for a successful commercial orcharding industry. At Bokrijk Arboretum in eastern Belgium there is a significant planting of deciduous hollies in a moist site; these plants fruit dependably, which may be the result of the climate there: it is more akin to that of parts of North America, with colder winters and hotter summers than along the western seaboard of Europe.

Ilex decidua (possumhaw) occurs entirely in the southeastern USA, from Maryland to Texas and southern Florida, and west as far as Illinois, Oklahoma and Kansas. Its hardiness is rated from Zone 5 to 9a, although careful cultivar selection and placement will be required at the lower end of this range. The species naturally occurs mainly by streams and in swampy areas, but it is also reported as occurring on dry rocky hillsides in southern Illinois, which would help to explain its reported tolerance of a wider range of soil conditions than other deciduous hollies.

Essentially shrubby in form, it varies in size from 1.5M to 7.5M or more, with a multi-stemmed, upright and spreading habit. With training it can be grown into a shapely single-stemmed small tree. The smooth grey bark is another distinctive and attractive winter feature of this species. The leaves are deep lustrous green, 3.75–7.5CM long. Creamy white flowers are borne from late April to May, on new growth and on numerous short spurs formed on older branches. In the absence of male plants, possumhaws can be pollinated by nearby males of *Ilex opaca* (American holly), with which it has produced hybrids. The fruits are rounded, glossy, 7–10MM in diameter, and range from

Ilex decidua 'Byers Golden', a free-fruiting plant of excellent habit.

Right: 'Byers Golden' fruits.

dark red through orange-scarlet to (rarely) yellow in colour. They are among the most persistent of all deciduous hollies, sometimes remaining on the plants for a year or more.

Most of the cultivars listed here are vigorous plants. The selections that have been made from this valuable species are excellent choices for those who wish to create a rapid impact with a fast-growing large shrub or small tree, which will provide colour and interest in the garden for twelve months of the year.

'Byers Golden' (female). This cultivar dates back to c.1959, a chance wild seedling introduced by the Byers Nursery Company of Alabama and named for its yellow fruits. It will grow to 2.4M tall by up to 3.6M wide. Fruit persistence is excellent, lasting until February in good condition. This desirable form is available but challenging to propagate and so difficult to obtain.

'Cascade' (female). Synonym 'Red Cascade'. Of more rounded habit, growing to 7.5M high by 6M wide, this vigorous, hardy (Zone 6) cultivar is distinctive for its wide-spreading, sinuous, strikingly silver-white stems. The deep reddish orange berries persist until spring, and are among the largest of the possumhaw cultivars.

Ilex decidua 'Council Fire' in winter.
Photograph by Susyn Andrews.

'Council Fire' (female). A hardy, vigorous cultivar, well established and available in cultivation. Its habit is initially upright, then rounded and compact, to over 4.5M tall and 3M wide. The deep red fruits are borne freely in tight clusters along the stems, and may persist for a year: it is recommended by Ecker and Larson for northern gardens.

'Finch's Golden' (female) is a more recent yellow-fruited selection (1989), again arising in a wild population in Alabama. Upright and multi-stemmed in growth, 3M tall by 1.5–3M wide. The brilliant yellow fruit is said to be a better colour than 'Byers Golden'. Although it is reputedly easier to propagate, it is still making its way into cultivation, and not yet widely available.

'Pocahontas' (female). Arising from a chance seedling in a garden in Pocahontas, Missouri, this is a vigorous upright selection capable of reaching 5.9M tall by 3.7M wide in just fifteen years. The glossy bright red fruits are retained well, and the autumn leaf colour is yellow.

'Red Escort' (male). A vigorous, hardy (Zone 6) pollinator, with a rounded habit to 7.5M tall by 6M wide and good dark green foliage.

'Sentry' (female). One of the most columnar of the possumhaws, this hardy (Zone 6) plant will grow twice as high as wide, 6M by 3M in twenty-five years. It is recommended for training as a single-stemmed specimen, and loses its leaves early to expose the 8mm-wide vivid orange-red fruit.

'Warren's Red' (female). The oldest cultivar generally available, which has been proving its worth since its introduction in the late 1950s. This selection has an upright habit, growing to over 7.5M tall and 6m wide, with intense silver bark and glossy, abundant vivid red berries that persist well.

Ilex serrata (Japanese winterberry, finetooth holly). This species occurs in China and Japan; it has been long cultivated in the latter, where its uses range from gardens (especially by water) through bonsai to winter house decoration. First introduced to the USA c.1866 and to Britain in 1893 (at the Royal Botanic Gardens, Kew), this graceful and delicate plant is finer in all its parts (as its name suggests) than the two principal North American species of deciduous holly. This delicacy continues into its constitution, which is not as hardy or as vigorous as many, and the shorter persistence of its fruits. Its hardiness is rated at Zones 5b to 8; at the lower end careful choice of site would be important, and the fruit might be liable to damage from unseasonal cold. Likewise it will not tolerate prolonged high temperatures; shade and adequate moisture would assist here. Although not as robust as its American relatives, its other qualities make it a distinctive and valuable garden plant in its own right, added to which it is a parent of a group of hybrids with *I. verticillata* which are of growing importance.

Ilex serrata will achieve around 3.6M in height and as much or more across. The branching habit is essentially horizontal, with slightly pendent young shoots, especially when laden down with fruit. The foliage is like a slimmed-down *I. verticillata*, thinner and more finely toothed, pubescent (slightly hairy) on the underside and mid-green in colour. The young branches are also pubescent, a character which sets it apart from its close American cousin. Continuing this more gracile theme, the white to pale pink to purple flowers are followed by profuse smaller red fruits, around 5MM across, which typically colour in August and persist until the turn of the year—by any normal standards a worthwhile contribution to the garden scene! If you cannot find a male *serrata* then male *verticillata* plants will serve as pollinators—and have the advantage of greater availability.

The small red fruits of the Japanese winterberry, *Ilex serrata.*

There are numerous Japanese cultivars of *Ilex serrata*, some of which, following a long gardening tradition, were rechristened with latinised cultivar epithets when they were introduced to Western horticulture. Those we grow are very distinctive and stand out among the entire range of deciduous hollies. All *serrata* forms are well worth seeking out, although recourse to specialist nurseries will almost certainly be necessary.

'Leucocarpa' (female). Synonyms *Ilex serrata* f. *leucocarpa*, 'Shimo-ume-modoki', 'Inu-ume'. This is a distinctive and beautiful form, with fruits of the palest creamy white. The fruits are unique among deciduous hollies; where the majority are stridently colourful, 'Leucocarpa' is subtle. Its graceful habit accentuates and complements this, striking a welcome note in the winter landscape.

The pale berries of *Ilex serrata* 'Sundrops' show well against the foliage.

'Longwood Firefall' (female). This cultivar originated from a collecting trip made by staff from Longwood Gardens, Pennsylvania, and the US National Arboretum to Japan in 1985. It was selected from plants at the Shimabichi Nursery in Honshu for its mounded, semi-pendulous habit of growth, reaching 1.5M high by 3M wide after fourteen years. Its red berries are typical of the species. Registered in 1999, its hardiness is rated at Zone 5.

'Sundrops' (female). A seedling from a yellow-fruited Japanese cultivar, raised and introduced by the US National Arboretum in 1993. The flat-topped wide-spreading plant will grow to over 2.4M high by 5M wide, and becomes weighted down with cascades of primrose-yellow fruits. Stronger in colour than 'Leucocarpa', and very striking in its own right, it is still a quietly attractive plant rather than an attention-seeker.

Other forms we know of sound very intriguing: 'Rakusogu' is described as having bicoloured fruits of red and pale yellow, and 'Koshobai', a dwarf form used in bonsai in Japan, has purple new growth and sets its abundant red berries without the need for a pollinator.

Ilex verticillata (winterberry, black alder). First described by Linnaeus as *Prinos verticillatus* in 1753, this species has a long history in cultivation, having been introduced to Britain in 1736. A very widespread plant, from its northern outpost in Nova Scotia it ranges south to Florida and west to Ontario, Minnesota and Texas; its wide occurrence gives it a correspondingly wide hardiness range, Zones 3 to 9. The chosen habitat, however, remains the same throughout its range: swamps, streamsides, wet woodlands—in fact, any area that can be relied upon to remain good and wet all year round. Dirr (1988) '*delighted in chancing upon masses of* I. verticillata *in boggy areas and … observed plants* *growing submerged in kettle ponds on Cape Cod'*. This tolerance of boggy conditions up to and including compete inundation reflects both a very tough constitution and is a potentially valuable horticultural characteristic.

The winterberry is highly variable in size, growth habit, leaf size, shape and colour, and many other finer botanical characteristics. Capable of growing to 6M tall by 4.5M wide, it has a tendency to sucker and can form large, rounded thickets of dark grey winter stems. The leaves vary in length from 3.75CM to 7.5CM, sometimes more, and in colour from mid to dark green. Typically there is no appreciable autumn colour (usually yellow or slightly purple-tinted) before leaf fall; if frosted before natural abscission the leaves tend to fall dark brown or black.

Winter fireworks from *Ilex verticillata*.

For horticultural purposes the long-recognized division of this species into 'northern' and 'southern' types creates a useful, if informal, classification. The differences extend further than flowering times. Northern types essentially hail from New England and points north. They are typically smaller, less vigorous in growth, with a more compact habit, light to mid-brown twigs, and smaller leaves. Their southern cousins are more vigorous, growing into plants which are more open in habit, with darker stems and larger, more lustrous and thicker leaves. This broad division assists in deciding which plants might be chosen for specific purposes or areas, and becomes critical at flowering time.

Winterberries produce greeny white flowers in May, June and July, after the leaves have unfurled. Male plants are required for pollination; it is advisable to plant the male cultivars recommended for your location or the female cultivars grown, to coincide with their 'northern' or 'southern' flowering times. (This advice holds true for most situations, although Dirr comments that pollination by other holly species has been observed on isolated plants.) The size of the bright red fruit is variable, usually 6–8MM in diameter in the wild. Larger-berried forms have been selected, as have orange and yellow cultivars. Fruit persistence is generally good to excellent, although they may be more palatable and thus more susceptible to animal attack than those of *Ilex decidua*.

Fruit persistence is also of note when using winterberry for indoor decorations. Simpson reports that the cultivar 'Winter Red' is able to retain its berries as part of a dried arrangement for several months. They shrivel, as would be expected, but the trusses of fruit do not shatter, thus remaining a colourful element of a dried bouquet.

Before moving on to look more closely at the wealth of cultivars and hybrids of the winterberry, the horticultural potential of the species is well summed up by Michael Dirr, when commenting upon the variability in all its plant characteristics. He noted, '*What I found vividly evident, even from dried specimens, were the opportunities for making superior selections*'. These comments date back to 1988; since then some of this potential has been realised, as has the commercial potential of this excellent species. This is certainly reflected in the numbers of *Ilex verticillata* cultivars and hybrids now available, making it the most important deciduous holly in cultivation. The selection below notes whether the cultivars are of the northern (N) or southern (S) persuasion with regard to flowering times.

'Afterglow' (N) (female). Introduced by Simpson Nursery in 1976. A compact, rounded plant, slowly growing to 3M high and wide in twenty-five years (but may be maintained at a lower height) with excellent small glossy leaves. Orange-red fruits are produced in abundance, changing to orange as the season progresses and persisting until spring. Hardy to Zone 4.

'Aurantiaca' (N) (female). This cultivar name is often used instead of the more correct *Ilex verticillata* f. *aurantiaca*. Collected from a wild plant in Morris County, New Jersey, in 1938, this is a plant of upright spreading habit, slow-growing to 3M tall. The abundant and persistent orange fruit of this unique selection is superbly effective; as it ages it may develop a yellow flush, but will remain untroubled by birds.

'Bright Horizon' (N) (female). Raised from seed collected in Massachusetts and introduced by Polly Hill. A compact, bushy plant, growing to 1.8M tall by

The warm orange berries of *Ilex verticillata* 'Aurantiaca'.
Photograph by Susyn Andrews.

0.9M wide in twelve years; the fruits are red, and the plants are hardy to Zone 4. 'Earlibright' (N, female) is a sibling, similar in growth but with lighter orange-red berries, which ripen earlier.

'Cacapon' (N) (female). A popular cultivar, a selection of wild origin from West Virginia. It is upright in growth, reaching 3.6M tall by 2.4M wide in fifteen years, with glossy dark green foliage and prolific small vivid red fruits.

'Jim Dandy' (N) (male). Synonyms 'Dwarf Male', Dwarf Male Selections. This compact plant was one of two selected as pollinators for northern and southern types by Bob Simpson in 1985. Slow-growing to 3M tall by 2.1M wide, with a dense twiggy habit, abundant flowers and a prolonged flowering season. Widely available and hardy to Zone 4.

'Oosterwijk' (female). A Dutch selection dating back to 1950, originally by P. Oosterwijk of Boskoop in Holland, which has recently been introduced into cultivation in the USA. This is the first *verticillata* cultivar to be named in Europe, and is a vigorous plant, with abundant 8–9MM wide berries which persist well both in the garden and in cold storage. It has been developed for the cut holly trade, with cut stems exported to a number of countries including, apparently, the USA!

Although small in stature, *Ilex verticillata* 'Red Sprite' packs a colourful punch.

'Red Sprite' (N) (female). Also known as 'Nana', this cultivar brings deciduous hollies of true dwarf stature to gardens that cannot accommodate the larger-growing forms. Mature plants slowly reach 1–1.5M tall by 1.5M wide, with good dark green leaves. Although dwarf it has large, vivid red fruits, approaching 12.5MM in diameter, borne abundantly. An invaluable selection, described by Simpson as '*a real gem*', widely available and hardy to Zone 4.

'Southern Gentleman' (S) (male). Misleadingly originally called 'Early Male' (which is strange as it was selected to pollinate the later-flowering southern types; it has also been called Late Male Selections). This pollinator was also introduced by Simpson Nursery. It is widely available and will pollinate the remaining three selections (all Simpson introductions).

'Sunset' (S) (female). A vigorous, upright-growing cultivar, growing to 2.4M tall by 2.7M wide in thirty years. The leaves are long for the species, at 12.5–15CM, and a good glossy green. Large red fruits are borne with great freedom, almost reaching the very tips of the branches, which droop under their weight. Ecker and Larson consider it one of the best-fruiting forms.

'Winter Gold' (S) (female) is a branch sport of 'Winter Red', discovered in 1983 and introduced in 1987; it is similar in every way except for its orange-yellow berries, which have a distinctive pink cast and seem to be immune to the attentions of birds.

'Winter Red' (S) (female). Since its introduction in 1977 this has proved one of the most successful and popular of all deciduous hollies; Galle refers to it as having set the standard for other selections. Rounded in shape, growing 3M

Ilex verticillata 'Winter Gold'.

A plant of great historical importance, the original *Ilex verticillata* 'Winter Red', remarkably vibrant after leaf fall, that sported to produce 'Winter Gold', on the left.
Photograph by Susyn Andrews.

tall by almost as much wide, with dark green, glossy leaves which turn bronze before falling. Prolific vivid red berries 8–10MM in diameter persist well, and cut stems remain in excellent condition in cold storage for months. Hardy to Zone 4.

Hybrids between *verticillata* and *serrata*. The oldest of these, 'Bonfire' (selected c.1957 at the Simpson Nursery), arose serendipitously from a batch of seedlings and masqueraded for some time as a selection of *I. serrata*. This is understandable as the group tends to follow that species in its slender branching habit and prolific but small fruit, which colour early, and whose persistence and hardiness sit somewhere between straight *I. serrata* and *I. verticillata*. Galle reports fruit discoloration at around −12C; the plants, however, are hardy to Zone 5 and possibly below. In the 1960s controlled hybrid crosses were made at the US National Arboretum by Kosar and Vos, and at Rutgers University by Dr. Elwin Orton, from which most of the cultivars are derived.

Ilex 'Apollo' (male). This selection from the US National Arboretum was introduced in 1978 to pollinate 'Sparkleberry', an important task given the growing ubiquity of that cultivar. A vigorous plant to 3.6M tall and wide, the young growths are red-flushed, and the light green leaves turn straw-yellow in autumn.

Ilex 'Bonfire' (female). A vigorous-growing hybrid, which Ecker and Larson report as achieving 1.8M tall and wide in six years at the Dawes Arboretum, and the original plant 3.6M tall and wide after three decades. It bears well as a young plant, with masses of small vivid red berries colouring early in the autumn.

Ilex 'Harvest Red' (female). An Orton hybrid, with upright arching growth to 4.5M, reported as 2.4M tall and wide in eighteen years at the Dawes Arboretum. The foliage is dark lustrous green, and may turn purple before falling. A prolifically fruiting clone, with berries persisting until December and less liable to sun scorch; given the Styer Garden Award in 1991.

Ilex 'Raritan Chief' (male). A compact plant introduced by Orton to pollinate 'Harvest Red'. Growth is compact and broad, achieving 1.5M tall by 2.4M across in ten years.

Ilex 'Sparkleberry' (female). A US National Arboretum introduction in 1973 which has proved highly successful and is widely grown. Its habit is upright and spreading, to 4.5M tall in sixteen years. The *serrata* influence is shown to a

The aptly named *Ilex* 'Bonfire' (*serrata* × *verticillata*).
Photograph by Susyn Andrews.

Below: A fine plant of *Ilex* 'Harvest Red'.
Photograph by Susyn Andrews.

degree in its purple-flushed young foliage, but *I. verticillata* shows its hand in its profuse mid-size vivid red fruits, which hold until the end of the winter. The eminent holly expert Polly Hill is quoted as saying that if she could have but two deciduous holly cultivars, her choice would be 'Sparkleberry' and its consort, 'Apollo': praise indeed, echoed and amplified by the Styer Garden Award to 'Sparkleberry' in 1987.

Other deciduous holly species. Numerous deciduous hollies have not yet been introduced into cultivation, or are only sparsely represented in specialist or enthusiast's collections. Undoubtedly there is potential among them for new directions in selection and breeding, awaiting the creativity and enthusiasm of collectors, gardeners, commercial growers and researchers. The species listed below are of real garden merit, and may be met with in botanic gardens or specialist collections.

The soft yellow autumn tints and red berries of *Ilex amelanchier*. Photograph by Susyn Andrews.

Ilex amelanchier (serviceberry, swamp holly) is a rare but quietly attractive large shrub with quite sparsely borne velvety red fruits and straw-yellow autumn colour. It occurs from Virginia to Mississippi and is cultivated in specialist collections only.

Ilex laevigata (smooth winterberry) is allied (and very similar) to *I. verticillata*, occurring in similar habitats from Maine to the Carolinas, but apparently not hybridising with it. It is smaller in growth, leaf and fruit than the winterberry. The red fruit ripens and falls earlier, but the yellow fall foliage is attractive. Dirr hazards that some *I. verticillata* forms described from cultivation may well be *I. laevigata*.

The large black berries of *Ilex macrocarpa* (**left**) are borne on a stately, deciduous tree (**right**).

Ilex longipes. Occurring throughout the southern USA west to Texas and Mississippi, this attractive large shrub bears its fruits singly on stalks that may reach up to 5CM long. Its chosen habitat of woods or rocky slopes could one day be of interest to breeders, as also its relation to *I. decidua*, with which some argue that it may be conspecific.

Ilex macrocarpa. One of the most distinctive of all the hollies, forming a medium-sized tree capable of 20M in height in cultivation, perhaps half as much again in the wild. A native of south and southwest China and possibly Vietnam, it was introduced by Ernest Wilson in 1907. It has proved hardy at both the Royal Botanic Gardens, Kew, and the Arnold Arboretum, and a plant of over 12M grows at the Westonbirt Arboretum in England. The 5–15CM leaves are handsome, but the most arresting feature of this tree are the large black fruits, around 13MM wide, flattened at the top and bottom. They are very similar in appearance to a blackcurrant or small cherry, and look every bit as edible; Dudley (1986b) reported them as tasting '*rather sweet, not at all undesirable, though a bit astringent*'.

Evergreen Holly Species, Hybrids and Cultivars

In contrast to their deciduous cousins, the evergreen hollies enjoy wide acceptance wherever hollies are grown as plants of great merit and usefulness, whose value in the garden has been appreciated for centuries, if not millennia. They are a remarkably diverse group, one which is still developing rapidly as new selections of species and hybrids are introduced. The plants listed in the Directory reflect the range of evergreen hollies for all climates and conditions, with particular emphasis upon plants in cultivation and available to gardeners, blending those with a long track record in gardens with newer introductions.

***Ilex* 'Accent'** (male). An interesting hybrid between *I. integra* from Japan and the Chinese *I. pernyi*, made by William Kosar at the US National Arboretum and named in the mid 1960s. A plant of neat, upright pyramidal habit, with mid-green small-spined leaves around 3CM long by 1.8CM wide. It was introduced as a pollinator for its sister seedling, 'Elegance'. Hardy to Zone 7.

***Ilex* 'Adonis'** (male). One of two hybrids raised at the US National Arboretum from a cross made by William Kosar of the popular *I.* 'Nellie R. Stevens' (*cornuta* 'Burfordii × *aquifolium*) with *I. latifolia*. Broadly pyramidal in habit, it is capable of an average growth of 30CM a year, reaching over 6M tall in twenty years, and remaining well furnished to the ground. The dark green, glossy leaves are distinctly undulate (wavy) with spiny margins, around 11.5CM long by 5CM wide. A superb foliage plant in its own right, whose other key role is to pollinate its sister seedling, 'Venus'. Hardy to Zone 7, possibly 6b with shelter.

***Ilex* 'Agena'**. See *Ilex ×koehneana*

Ilex 'Ajax'. See *Ilex ×koehneana*

Ilex ×altaclerensis (*aquifolium* × *perado*). The Highclere hollies form a distinct group of hybrids, described by Bean as '*some of the finest of hardy evergreen small trees and shrubs*'. An epithet often (and fittingly) bestowed upon them is 'handsome', and they combine this quality with great vigour and the ability to thrive in polluted areas and exposed seaside locations. For maritime Western Europe and similar conditions on the East and West Coasts of the USA (broadly Zones 6 to 8 in the East, up to 9 and 10 in the West), they provide some of the most imposing holly cultivars available to use as specimen plants, in high hedges and avenues, and in the wider landscape. As the great English plantsman Graham Stuart Thomas (1992) says, '*Apart from* I. dipyrena *and* I. macrocarpa, *the Highclere hollies are most vigorous and tree-like, with stout branches and large leaves and generally few prickles. The tallest are too coarse in growth for the average garden, but admirable for an avenue, and will achieve 17M/50FT or more*'. While the largest of the ×*altaclerensis* hollies will quite rapidly grow into medium-sized trees, the tallest of which in Britain now exceed 20M in height, the size range includes more compact-growing shrubs for smaller gardens, and several cultivars which are popular subjects for trimming into hedges and topiary.

Many of the Highclere hollies were originally (and understandably) considered to be varieties of the highly variable *Ilex aquifolium*. The early history of how this valuable group of plants arose is unclear; however, the name *altaclerensis* was first used by Loudon in his *Arboretum et Fruticetum Britannicum* (1838) as a variant of the common holly (*I. aquifolium* var. *altaclerensis*), in his description of a plant growing in the gardens of the Highclere estate near Newbury in southeast England. For many years the name was misspelt as *altaclarensis*, a situation corrected by Susyn Andrews (1983a, 1983b, 1984a).

While Loudon's was the first formal recognition of the group, plants of hybrid origin had in all likelihood arisen independently on a number of occasions. This is unsurprising, given that their 'exotic' parent, *Ilex perado*, had been in cultivation since as early as 1760; and William Paul, in his address to the RHS Floral Committee in 1863, confirmed that hybrids between *I. perado* and *I. aquifolium* had knowingly been grown for some time in Scotland: '*Some years ago I met with a beautiful holly, with broad prickly leaves, in the Botanic Gardens of Edinburgh, which the late Mr. McNab informed me was raised from the Ilex perado hybridized with the English Holly*'. He had also seen leaves from other seedlings at Edinburgh '*raised from the* Ilex perado, *supposed to be fertilized with the English Holly*'. In his subsequent notes he described a number of cultivars that we now know to be of hybrid origin (and place under *Ilex ×altaclerensis*), demonstrating how well they had already established themselves in cultivation. Thomas Moore's review of the range of hollies available to gardeners in the latter part of the 19th century, 'The common holly and its varieties', published in *The Gardeners' Chronicle* between 1874 and 1876, also included plants we would now recognise as *Ilex ×altaclerensis* cultivars.

At the turn of the 20th century Dallimore (1908) dealt with the plants we now know as *Ilex ×altaclerensis* in a chapter entitled *I. platyphylla*. He recognised their distinctiveness: '*The set of large leaved, garden Hollies typified by this plant are essentially different from the varieties of* I. aquifolium, *under which species they are usually included. Without doubt some of the sorts that approach the type in appearance are hybrids, and* I. platyphylla *and the 'Common Holly' doubtless cross readily*'. Dallimore's *I. platyphylla* (of gardens) was principally a group of large-leaved cultivars we now recognise mainly as *Ilex ×altaclerensis* , although he considered that it might be a Canary Island species whose '*nearest ally appears to be* I. perado'. Importantly, he did describe what he spelt '*I. altaclarensis*' as a member of a group of '*Broad-Leaved Hollies that are apparently of Hybrid Origin but approach Platyphylla most closely*'. Thus for the first time he established the hybrid as a separate entity from the common or English holly.

The plants we now recognise under the name *Ilex ×altaclerensis* are the result of a series of unrecorded crosses and backcrosses involving the common holly, *I. aquifolium*, with *I. perado* subsp. *perado* (originally called *I. maderensis*), *I. perado* subsp. *platyphylla* var. *platyphylla* and (according to Susyn Andrews) *I. aquifolium* in its Balearic race (once known as *I. balearica*). The progeny of further backcrossing with the common holly has resulted in a group of plants that can sometimes only with difficulty be distinguished from *I. aquifolium*, which makes the recognition of cultivars something of a challenge. Bean puts it well: '*The fact that some of the early hybrids were named as varieties of* Ilex perado *… suggests that this species was the seed-parent of the first-generation hybrids. Once these first-generation hybrids … had become established in gardens, back-crosses would have been raised from females such as 'Hendersonii', pollinated by the Common holly, and certainly some of the hybrids are the result of deliberate crossing. In this way a diverse assemblage of hollies has arisen, and the boundary between* Ilex ×altaclerensis *and* I. aquifolium *has become somewhat blurred* '. The inter-fertility of the hybrids and the original parents also suggests that the original parent species were closely related, and indeed Andrews proposes that they share a common ancestor.

In her *Plantsman* articles (1983b, 1984a), Susyn Andrews grouped a number of the Highclere hollies into distinct groups, derived either from their characteristics or from how they arose, as follows (some of these cultivars are not described in the Directory: several popular and widely grown cultivars do not fit into this classification):

1 Camelliifolia Group. These are all female, and share the principal characteristic of having large leaves, which are typically entire and only rarely very spiny. The cultivars included here are 'Camelliifolia', 'Camelliifolia Variegata', 'James G. Esson' and 'Marnockii'.
2 Hendersonii Group. All these cultivars, including 'Golden King', 'Howick' and 'Lawsoniana', arose as branch sports from 'Hendersonii'.
3 Hodginsii Group. This group arose as branch sports of 'Hodginsii'; cultivars include 'Hodginsii' and 'Nobilis Picta'.
4 Balearica Group. All the members of this group are vigorous, female plants with variably spiny leaves and large berries; cultivars include 'Balearica', 'Moria' and 'Purple Shaft'.
5 Belgica Group. Again, an all-female group, with leaves that are longer and narrower than the Balearica hybrids; cultivars include 'Belgica' and 'Belgica Aurea'.
6 Maderensis Group. An all-male group, tall trees of upswept branch habit; cultivars include 'Atrovirens'; 'Jermyns', 'Maderensis' and 'Nigrescens'.

The Highclere hollies generally share the robust constitution of *Ilex aquifolium*, but with greater vigour. They are typically fast-growing, making large shrubs or small- to medium-sized trees, conical and upright to broad and spreading in habit. As a rule they are larger in leaf, flower and fruit than their *aquifolium* ancestors. They are of particular note for their bold, typically glossy deep green leaves, which are often sparsely spined or spineless. In hardiness they are very similar to the common holly, thriving in temperate maritime conditions, appreciating neither intense cold nor great heat; in general Zones 7 to 9 will suit them best, 6 with protection. They may do well in a few parts of the East Coast of the USA but are more at home and will achieve their full potential in the Pacific Northwest. Cultivars of *Ilex ×altaclerensis* may be grown in neutral to slightly alkaline soils, sharing the wider tolerance of *I. aquifolium*.

'Atkinsonii' (male). A vigorous cultivar introduced in the early 1900s by the British nursery Fisher, Son and Sibray. It has green stems that bear particularly large, ovate black-green glossy leaves up to 12.5CM long by 7CM wide, which have distinctively corrugated surfaces and small spines.

'Balearica' (female). A vigorous, upright-growing, free-fruiting cultivar dating back to the mid 1800s. Green young stems bear ovate, leathery, flat dark glossy green leaves, varying from spiny to entire, up to 9.2CM long by 5.6CM wide. The large red berries are freely borne. 'Purple Shaft' is a sport from this cultivar, named by Roy Lancaster in 1965 and introduced by Hillier Nurseries. Chiefly distinguished by its deep purple young stems, it is vigorous, upright in growth, free-fruiting, and forms a fine specimen tree.

'Barterberry'. See 'Camelliifolia'.

'Belgica' (female). An old cultivar (recorded as being offered for sale first in 1874) and not common in cultivation. A tree of upright pyramidal growth with dark, glossy green leaves up to 10CM long by 4.5CM wide, typically entire (spineless) or occasionally lightly spined; berries bright red, around 10MM wide.

'Belgica', showing the classical *Ilex ×altaclerensis* characters of dark, glossy, almost spineless leaves and brilliant red berries.

'Belgica Aurea' AGM (female). Synonym 'Silver Sentinel'. An important and distinctive cultivar, introduced by the Dutch nursery firm of Koster in 1908, when it was awarded a First Class Certificate; this high accolade has since been joined by the RHS Award of Garden Merit. Described by *The Hillier Manual* as '*one of the most handsome variegated hollies*', it grows into an upright medium-sized broadly conical tree of up to 10M. The green stems may be yellow-streaked, and bear glossy flat leaves, usually spineless, around 10CM long

by 3.8CM wide. The leaves are variably margined in yellow to cream, sometimes to as much as half of the entire surface; their centres are mottled with green and grey-green. While sometimes reported to be sparse or rarely fruiting, the bright orange-red fruits may be freely borne—it may be that there is more than one clone of this selection in cultivation.

The superb conical habit of *Ilex ×altaclerensis* 'Belgica Aurea' AGM, whose spineless leaves are edged creamy yellow (**right**).

'Camelliifolia' AGM (female). Undoubtedly one of the finest of this group, and arguably one of the handsomest of all large-growing hollies, this cultivar was first recorded as being offered for sale in 1865. It is vigorous in growth and forms a medium-sized tree, described by Susyn Andrews (1983b) as '*a superb plant with its narrow pyramidal growth of dense foliage well furnished to the ground*', capable of reaching over 15M in height. The purplish stems bear large, flat, spineless glossy dark green leaves up to 12.5CM long by 5cm wide, bronzy purple when young; the substantial scarlet berries, around 12MM wide, are abundantly borne. A fine plant, well deserving of its RHS Award of Garden Merit. The American selection 'Barterberry', occasionally available in the USA, is described as very similar to 'Camelliifolia' by Fred Galle, but of particular note for its freedom of cropping.

Left: Good upright habit, superb foliage and generously borne red berries make *Ilex ×altaclerensis* 'Camelliifolia' AGM one of the finest of the Highclere hollies.

Rarely seen, but deserving to be more widely grown, the elegant *Ilex ×altaclerensis* 'Camelliifolia Variegata'.

'Camelliifolia Variegata' (female). A sport of 'Camelliifolia', which is very rare in cultivation. This is a distinctive selection, an attractive, slow-growing broad spreading shrub without the vigorous upright habit of 'Camelliifolia'. It has large, flat, sparsely spiny leaves up to 11.3CM long by around half as wide, generously and irregularly margined in cream. Berries are only rarely produced.

'Eldridge' (female). Discovered on Long Island, New York, in around 1900, this cultivar's chief claim to fame is as the parent of 'James G. Esson'. It has green-purple stems, relatively small deep green leaves up to 7.5CM long, typically spineless, and red berries 10MM wide.

'Golden King' AGM (female). One of the brightest and most popular variegated hollies, which arose as a sport of 'Hendersonii' at the Bangholm Nurseries in Edinburgh, in 1884. This plant created something of a sensation when first distributed in 1898, and within the same year received the Award of Merit and First Class Certificate from the RHS, a double accolade which places it in a very small and select group of plants (it now holds the RHS Award of Garden Merit also). A vigorous-growing, medium-sized upright spreading shrub to over 7.5M in height. Purple-flushed young stems bear glossy, typically spineless rounded leaves up to 10CM long by 6.3CM wide, with dark green centres splashed grey-green and generously margined in bright creamy yellow. The reddish brown fruits are a further bonus with this highly decorative plant. Although the leaves are quite large, its dense habit lends itself well to trimming into topiary and hedges.

Opposite: Deservedly one of the most widely grown and adaptable of the Highclere hollies, *Ilex ×altaclerensis* 'Golden King' AGM, densely leafy and generous in fruit.

'Green Maid' (female). A vigorous clone of dense habit, introduced by Brownell in 1940. Green-stemmed with dark olive-green leaves that are quite small for an *×altaclerensis* cultivar at around 7.5CM long by 3.1CM wide, and distinctly twisted, either smooth-edged or with one or two spines; glossy red berries.

'Hendersonii' (female). A very vigorous cultivar, making a good specimen of around 15M and capable of reaching over 18M. Raised in the early 1800s by Edward Hodgins in County Wicklow, Ireland, and introduced around 1846, it has essentially spineless broad dull green leaves, up to 11.3CM long by 6.3CM wide. Brownish red fruits are freely borne. It is not in the first rank of *×altaclerensis* cultivars, mainly on account of the dull leaves, reflected in Bean's comment that its '*chief claim to fame [is] that it is the parent by sporting of 'Lawsoniana' and 'Golden King'* ', to which should now be added the cultivar 'Howick'.

Not as shiny in leaf as some of its tribe, but bearing abundant fruits, *Ilex ×altaclerensis* 'Hendersonii'.

'Hodginsii' AGM (male). Synonyms 'Nobilis', 'Shepherdii'. Of the same origin as 'Hendersonii', this is one of the finest large-growing green-leaved hollies. Bean remarks that after its introduction it '*soon became common in the industrial Midlands [of England] because of its ability to withstand a heavily polluted atmosphere*'; this also makes it a good selection for coastal planting. Susyn Andrews (1983b) says of this cultivar that it '*can grow into a magnificent specimen*', capable of forming a pyramid of well over 15M in height, and Graham Stuart Thomas (1992) says it is '*imperturbably hardy; a great, dense bushy tree [and] makes a superlative windscreen or hedge*'. The purple stems bear deep glossy black-green leaves that are large, 10CM long by 6.3CM wide, broad, flat and typically almost spineless. The RHS Award of Garden Merit has been bestowed upon this fine cultivar.

'Howick' (female). A sport from 'Hendersonii', named by Susyn Andrews for the English arboretum where the finest specimen is to be found. While rare as a mature plant it is now making its way into cultivation. A large tree which remains well-furnished with age, it has green stems which bear almost spineless leaves up to 9CM long by 5CM wide. The leaves are dark green, glossy, with a narrow creamy white margin and some central grey-green blotching and streaking. Red fruits are borne, although not abundantly; Andrews considers that this cultivar is of potential interest to flower arrangers.

'James G. Esson' (female). A vigorous upright tree, an American selection which originated from seedlings of *Ilex ×altaclerensis* 'Eldridge', named for its finder by Thomas Everett of the New York Botanical Garden in 1949. Purple stems bear dark green glossy leaves up to 11CM long by 5CM wide, with undulate (wavy) margins, very variably spiny from well armed to smooth, even on the same shoot. Scarlet fruits are abundantly borne; Susyn Andrews distinguishes this plant from 'Camelliifolia' by its relatively open habit, and smaller more spiny leaves.

'Jermyns' (male). Named for Jermyns House by Hillier Nurseries, where the original plant was discovered in 1952, this is a dense-growing vigorous columnar form, recommended for hedges. The very glossy dark green leaves are almost spineless, up to 10CM long by 4.8CM wide.

A sport from *Ilex ×altaclerensis* 'Hendersonii', 'Lawsoniana' AGM is one of the finest centrally variegated hollies.

'Lawsoniana' AGM (female). A boldly variegated branch sport of 'Hendersonii', an introduction from the nursery of William Hodgins at Cloughjordan, County Tipperary, Ireland, first named and made available for general sale through the Lawson nursery in 1874. It was awarded a First Class Certificate by the RHS in 1894, and has the Award of Garden Merit. Elwes and Henry described it well as '*one of the handsomest of the golden hollies, but often reverts to the green state*'; and it is indeed given to sporting back to 'Hendersonii', although the need for occasional vigilance with the secateurs should not dissuade gardeners from growing it! Upright and broadly pyramidal in growth to over 6m, with green stems streaked with yellow, and spineless leaves similar in size and shape to its sister 'Golden King', but very colourfully blotched with bright yellow and light green at their centres. The brownish red fruits are not generously produced in most years.

'Maderensis' (male). A strong-growing, vigorous cultivar capable of reaching over 9m, creating a superb high screen, which was first recorded in 1854. Green stems bear broad leaves, variably spiny to spineless, dark glossy green, which can be over 10CM long by 6.5CM wide.

'Moorei' (male). A vigorous cultivar from Fisher, Son and Sibray's nursery dating from the 1930s or early 1940s. Green-purple stems bear dark green lustrous leaves around 10CM long by 6CM wide, with pronounced spines.

'Nigrescens' (male). Similar to 'Maderensis', forming an upright well-furnished tree to 13M tall. Its leaves are typically spineless and glossy, up to 10CM long by 6.3CM wide. It has been in the trade since around 1845.

Most *Ilex ×altaclerensis* cultivars are a century or so old, but 'Ripley Gold' is a mere stripling dating back to 1980.

'Platyphylla' (female). This name was previously used to cover a range of cultivars of what we now recognise as *Ilex ×altaclerensis*, but now is more correctly applied to this plant, which is thought to be one of the earlier introductions of Fisher, Son and Sibray from the mid 1800s. It is a typical early Highclere holly cultivar, making a large, well-furnished and vigorous tree with green stems, bearing broad, spiny dark glossy green leaves, up to 10CM long by 6.6CM wide, and red fruits.

'Purple Shaft'. See 'Balearica'.

'Ripley Gold' (female). A sport from 'Golden King' which arose in the village of North Ripley, Hampshire, England, in 1980. This is superficially very similar to 'Lawsoniana' in its glossy, generously centrally variegated foliage, whose chief distinguishing factor lies in the distinct twist to their leaf blades. A plant of compact habit, bearing scarlet fruit.

Bold and broad in leaf, with large red fruits, *Ilex ×altaclerensis* 'Wilsonii' is a vigorous spreading cultivar.

'Wilsonii' (female). A strong-growing selection, forming a tall, compact dome of over 9M, well furnished to the base. This cultivar arose as a chance seedling at the Fisher, Son and Sibray nursery in the early 1890s. It made quite an impression very early on, and was awarded a First Class Certificate by the RHS in 1899. Elwes and Henry speak of this cultivar as '*one of the most ornamental of the hollies … producing an abundance of large berries*'; The Hillier Manual says it is '*deservedly one of the most popular of this group*'. Purplish green stems bear large, spiny, broadly oval burnished dark green leaves, around 10CM long by 7.5CM wide. Glossy scarlet berries are freely produced.

Below: *Ilex ×altaclerensis* 'W. J. Bean', smallest of the Highclere hollies, can fruit profusely.

'W. J. Bean' (female). An atypical *×altaclerensis* selection, named for the curator of the Royal Botanic Gardens, Kew, in the early 20th century, the original author of one of the most important reference works on trees and shrubs for temperate regions. This cultivar is slow-growing, forming a

compact mound, effectively a plant with Highclere holly characteristics for the smaller garden. The comparatively large, markedly wavy, lightly spined deep glossy green leaves are around 9CM long by 3.7CM wide; the bright red fruits are of good size.

Opposite: With berries of clear orange, *Ilex aquifolium* 'Amber' AGM is a distinctive selection.

Ilex aquifolium AGM (common holly, English holly). '*I have often wondered at our curiosity after foreign plants, and expensive difficulties, to the neglect of the culture of this vulgar, but incomparable tree*'; the high esteem in which *I. aquifolium* has long been held among the most discerning gardeners is amply demonstrated by this quote from John Evelyn's *Sylva, or a Discourse on Forest Trees* (1664). In this context the word *vulgar* means common, and Evelyn's charge—that gardeners regularly overlook the qualities of familiar plants in their quest for exotic novelties—holds as true now as it did then.

Thomas Moore echoed the thought in the introduction to his series of articles, 'The common holly and its varieties', in *The Gardeners' Chronicle* of October 1874: '*There are, we suppose, few persons comparatively, amongst those who take an interest in hardy shrubs, who are fully aware of the wealth of variety which the common Holly* (Ilex aquifolium) *affords. Whether as a specimen plant, a shrubbery plant, or a hedge plant, the Holly, if it has any equals, has no superiors, and therefore we need not wonder at its popularity*'. William Robinson (1900) concurred wholeheartedly with this opinion, calling the hollies '*beautiful evergreen shrubs ... of which the most precious is our own native holly. It would be difficult to exaggerate the value of this plant, whether as an evergreen tree, as the best of all fence-shelters ... or as a lovely ornament of our gardens*'.

Bringing this high praise up to our own time, Bean's monumental *Trees and Shrubs Hardy in the British Isles* refers to the common holly as '*on the whole the most useful of evergreen trees and shrubs.... During the dark months a holly tree well laden with its bright red fruits is one of the handsomest and most cheerful objects our winter landscape provides. It makes the best of all evergreen hedges*'. *The Hillier Manual of Trees and Shrubs*, speaking again of plants growing in Britain (and we should bear in mind the wealth of plants from which British gardeners can choose), boldly states, '*There is no more beautiful or useful evergreen for this climate*'.

Among American writers Fred Galle, in his seminal work *Hollies*, accords the English holly the accolade of being '*the best known and most useful of all hollies*', and the English plantsman Roy Lancaster (2001) writes, '*Although there are hundreds of other holly species ... many of which have ornamental merit, none in my experience excels the English holly in berry and leaf*'. I hope the reader is now prepared for further encomiums for this distinctive plant, the source of a tremendous variety of hybrids and cultivars, which may justifiably be claimed to have laid the foundation of the modern world of hollies.

Ilex aquifolium is an evergreen tree that may grow as high as 25M in ideal conditions, although typically rather less. Its natural habit of growth is pyramidal, with grey bark and green or purple young stems densely clothed with glossy green foliage that typically is retained close to the ground. The leaves are very variable in their size, shape and the number of spines they bear. Plants raised from seed are usually furnished with wavy-edged spiny leaves lower down; they become progressively less well-armed as the plants gain height, until at the very top of a mature plant they may be virtually spineless, and almost completely lose their wavy margins.

The upper leaf surfaces are highly burnished, deep green, 2.5–10CM long and 1.8–6.2CM wide. Small, slightly fragrant white flowers are borne in clusters in the leaf axils in May and June. Female plants then bear glossy red berries of around 6mm in diameter. This combination of excellent horticultural characteristics has led to the Royal Horticultural Society awarding this species the Award of Garden Merit.

The distribution and habitat choices of *Ilex aquifolium* provide useful pointers toward its requirements and adaptability in gardens. Despite one of its common names, *I. aquifolium* is by no means solely 'English' in its range; rather it is widely distributed from northwest Europe south and eastward to North Africa and western Asia. Its northern distribution is largely along the western fringes of the European continent from Norway southward, venturing inland where the maritime influence tempers winter temperatures. This distribution demonstrates its intolerance of extremes of cold; however, recent research at the University of Hannover has shown that the common holly has quite rapidly extended its range both northward and eastward over the last half century. Taking as a comparison data collected in 1944, it has been found growing over 200KM further north along the Norwegian coast, and to have moved east into coastal regions of Sweden. It has also extended around 170KM to the east in parts of continental Europe, for example moving across Germany from 120KM west of Berlin to 50KM east of that city. This extension is almost certainly a consequence of milder winters and the recent warming trend. The 1944 study concluded that fertile common holly occurred only where average January temperatures were above 0C.

This does not mean that the common holly has become hardier in cultivation. It is still largely restricted to areas with maritime climates: even in its horticultural 'home territory', the British Isles, it can be stripped bare by an occasional (but thankfully rare) 'Siberian' winter. Excessive heat can also be problematical to *Ilex aquifolium*; in more southerly and warmer latitudes, it occurs only in the more temperate conditions found at higher altitudes. These predilections suit it best for Zones 6 to 9, although some very tough cultivars are recommended for Zone 5; leaf variegation can also affect cold hardiness, typically rendering plants less hardy.

In North America *Ilex aquifolium* finds its home from home in the Pacific Northwest (to the point of invasiveness: see under "Distribution" in Chapter 1). It may thrive in some parts of the eastern seaboard, although it is always limited by extremes of both cold and summer heat. Selections capable of tolerating these more continental conditions have been made over the years; they may well prove more successful than English cultivars in the eastern USA and continental Europe. In less than ideal conditions English holly may grow quite well, but achieve only half to two-thirds of its potential size.

Otherwise, the English holly has a robust constitution and grows well in a wide variety of habitats, which is the key to its adaptability in our gardens. Over much of its range it is a classic understory and woodland edge plant, tolerating deep and partial shade with equanimity. It can also grow well in exposed situations and maritime areas, showing a high degree of resistance to salt winds. It is only to be expected that it will thrive and fruit best in good light, but it does not demand day-long sunshine to provide a dependable display. Its adaptability is also reflected in the range of soils it will grow in, from acid to moderately alkaline. It does not grow well in waterlogged conditions, doing best in a moist but well-drained loam. *The Hillier Manual* puts it succinctly when it says of *Ilex aquifolium* that it is '*adaptable to most soils and indifferent to sun and shade*'.

Over the centuries of mankind's close association with *Ilex aquifolium* a great number of cultivars have been selected, and indeed this plant is remarkably prone to throwing sports and mutations, whether from seed or spontaneously upon mature plants. In the 18th century, as hollies became more popular, the Wrench family (nurserymen of Parsons Green, Fulham, London) are reported by Miles Hadfield (1969) to have given rewards to '*people spotting remarkable kinds*'.

William Paul described the propensity of hollies to sport spontaneously in his address to the Floral Committee of the RHS in 1863: '*It is worthy of remark that the green varieties seem in many cases to repeat themselves as to form in both a gold and silver dress*'. Thomas Moore (1874–76) also remarked upon this, saying, '*It is, however, on the ground of variety that we now invite special attention to the Holly, and from this point of view no evergreen whose beauty is derived from its foliage, not its flowers, can compare with it*'. While the great diversity of the English holly undoubtedly lies in its foliage, yellow- and orange-berried variants have spontaneously occurred on a number of occasions, although for the present the oft-reported white-berried forms remain an unrealised myth.

This remarkable diversity of leaf shape and variegation sets the English holly apart from all other evergreens. To the layman there may appear to be a plethora of variegated cultivars, and it would be accurate to say that there are more names than there are distinct plants. This may be due to the meeting of the propensity of *Ilex aquifolium* to throw sports with the enthusiasm of many gardeners to put names on their chance discoveries, even though in the greater picture they may be of questionable individuality (an observation that holds true for other horticulturally important groups of hollies).

The lustre or gloss of holly leaves develops over the season. The emerging young shoots of many cultivars are purple- or pink-flushed, and relatively matt when young. Tracking the changes of the foliage can be fascinating, and some cultivars are particularly striking in their early growth stages (for example, the pink-flushed young leaves of some silver-margined cultivars). Once holly leaves are fully expanded it takes a few weeks for their full gloss to express itself; some gardeners observe that the final shiny finish does not fully develop until after a number of frosts. Also, the arrival of winter changes the angle at which the sun strikes the leaves, as it does the colour of the sun's rays, which become more yellow. All these factors exert their subtle effects, making the already glossy foliage of the common or English holly even more striking.

There has been much renaming of English hollies over the centuries. Old colloquial English names (many quite charming, such as Glory of the East Holly and Painted Lady Holly) were 'upgraded' to more fashionable descriptive Latin epithets in the 18th and 19th centuries. Now the wheel has turned full circle, and Latinised cultivar epithets are no longer allowed under modern nomenclatural rules (unless retained because changing them would create undue difficulties). A few cultivars of *Ilex aquifolium* have been returned to their original names, for example, the expressive 'Silver Milkmaid', which conjures up much more of a picture to the layman than the admittedly descriptive 'Argentea Medio-Picta'.

'Alaska' (female). A handsome, narrowly conical small tree that berries abundantly. The spiny leaves are around 5CM long by 3.7CM wide, dark glossy olive-green, with distinctively paler reverse. Brilliant red fruits are borne in dense clusters along the green shoots. A hardy selection, recommended for formal situations as it clips well; also good in containers as it fruits well when young.

'Amber' AGM (female). One of a small number of orange-fruited cultivars, this plant was introduced by Hillier Nurseries. It has a neat pyramidal habit and dark almost spineless glossy green leaves, around 5CM long by 3.7CM wide. The distinctive, large and glossy orange fruits are generously borne and persist well if they escape the attentions of birds.

'Ammerland' (female). A hardy selection by Heinz Bruns, of Westerstede, Germany, in 1970. It is narrowly conical in habit, with upright shoots and dark purple stems, and distinctive large, spiny, dark glossy green leaves up to 8CM long by 4CM wide. Large dark red berries are freely borne. This plant is hardy under continental European conditions to –22C.

'Angustifolia' (male and female). This old British cultivar, dating back to the late 18th century, exists in both sexes. It makes a neat, small, conical plant, good in formal situations or trimmed in containers. The purple stems bear leaves that are relatively narrow and variable in size, reaching around 5CM long by 1.5CM wide, with slender marginal spines; female plants bear red fruit. 'Hascombensis' is a similar-looking clone, growing to around 0.9M tall by 1.2M wide.

'Angustimarginata Aurea' (male). This old cultivar has been grown under a number of synonyms including 'Angustifolia Aurea Marginata', 'Aurea Angustifolia' and 'Myrtifolia Elegans'. The current name was given by Susyn Andrews to clear up the longstanding confusion. This is a handsome, small, broadly pyramidal plant; purplish stems bear small, neat, dark green leaves

3.8–5.5cm long by up to 2.5cm wide, with distinctive yellow margins. It should make a neat and elegant variegated hedge.

'Apricot Glow' (female). Synonym 'Wieman's Apricot Glow'. Raised by J. S. Wieman, this orange-fruited American selection is conical in habit, and said by Galle to be '*very distinct and effective in the landscape*'. A moderately vigorous grower, with relatively lush, spiny, glossy dark olive-green leaves that can reach over 12.5cm long by 7.5cm wide. The orange fruits have a red blush and are freely borne on purplish stems.

'Argentea Marginata' AGM (female). The broad-leaved silver holly is one of the oldest variegated hollies; its exact ancestry is lost, but it certainly goes back to the 18th century. Over the years a number of synonyms have been bestowed upon this valuable cultivar (in the USA this and very similar plants may be sold under the synonyms 'Silvary', 'Silver Beauty' and 'Silver Princess'); these are testimony to its quality and desirability, as is the RHS Award of Garden Merit. It is quite vigorous, growing after many years into a large spreading bush or small tree of 10m or more. Very amenable to trimming, it has a long history of being worked into topiary and hedges. The spiny leaves, borne on green stems, are 5–7.5cm long by around half as wide and have a generous creamy white margin enclosing a dark olive-green centre. This cultivar gives several distinct displays as the season progresses. In early summer the young growths are distinctively flushed pinky red; this attractive effect is then followed in autumn by handsome bright red glossy fruits.

Ilex aquifolium 'Argentea Marginata' AGM combines handsome variegated leaves and glossy red fruits.

Opposite: The small pointed leaves of *Ilex aquifolium* 'Angustimarginata Aurea' have distinctive golden edges.

'Argentea Marginata Pendula' (female). Another plant with numerous synonyms, one of the oldest being 'Perry's Weeping' (its common name), this graceful cultivar was introduced in 1859 by Perry's Nursery, of Banbury,

The weeping *Ilex aquifolium* 'Argentea Marginata Pendula', with cascading purple stems that complement the boldly variegated leaves (**right**).

Oxford, England. Left to its own devices, this steadily forms a mounded creamy white and green dome, whose pendent purplish lateral branches bear spiny leaves, similar to those of its upright namesake, with attractive creamy yellow marginal variegation. For quicker effect in the landscape this cultivar can be trained upward to the height required, and then allowed to weep in order to show off its distinctive habit. Bright red berries are freely borne.

'Aurea Marginata' (female). Similar to 'Argentea Marginata', distinguished by its purple stems and yellow-margined leaves. This name has probably been applied to many cultivars over the years. Not free-fruiting. 'Aurea Marginata Pendula' has a weeping habit, yellow leaf margins and can fruit well.

'Aurifodina' (female). Synonym 'Muricata'. This is a distinctive and attractive golden variegated selection, forming a broadly conical large shrub to around 4.5M tall. The leaves are relatively flat for an English holly, very dark green in the centre with some lighter streaking, variegated with yellow-green and margined in yellow. It bears vivid red fruits.

A centuries-old yellow-berried cultivar, *Ilex aquifolium* 'Bacciflava'.

'Bacciflava' (female). Yellow-berried English holly cultivars have been remarked upon in the literature since the 17th century. This is the best established yellow form in cultivation, listed in catalogues since the late 18th century. It is effectively synonymous with 'Fructu Luteo' and cannot be told apart from it. Upright and quite vigorous in habit, it has glossy dark green leaves that are nearly spineless, around 7.5CM long by 2.5CM wide. The berries are generously produced, around 8MM across, of a clean, slightly acid yellow, and typically left alone by birds until after the red- and orange-fruited varieties have been exhausted.

'Balkans' (female). An interesting cultivar developed from seed collected in the wild in Yugoslavia in 1934 and introduced by A. Brownell of Oregon. It has wavy margined, spiny, dark green, glossy leaves up to 7.5CM long by 4CM wide. The bright red berries are around 8MM wide, and borne abundantly; this is reputedly a hardy selection. 'Marshall Tito' is a male from the same provenance. These selections have been included under *Ilex* ×*altaclerensis* by some authorities.

'Beautyspra' (female). One of a number of fine *aquifolium*-type hollies developed and introduced by the Wieman Nursery of Oregon, testimony to the importance of the English holly on the West Coast of the USA. This is a vigorous grower, as befits a plant used for holly orcharding; it is recommended by Galle for landscape use. The very spiny dark olive-green leaves are up to

6.3CM long by 2.5CM wide, and distinctly wavy. The bright red berries are freely borne and ripen early.

'Betty Brite' (female). Another Wieman introduction, a variegated sport from 'Early Cluster'. The leaves are large, oval in shape, and quite large-growing to around 12.5CM long by 7.5CM wide with an irregular generous yellow margin enclosing the light grey-green central area. Red fruits are borne in generous clusters. This cultivar is recommended for tubs and patios.

'Brownell's Special' (female). A recommended clone for growers on the East Coast, noted for its generous fruiting habit. Dark olive-green leaves, around 6.3CM long by 3.2CM wide, are borne on purple stems. The vivid red fruits are quite large, up to 12MM in diameter.

'Crassifolia' (female). Known as the leather-leaf holly, this old selection from Britain is one of a number of cultivars that fall into the category of being more curious than beautiful. Slow-growing but capable of reaching over 4.5M, the purple shoots bear dark green leaves, which are thick, spiny and relatively narrow, around 5CM long by 1.2CM wide; the red berries are distinctly flattened at their ends. A plant for the enthusiast.

'Crispa' (male). Synonym 'Contorta'. Another curiosity, this is known under the descriptive name of the screwleaf holly. First described in the early 19th century, it may have arisen as a sport of 'Scotica'; in common with that cultivar it bears comparatively thick leaves, which are glossy, variable in shape, around 5CM long by 2.5CM wide, almost spineless save for a bold apical spine, with a marked twist that shows off their paler undersides. Under ideal conditions plants can reach 7.5M or more in height. 'Crispa Aurea Picta' is of similar antiquity, virtually identical in its growth, with bold yellow splashing and markings in the centre of the leaf.

'Deletta' (female). A hardy selection ideal for the eastern USA, this is a heavy-fruiting compact conical plant of steady growth, capable of reaching over 1.8M tall by 1.2M wide in ten years. Its spiny, glossy dark green leaves, borne on reddish shoots, are around 6.3CM long by 2.5CM wide. Vivid red berries are freely produced. Hardy to Zone 6.

'Donningtonensis' (male). A distinctive and handsome selection, conical in habit and capable of growing to 7.5M tall. The dark purple stems bear glossy, usually spineless very dark green leaves, purple-flushed when young, around 5cm long by up to 1.8CM wide.

'Dude' (male). Another Wieman selection, as with so many variegated hollies arising through the chance discovery of a variegated shoot. The relatively flat lightly spined leaves have a generous yellow margin surrounding a dark green centre, up to 9CM long by a third as wide. Galle notes it as a plant capable of producing abundant pollen.

The generously white-margined leaves of *Ilex aquifolium* 'Elegantissima'.

'Early Cluster' (female). Introduced by Wieman, this cultivar has spiny leaves around 6cm long and half as wide and, as its name describes, bears good clusters of bright red fruit. It is of importance as the parent by sporting of the distinctive variegated 'Pinto'.

'Earlygold' (female). One of numerous introductions from G. Teufel of Oregon, this is a variegated sport from 'Zero', another Teufel selection. It is worth trying in locations where other marginal-variegated plants may be of doubtful hardiness, as it is reputed to share its parent's toughness. Pyramidal in growth, the original plant was described in 1959 as being 3.6M tall by 4.5M wide at around fifteen years old. It has a handsome combination of deep purple stems and undulate leaves, around 6.3CM long by 3.2CM wide, with spiny margins and generous creamy yellow borders enclosing a dark olive-green centre. The glossy red berries ripen early.

'Elegantissima' (male). An old cultivar dating back to before the mid 19th century, broadly similar to 'Argentea Marginata', with handsome distinctly spiny white-margined, smaller leaves of more delicate effect, around 5CM long. The young growths are pink-flushed. 'Elegantissima' is a broad, upright-growing shrub that is particularly useful for trimming and topiary.

'Ferox' (male). The hedgehog holly, claimed to be one of the oldest cultivars in continual cultivation (since at least the early 17th century, when John Parkinson described it, unmistakeably, as '*a holly with leaves wholly prickly*'). It can certainly lay claim to being the most distinctive of all hollies, and (with its variegated siblings) is arguably unique among evergreens. 'Ferox' forms a rounded shrub of moderate vigour, although capable of growing to around 4.5M in time. The purple stems bear relatively small leaves, around 5CM long by half as wide, heavily spined along the margins, with further small spines clustered along the upper surface, particularly toward the tip. 'Ferox' and its coloured variants may flower prolifically, but the flowers are sterile, so it should not be used for pollination. Several variegated cultivars exist. The first of the two most common is 'Ferox Argentea' AGM, a very effective plant whose deep purple stems and flower bud clusters set off the white-margined leaves superbly; the leaf blade spines are particularly showy, as they are also mainly white. Well deserving of its RHS Award of Garden Merit. The second, 'Ferox Aurea', is broadly similar to its namesakes, although not quite as spiny on the leaf surface, bearing a bold golden yellow central splash in the leaf.

Uniquely spined on the upper surface and the leaf edges, *Ilex aquifolium* 'Ferox Argentea' AGM.

Left: A distinctive golden yellow cone, *Ilex aquifolium* 'Flavescens'.

'Flavescens' can fruit well, but is most valued for its pale creamy foliage.

'Flavescens' (female). The moonlight holly, an old cultivar from the mid 19th century. While sometimes referred to as variegation, the effect of the leaf colouring of this plant might best be described as suffusion or shading rather than true variegation. However described, it is a distinctive and effective plant in the landscape. The foliage is typical of the species, but softly and variably suffused with yellow. The effect is strongest on the young leaves and in good light, so for maximum colour place in a sunny position. Elwes and Henry call it a '*beautiful variety*' whose '*dark central mass of foliage with light yellow terminal shots [give] the effect of a shrub seen by moonlight*'. The drama of this plant is further increased when it bears its bold red fruits. The leaf colour does not seem to affect the vigour of this plant greatly; it is certainly capable of reaching 4.5M and much more over time. Unlike truly variegated plants the yellow leaf suffusion can be passed on to offspring, and in the USA Wieman has produced hybrids of 'Flavescens' with 'Dude', yielding the cultivars 'Wieman's Moonbrite' (male) and 'Night Glow' (female), which share the distinctive golden suffusion of 'Flavescens'. 'Phantom Gold' (male), a Brownell introduction, is another similar cultivar. Of these selections Brownell says, '*On moonlit nights these hollies serve as phantasmal beacons illuminating the landscape with their pale yellow glow*'; beautifully put!

'Friesland' (female). Discovered growing in the wild in Friesland, northern Germany by Hans-Georg Buchtmann in 1988. It is erect in growth, with undulate, spiny, dark olive-green glossy leaves, distinctively long and narrow, at up to 9cm by 3.5cm wide. Bright red berries are freely borne, and the plant is reportedly very hardy, as might be expected from its provenance.

'George Daniel' (male). A very hardy cultivar, introduced by Bull Valley Nurseries, Pennsylvania, with dark green spiny leaves 5–7.5CM long by up to 3.7CM wide. Reported by Galle to be hardy to –18C in Zone 6.

GOLD COAST = 'Monvilla' (male). A variegated sport from 'Little Bull', an upright-growing shrub of compact and dense habit to 2.4M tall by 1.8M wide. The spiny leaves are small, with slightly wavy margins, up to 4.5CM long, vividly and boldly margined with bright creamy yellow, standing out well against the dark purple stems. It is reputed to be a good pollinator, recommended for hedges and would make a good subject in a container. Hardy to Zone 6.

'Golden Milkboy' (male). The Milkboy and Milkmaid (golden and silver) hollies are among the most distinctive of the variegated hollies, all bearing leaves with bold central blotching in various shades of white and yellow. 'Golden Milkboy' is a striking cultivar, among the brightest of all variegated plants. The lightly spined leaves are quite large, flat, up to 7.5CM long by 3.8CM wide and variable in their markings, with the most heavily variegated having their green edges reduced to a narrow margin. Despite its lack of green tissue this plant is moderately vigorous, but quite prone to reverting to its green-leaved forebear.

'Golden Milkmaid'. An old selection with a rather confused life history: the name has probably been applied to numerous plants within a broad group over the years. The plant we now recognise under this name is superficially very similar to 'Golden Milkboy', with purple stems bearing slightly smaller leaves with wavy margins, which are not quite as heavily marked. The drama of this cultivar is increased tremendously by its red berries, which show up superbly against the pale variegation. A vigorous plant, which can reach over 9M tall. 'Weeping Golden Milkmaid' is effectively a weeping form of 'Golden Milkmaid', bearing good quantities of glossy red fruit. There is some confusion in the trade among the Milkmaid and Milkboy types, with matters complicated even more by 'Silver Milkboy' having begun to bear fruit after

Left: *Ilex aquifolium* 'Golden Milkboy', one of a number of handsome centrally variegated cultivars.

Ilex aquifolium 'Golden Milkmaid' combines bold variegation and brilliant berries.

masquerading initially as a male; however, where they can be found, they remain distinctive and desirable clones for those who appreciate bright variegation.

'Golden Queen' AGM (male). Synonym 'Aurea Regina'. Another holly with gender identification difficulties! This striking selection has been in cultivation for over a century and a half, and is considered one of the finest of the gold-margined cultivars (hence the RHS Award of Garden Merit). Of vigorous habit, it grows into a broad pyramidal tree 7.5M tall or more. The large leaves are spiny, with distinctly wavy edges and quite broad, around 7.5CM long by 5CM wide. They are boldly margined with yellow, and marked and splashed with pale green and grey overlying dark green. Hardy to Zone 7b, but in colder regions it may be replaced by 'Madame Briot'.

'Golden van Tol' (female). Discovered by the Dutch firm of Ravestein and Sons in 1960, this is a very handsome variegated sport of 'J. C. van Tol', sharing its ability to set prolific red fruit without need of a male, and its pyramidal habit. The leaves are dark glossy green, with striking yellow margins. Now reputedly one of the most commonly grown variegated hollies in continental Europe, it was awarded the First Class Certificate by the Royal Boskoop Horticultural Society in 1969. Hardy to Zone 6.

'Gold Flash' (female). Synonym 'Bosgold'. Another Dutch introduction, again a sport of 'J. C. van Tol'. The leaves are almost spineless, bearing irregular bold yellow splashes in the centre, which creates a very bright effect. 'Gold Flash', with other centrally variegated cultivars, is rather prone to reversion. The tendency to revert can be easily managed, especially on plants kept within bounds by trimming. Hardy to Zone 6.

'Goldfrucht' (female). A very hardy yellow-fruited selection found in 1958 on the Carstens Nursery, Varel, Germany. A compact conical plant to 5M tall in around thirty years, with dark purple stems. The dark glossy leaves bear prominent spines, and are around 6cm long by half as wide. Yellow fruits with a red blush on the side exposed to the sun are freely borne. A very hardy cultivar, which has survived –28C.

Ilex aquifolium 'Gold Flash' shows the generous fruiting characteristic of its distinguished forebear.

'Green Pillar' (female). Selected and introduced by Hillier Nurseries in England, this cultivar is grown for its narrowly conical habit to 7.5M tall. The branching habit is upright, and the spiny, wavy-edged deep green leaves are up to 7.5CM long by 5CM wide, with typical bright red fruit borne freely. This selection is highly recommended for use as a specimen plant or in a screen, and is suitable for growing in containers.

'Handsworth New Silver' AGM (female). One of the most successful and widely grown variegated cultivars, introduced by Fisher, Son and Sibray before 1850, and awarded the RHS Award of Garden Merit. It grows into a broad pyramidal tree over 7.5M tall, with dark purple young stems that set off

the variegated foliage superbly. The leaves are around 7.5CM long by 3.1CM wide, dark lustrous green with grey mottling in the centre, and generously bordered in white or pale cream. Free-fruiting with abundant red berries.

Opposite: *Ilex aquifolium* 'Handsworth New Silver' AGM, a fine combination of dark green and cream with freely borne red berries.

'Harpune' (female). A distinctive, dainty cultivar of narrow upright habit, which arose as a sport of 'Alaska' in 1978, introduced by H. Hachmann in Germany. The dark green glossy leaves bear few or no spines, and are very narrow, around 5CM long by only 10MM wide. Fruiting is more generous on older plants, with the glossy red berries showing well among the delicate foliage. A good plant for containers; considered to be very hardy.

'Hastata' (male). This is another plant for the devotee of the strange, one of a number of old holly curiosities maintained in cultivation for many years (in this case since its introduction by Fisher and Holmes in 1863). A slow-growing

An architectural curiosity, *Ilex aquifolium* 'Hastata'.

shrub with deep purple young stems, the thick dark green leaves around 2.5CM long by 1.3CM wide bear one to three large spines on each side, but have unique rounded, spineless apices. The effect is architectural rather than ornamental.

'Ingramii' (male). Synonym (in the USA) 'Silver-dust'. Another holly with a unique character, this old (pre-1875) English cultivar is fascinating, although perhaps an acquired taste to the layman. Of moderate vigour, it grows into a broadly upright shrub of 3M or more, with purple shoots and small, flat, spiny dark green leaves scarcely 3.7CM long, each uniquely speckled and margined with white and grey-green. This silver dusting is distinctive, and even more so when combined with the strong purple flushing of the young leaves. May be prone to reversion if not watched. 'Ingramii' is a remarkable plant, very suitable for small gardens or containers, whose strong but erratic variegation makes it slightly less hardy (Zone 7b).

'Integrifolia' (female). A very distinctive cultivar, dating back to before 1817. A plant of upright growth, with green stems bearing handsome, scarcely spined dark glossy green leaves around 7CM long by 3CM wide. The bright red berries show well against the neat foliage. A useful plant for those who prefer their hollies to be more user-friendly.

Above: Another distinctive variegated cultivar, *Ilex aquifolium* 'Ingramii', with deep purple new growths.

Opposite, top: Small, entire leaves are the main feature of *Ilex aquifolium* 'Integrifolia'.

Opposite: *Ilex aquifolium* 'Lichtenthalii' slowly forms a mound of linear leaves with sparse red berries.

'J. C. van Tol' AGM (female). An old (around 1895) Dutch selection, selected and introduced by van Tol. This is generally considered to be one of the best and most valuable cultivars available for its foliage, hardiness, free-fruiting habit, and the priceless ability to set fruit without need of a pollinator, all of which contribute to the RHS Award of Garden Merit, and its popularity on both sides of the Atlantic. A vigorous-growing plant of broadly conical habit to over 4.5M tall, with almost spineless dark glossy green leaves around 5CM long by 2.5CM wide. Glossy brilliant red fruits are very freely borne. Hardy to Zone 6.

'Larry Peters' (male). A compact selection, the original plant formed a broad cone 0.75M tall after ten years. The leaves are very dark olive-green and glossy, borne on reddish young stems, around 6.3CM long by 3.8CM wide, undulate and spiny-edged, taking on distinct bronze tones in winter. Reputed to be hardy to Zone 6.

'Lewis' (female). A vigorous, hardy clone of upright habit originating in the happily named town of Delight, Maryland, introduced by S. McLean. The leaves are quite small, dark olive-green, undulate, around 5CM long by 2.5CM wide and moderately spiny. Dark red fruits are freely produced. Hardy to Zone 6b.

'Lichtenthalii' (female). Another of those strange-leaved cultivars which seem to hold a lasting fascination for gardeners. This plant initially arose in Austria, and was introduced in the late 1880s. It forms a slow-growing mound with dark purple stems and relatively long narrow leaves of glossy dark green with prominent pale midribs and margins, variably spiny. Very shy-fruiting.

'Madame Briot' AGM (female). An old (pre-1866) French variegated selection, which has deservedly carved itself a niche as an outstanding example of the gold-margined variegated hollies, this is an excellent performer in many regions (recognised by the RHS Award of Garden Merit). A large, broad-growing

Ilex aquifolium 'Madame Briot' AGM in full winter garb, with prolific red berries.

shrub to 7.5M high, with purplish young stems bearing quite large wavy-edged and spiny leaves, around 7.5CM long by 3.7CM wide, whose dark olive-green centres are very generously margined in rich butter-yellow, creating the perfect setting for the vivid red fruits. Considered to be more hardy in continental conditions than the similar 'Golden Queen' (Zone 7a), this comes with the added advantage of berries.

'Marshall Tito'. See 'Balkans'.

'Mary Peters' (female). Another tough introduction from R. K. Peters, reported to have survived –34C. A broad-growing shrub, the original plant taking fourteen years to reach 2.7M tall by 2.1M wide. Dark glossy green spiny leaves around 5CM long by half as wide, with pinky red fruit. Reportedly hardy to Zone 5.

'Monstrosa' (male). An unusual and slightly hyperbolic name for a plant which while unusual is by no means monstrous! This old cultivar (listed in catalogues as long ago as 1845) has a broad and dense habit of growth. The green stems bear very spiny, deep glossy green leaves, 5–7.5CM long by up to 2.5CM wide, some with such a distinct inward curve that the marginal spines virtually cross in the middle, to give a distinctive and fascinating textural effect.

'Myrtifolia' (male). A small-leaved clone of great age (pre-1830), slowly forming a small shrub. The leaves are flat, glossy dark green, up to 3.8CM long by half as wide, with numerous small spines. This cultivar is best known as the parent by sporting of two distinct variegated forms, which follow.

'Myrtifolia Aurea' (male). Synonym 'Myrtifolia Aurea Marginata'. This is a handsome, neatly variegated small pyramidal shrub, dating back to 1863.

Upright in growth to 2.4M tall, the leaves are very similar in shape to 'Myrtifolia', with a distinct and attractive yellow margin. An excellent plant for a container or patio.

Left: *Ilex aquifolium* 'Monstrosa' is a striking selection with distinctively spiny leaves.

'Myrtifolia Aurea Maculata' AGM (male). Another small, pyramidal shrub, which dates back to the 19th century. This cultivar has wider leaves than its parent, distinctly spiny and bearing bold central splashes of yellow; it is occasionally prone to revert to 'Myrtifolia'. A bright, small shrub ideal for containers, small gardens, low hedges and topiary, this is becoming more popular in the trade in Britain and has been awarded the RHS Award of Garden Merit.

A bright subject for winter effect or a colourful low hedge, *Ilex aquifolium* 'Myrtifolia Aurea Maculata' AGM.

'New Brunswick' (male). Another introduction from the cold-hardy stable of R. K. Peters. This cultivar has dark glossy green leaves, up to 7.5CM long by 3.7CM wide, with spiny undulating edges. A good pollinator, it is hardy to Zone 6.

'Pendula' (female). A number of pendulous hollies have been selected over the years. The plant we now grow under this name was selected in 1842 in a garden in Derby, England. It develops over time into a graceful, free-fruiting deep glossy green mound with pendent lateral branches, capable of growing up to 3M or more, and usually wider than tall. The purple stems bear spiny leaves up to 7.5CM long by 3.7CM wide, and generous quantities of vivid red fruit.

'Pinto' (female). Synonym 'Wieman's Pinto'. This variegated selection arose as a sport of 'Early Cluster' and was discovered in 1935. It has purplish stems bearing lightly spined, variegated dark olive-green leaves with a bold central splash of vivid yellow which ages to cream, around 7CM long by 3CM wide. Vivid red berries up to 10MM wide are freely borne in generous clusters.

'Pyramidalis' AGM (female). An excellent cultivar which may bear spiny and entire leaves on the same plant, originally selected in the late 19th century by

Ilex aquifolium 'Pyramidalis' AGM offers deep glossy green spineless leaves and dependable fruit.

van Nes, a Dutch nurseryman. It has gone on to become one of the most useful and widely grown hollies, particularly in Europe. As its name suggests, this is an upright grower, forming a narrow cone of 9M or more tall. The leaves are usually nearly or entirely spineless, deep glossy green, around 7.5CM long by 2.5CM wide. It fruits very freely, with abundant shiny red berries which set without the need of a pollinator (i.e., it is parthenocarpic), further increasing its garden value, recognised by the RHS Award of Garden Merit.

'Pyramidalis Aureomarginata' (female). Broadly similar in habit and leaf shape to 'Pyramidalis', introduced from Holland in 1910. The glossy dark green leaves are slightly spiny or entire, handsomely edged with pale yellow, and red fruit is again borne freely.

'Pyramidalis Fructu Luteo' AGM (female). Originated at Hillier Nurseries in England in the 1960s, this distinctive selection is again similar to 'Pyramidalis' in habit and leaf, distinguished by its tremendous quantities of bright yellow berries. A plant of high quality, which has been given the RHS Award of Garden Merit.

Ilex aquifolium 'Pyramidalis Fructu Luteo' AGM, vigorous and dependable.

Left: The bright yellow berries of 'Pyramidalis Fructu Luteo' AGM.

'Rederly' (female). Originating in Oregon, this cultivar was selected mainly for its early colouring habit (the cultivar name combines 'red' and 'early'). A vigorous plant, with purple stems bearing undulate spiny-edged dark olive-green leaves of medium size, around 5CM long, and generous quantities of glossy red fruit.

Opposite: The dark stems and red fruits of *Ilex aquifolium* 'Rubricaulis Aurea' complement the handsome rounded leaves.

'Ricker' (female). A compact, columnar selection from the 1930s, discovered in Takoma Park, Maryland. Dark stems bear deep olive-green leaves around 7.5CM long by 3CM wide. The bright red fruits are quite large, up to 13MM wide; originally selected for winter hardiness.

'Rubricaulis Aurea' (female). Originating in continental Europe in the mid 18th century, this is a neat and distinctive cultivar. Of broadly upright habit, growing to 4.5M tall, it has dark purple stems and shoots, with small- to medium-sized flat rounded leaves around 5CM long by 3.7CM wide. They are dark olive-green, distinctively margined in rich golden yellow, flushing with crimson after cold weather; the berries are deep scarlet. It is a very handsome plant, quite hardy for a variegated holly, and recommended for Zone 6b.

'Scotica' (female). A vigorous, large-growing cultivar dating from before 1830, forming a broadly pyramidal plant to 9M or more high. This distinctive plant has purple stems bearing thick, lustrous spineless deep green leaves up to 7.5CM long, and red fruits. Two variegated cultivars exist: 'Scotica Aurea', with gold-edged leaves, and 'Scotica Aureopicta', with very twisted leaves bearing irregular central leaf blotches; the latter is a vigorous plant but needs to be watched for reversion.

'Shortspra' (female). Synonym 'Wieman's Shortspra'. Introduced by Wieman in the 1960s, this compact, erect-growing cultivar is recommended for landscape and orchard work, attesting to a vigorous and free-fruiting constitution. Green stems bear dark green, spiny, wavy-edged leaves up to 7.5CM long by half as wide, with vivid red fruit.

SIBERIA = 'Limsi' (female). A seedling apparently discovered growing by a hedge in a nursery in Boskoop, Holland, by Arie Blanken. Since its recent introduction it has shown great promise for continental Europe and the USA

Opposite: The palest of all the centrally variegated hollies, *Ilex aquifolium* 'Silver Milkboy'.

as a hardy, free-fruiting cultivar of very compact, upright pyramidal growth. The foliage is neat, dark glossy green, borne on purple stems, undulate and variably spiny, the leaves up to 7.5CM long by 5CM wide. Glossy vivid red berries are produced in abundance. Hardy to Zone 6.

'Silvary'. See 'Argentea Marginata'.

'Silver Lining' (female). A very distinctive recent introduction from Louise Bendall at Highfield Hollies in England, discovered as a chance seedling, and the first new holly to be registered by the Holly Society of America in the new millennium. Upright and vigorous in habit, over 3M tall so far, with purple stems bearing delicately white-margined leaves, variable in their size and spininess. The unique characteristic of this plant is the deep purple flush that it takes on as winter progresses, giving it a further distinct season of display. Red berries are borne, but not freely.

'Silver Milkboy' (female). Introduced by Hillier Nurseries in England, when well grown this is a cultivar of unique character. A dense-growing broad upright shrub to 3M or more tall by as much across, with very spiny wavy leaves around 5CM long. The green edges surround very large pale central patches of creamy white or palest primrose-yellow, giving the plant a very ethereal appearance from a distance. Although this was grown for many years as a male, it has recently shown its hand as an extremely sparse-fruiting female. With its pale variegation it remains a very distinctive cultivar, but one that is likely to be quite tender over much of continental Europe and the eastern USA. Hardy to Zone 7b.

'Silver Milkmaid' (female). An old British selection, dating back to before 1820. This cultivar is broadly similar in vigour and habit to 'Silver Milkboy'. Apart from its free-fruiting habit, it is distinguished by markedly curved and twisted small spiny leaves, which bear a bold central patch of slightly darker creamy yellow. It bears generous quantities of bright glossy red berries.

'Silver Queen' AGM (male). Synonym 'Argentea Regina'. An old British cultivar, dating back to before 1863, and one of the finest of the Argentea Marginata (silver-margined) Group. Moderately vigorous to begin with, it will in

Ilex aquifolium 'Silver van Tol', with dark leaves brightly picked out in creamy white.

time become a large shrub or small tree, exceeding 6M in height and over half again as wide; training a leader up a stake will help it to gain height. The brightly variegated leaves are broadly oval in shape, around 6.8CM long by half as wide, with dark green centres marbled grey-green and bold creamy white margins that contrast strikingly against the dark purple young stems. To round things off, the young growths have their own moment in the sun and are suffused with pink. This fine male selection, while superficially similar to others in the Group, is an excellent garden plant and earned the RHS Award of Garden Merit. It is considered to be slightly less hardy than 'Handsworth New Silver' and 'Argentea Marginata', at Zone 7b.

'Silver van Tol' (female). Another sport from the productive 'J. C. van Tol', introduced from Holland in 1977. The general habit of the plant is similar to its parent, although the lightly spined leaves are slightly more convex. The marginal variegation is of a particularly clean creamy white, which shows up very well against the dark glossy centres and purplish stems. Like its relations it will set fruit well without need of a pollinator. The Royal Boskoop Horticultural Society gave this clone an Award of Merit in 1977. Hardy to Zone 7.

SPARKLER = 'Monler' (female). An early-fruiting cultivar, introduced in the early 1960s by Monrovia. The foliage is quite small, with spiny leaves up to 5CM long, dark glossy green and slightly wavy. Bright red berries are freely borne from a comparatively early age.

'Watereriana' (male). Synonym 'Waterer's Gold'. A distinctive old English cultivar, named for the Waterer nursery at Bagshot in Surrey, this is a slow-growing broad-spreading shrub with a very dense habit. The stems are green with yellow stripes, and the glossy leaves are small, around 4.3CM long, relatively flat with a few small spines on each side, olive-green in colour mottled with lighter yellow-green and grey, with an irregular narrow yellow margin. From a distance the effect of this small shrub is bright and cheerful; its dense habit and small leaves should make it an ideal subject for a low hedge.

Small-leaved and bright, *Ilex aquifolium* 'Watereriana'.

'Weeping Golden Milkmaid'. See 'Golden Milkmaid'.

'Whitesail' (female). A seedling of 'Handsworth New Silver', introduced by J. S. Wieman in the 1960s. A broadly upright variegated cultivar with purple stems and flat, spiny, dark olive-green leaves up to 6.8CM long, which are conspicuously margined in creamy white or pale yellow. Dark orange-red fruits are produced sparsely.

'Wieman's Moonbrite'. See 'Flavescens'.

'Wieman's Yellow-pillar' (female). A chance seedling discovered in the 1960s, this columnar yellow-fruited cultivar was developed and named by Wieman in 1982. Upright in growth, forming a compact column, with spiny dark green leaves up to 7CM long by half as wide, and generous clusters of clear yellow berries.

'Winter Green' (female). A very hardy selection, discovered in the mid 1970s by R. K. Peters, another of his numerous introductions of hardy English holly cultivars. A conical plant, it is reported to grow to 2.4M high by half as wide in ten years. The leaves are dark glossy green, variable in shape, usually spiny, up to 7CM long by 5CM wide, and the fruits vivid red. A remarkably hardy plant, reportedly to Zone 5, which has survived temperatures as low as –32C.

'Zero' (female). Synonym 'Teufel's Zero'. A hardy selection, as its cultivar name implies. A strong-growing upright plant with weeping branches and purple young stems with spiny dark green leaves and freely borne dark red berries. Hardy to Zone 6.

Ilex aquifolium has proved itself a productive parent with an important role in a number of major hybrid groups. *Ilex ×altaclerensis*, the Highclere hollies, whose complex parentage was described earlier, is the oldest and most important of these, with a number of large-growing plants of high quality. Another such group, with the potential to rival the Highclere hollies, especially in warmer regions, is the splendid *I. ×koehneana* (*aquifolium* × *latifolia*), the Koehne hybrids. Intermediate-sized plants come from *I. aquifolium*'s union with *I. cornuta*, including the important 'Nellie R. Stevens'. Another Chinese species, *I. pernyi*, has been used with the English holly to create the compact-growing, elegant group of *I. ×aquipernyi* hybrids, of great value for the smaller garden. Also small, and extremely successful in extending the range of *aquifolium*-type plants to cooler regions, are the blue holly hybrids, *I. ×meserveae*, which arose from the crossing of *I. aquifolium* with *I. rugosa*.

Ilex ×aquipernyi. This group of cultivars is both distinctive and of great value, particularly for the modern smaller garden. Refer to the section on *I. pernyi* for further information on these hybrids.

'Aquipern' (female). The first recorded *×aquipernyi* hybrid, apparently from a chance crossing of *Ilex aquifolium* 'Pyramidalis' with *I. pernyi*, dating back to 1933. As might be expected, the result of this union is a compact shrub of densely conical habit. The foliage follows the *I. pernyi* parentage, deep green, glossy, up to 5CM long by 2.5CM wide. The berries are bright red, 7MM wide.

DRAGON LADY = 'Meschick' (female). A Kathleen Meserve hybrid, introduced by the Conard-Pyle Company. This cultivar produces an upright narrow column, which will grow to 6M high. The spiny dark olive-green leaves, borne on dark stems, are glossy, up to 5CM long by 3CM wide. It bears prolific vivid red berries around 7MM wide, which in true *pernyi* style are comparatively large. A good plant to grow in a container.

'Gable's Male' (male). Synonym 'Gable'. A handsome foliage plant, with small, spiny, dark olive-green leaves 3–4.5cm long by 1.3–2cm wide. This selection is naturally pyramidal, but with occasional formative pruning it can be shaped into an excellent cone.

'San Jose' (female). A plant of unknown origin which should not be confused with the ×*koehneana* cultivar of the same name. Popular in the southwest USA, compact, pyramidal and upright in growth to 6m tall, with ovate dark green leaves 3.8–5cm long by half as wide. The vivid red fruits are of typical ×*aquipernyi* size and generously borne. Hardy to Zone 6b.

Ilex **'Arthur Bruner'**. See *Ilex* 'Emily Bruner'

Ilex ×attenuata (topal holly). This distinctive group of garden plants has arisen principally from natural and man-made hybrids between *I. opaca* (American holly) and *I. cassine* (dahoon holly), although it is now thought that the dahoon's close relation, *I. myrtifolia*, might also have been involved. Although known to Loesener at the turn of the 20th century from a number of intermediate forms between the species, *I. ×attenuata* was not formally described until 1924, from specimens collected in Florida. It was first cultivated under its correct botanical name in 1933, although at least one cultivar (now known as 'Hume No. 2') was in cultivation several decades before: noted holly expert H. Harold Hume (1953) mentions it as being cultivated at the Hume nursery in 1909, at which time it was still listed as a cultivar of *I. opaca* (as was *I. ×attenuata* 'East Palatka').

Ilex ×attenuata occurs naturally where the ranges of its parents overlap, a strip encompassing the coastal areas of the Carolinas, extending south via Georgia and Florida, then west to Alabama, Mississippi, and Louisiana. There is no hard-and-fast description of *I. ×attenuata*: this is understandable considering that it is a widespread natural hybrid grex (or group of cultivars arising from multiple hybridizations), from parents which are themselves variable across their distribution.

Essentially, the topal holly follows its *cassine* (or *myrtifolia*) parentage rather than *opaca*. It is lighter-textured than the American holly, with smaller, softer,

Opposite: The only yellow-fruited topal, *Ilex ×attenuata* 'Alagold'.

less spiny (or spineless) leaves, variably glossy, on thinner and more flexible twigs. It is also faster-growing than *Ilex opaca*, more likely to be multi-stemmed, and often conical in habit. Mature plants are less rigid in habit than the American holly, and the most vigorous cultivars are capable of over 13.5M in height after thirty years. The fruit of the topal holly matures earlier in the season than the American holly but is not as persistent. The berries are typically slightly smaller; but, following the dahoon, they may be carried in twos, threes or more (rather than singly as in *I. opaca*) and are usually very generously borne.

Among the cultivars of the topal holly are numerous adaptable plants for the garden (as is further discussed in Chapter 2). Gene Eisenbeiss (1996) calls them '*valuable landscape plants when utilized under conditions favorable to their genetic heritage*'. He drew attention to the potentially variable hardiness of hybrid plants whose provenance varied so widely, and recommended that they be considered as reliably hardy only to Zone 7b. This conservative assessment is not generally shared, however, and current thinking has shifted their hardiness to Zone 6b (and maybe 6a, if very carefully sited). If in doubt, check whether there is a history of topal holly growing in your locality, and if so, that they are untroubled by the climate. Bear in mind that it's not just sheer survivability that is required of a plant, but the ability to thrive and achieve its potential. With *Ilex ×attenuata* at the northern edges of its range, it is particularly important to seek out cultivars that will do well in your locality.

It appears we have serendipity and sharp-eyed gardeners to thank for most of the currently grown cultivars of *Ilex ×attenuata*. Some deliberate crosses have been made, but they have yet to make their mark commercially. Most of the cultivars listed here are reasonably available, particularly from specialist nurseries.

'Alagold' (female). The only yellow-fruited topal holly in general cultivation arose as a chance seedling from 'Foster No. 2', discovered by J. A. Webb and introduced in 1979. It has the typical narrow conical habit to over 3M high by 1.2M wide, with narrow, almost spineless dark olive-green leaves around 3.8CM long by about half as wide. The fruits are 6–7MM in diameter, and bright yellow with a slight orange tinge. Hardy to Zone 7.

'Blazer' (female). A scaled-down *Ilex ×attenuata* for smaller situations, this 'Foster No. 2' seedling from the same stable as 'Alagold' grew only 1.8M high by 0.9M wide in fifteen years. The dark olive-green leaves are around 3.8CM

long by 2CM wide, and the berries are vivid red, typical in size and borne in groups of six or seven. 'Eagleson' (female) is another compact, dwarf red-fruited selection; Galle quotes it achieving 3.7M high by 2.7M wide in eight years.

'East Palatka' (female). Named and introduced by H. Harold Hume from a tree at East Palatka, Florida, in the mid 1920s. Hume appraised it thus: '*Few American hollies surpass this variety in the amount of fruit borne and the regularity of its bearing, and because the leaves are small the fruit shows to its advantage*'. These comments neatly encapsulate the difference between the topal and the American holly, even though, albeit unwittingly, Hume was not comparing like with like. Growth is upright, pyramidal, with spineless glossy olive-green leaves somewhat broader than other *Ilex ×attenuata* cultivars, around 5CM long and half as wide. The vivid red fruits are around 8MM wide, borne abundantly and, as Hume noted, highly visible, adding further to its brilliant display. Hardy to Zone 7.

'Foster No. 2' (female). One of a group of cultivars selected and introduced by E. E. Foster in the 1940s, this is the most successful of the group and among the hardiest of the topal hollies. Narrowly conical in habit, with dark olive-green leaves 3.8–7.5CM long by half as wide, sporadically one- to five-spined, quite glossy and slightly suggestive of its opaca ancestry. The prolific, brilliant vivid red 7MM-wide berries stand out superbly against their sombre background. A highly adaptable landscape plant, hardy to Zone 6b (or 6a), and particularly suited for restricted spaces.

The shiny foliage and generous red berries of *Ilex ×attenuata* 'Foster No. 2'.

Opposite, top: Brilliant yellow in good light, *Ilex ×attenuata* 'Sunny Foster'.

Opposite: The vivid foliage colour found on the outer parts of 'Sunny Foster' fades to green on older leaves.

'Greenleaf' (female). A distinctive and vigorous cultivar introduced by the Greenleaf Nursery in the 1970s. The foliage is paler than most topal hollies, just about a medium olive-green, with a definite curve of the leaf blade, matt (not glossy), and comparatively broad at around 5CM long by over half as wide. The fruit is typical in size and colour, abundant and highly glossy.

'Hume No. 2' (female). As far as can be deduced, the original *Ilex ×attenuata* to be bought into cultivation, with leaves of medium olive-green bearing only the occasional small rogue spine. The prolific vivid red fruit is typical in size, but may be borne in clusters of as many as eight. A fine plant with a long track record in cultivation. There is also a 'Hume No. 1', whose origin is unknown.

'Oriole' (female). Raised at the US National Arboretum by Kosar, a finer-textured plant with very slightly spined dark olive-green narrow leaves, up to 3.8CM long by about a third as wide. The vivid red fruits, although similar in size to other topal hollies, appear larger in the finer foliage. A compact, relatively slow-growing cultivar, which is capable of 4.5M in height by half as much across after a slow start.

'Savannah' (female). Discovered in the 1960s in Savannah, Georgia, this cultivar definitely leans toward the American holly in its character, more so than most of the topal hollies in cultivation. The distinctly spined leaves are substantial in texture, medium olive-green, around 7.5CM long by 3.8CM wide; vivid red berries are borne in clusters of two or three. As its name would suggest, this cultivar is particularly popular and widely grown in the southeastern USA. Hardy to Zone 7b.

'Sunny Foster' (female). When well sited and given good light, this is one of the most colourful and distinctive of all hollies, 'Sunny' by name and sunny by nature. It arose as a sport on 'Foster No. 2' at the US

Opposite: *Ilex* BECKY STEVENS = 'Wyebec' combines small leaves and prolific fruit to good effect.

National Arboretum in 1964, and unsurprisingly is almost identical in every character apart from the distinctive bright yellow flush that suffuses the leaves where they are exposed to good light. In shade this character is lost, and older leaves also lose their brilliance as the plant grows. In a good site this plant is a narrow pyramid of brilliant colour, accentuated by its reflective leaves, and further enhanced when bearing its vivid red fruit. The apparent lack of chlorophyll does not seem to adversely affect its growth, although it may be rather slower than the typical *Ilex ×attenuata* cultivar. While an open site is essential for the best colour, protection from possible leaf-burn from cold winter winds is advised. Hardy to Zone 7, possibly 6b.

'Tanager' (female). Included with *Ilex ×attenuata*, this is actually the product of a deliberate crossing of *I. myrtifolia* and *I. opaca*, made by Kosar at the US National Arboretum. The cross produced a red-fruited, upright, compact, slow-growing plant, with narrow dark olive-green leaves up to 4.5CM long by 1.3CM wide. Hardy to Zone 7a.

***Ilex* BECKY STEVENS** = 'Wyebec' (female). A chance seedling found at Wye Nursery in Maryland, this distinctive plant is described by Fred Galle as a superior hybrid of 'Nellie R. Stevens'. The male parent is most likely to have been the species *I. ciliospinosa*, whose potential in hybridising is discussed at its Directory entry. BECKY STEVENS is a plant of narrowly upright growth; Galle reports an eighteen-year-old plant as being only 3.6M tall by just over half as wide, making it an ideal subject for small gardens. The neat spiny leaves are quite small, around 5.5CM long by 2.5CM wide, and abundant orange-red berries wreathe the stems. Hardy to –26C.

Ilex bioritsensis. Synonym *I. pernyi* var. *veitchii*. This handsome plant has a confused nomenclatural history, perhaps in part due to its wide distribution, taking in Taiwan (from where it was first described in 1911), throughout south-west China including Hubei, Ghuizou, Yunnan and Sichuan, and possibly Burma. It is a member of that choice group of Chinese species including *I. pernyi* and *I. ciliospinosa*, and as *I. pernyi* var. *veitchii* received an Award of Merit from the RHS in 1930. A shrub or small tree of upright habit to around 10M high,

it shares the neat foliage characteristics of its close relations, combining angles with curves to interesting effect. The dark green leaves are typically around 3CM long by 2CM wide, attractively spined, with several spines on each side and a strong apical spine, persisting for up to four years. The red fruits, 8–10MM long, are held closely to the shoots on short stems. Should be hardy in Zones 7 to 9.

***Ilex* Blue Holly Group**. See *Ilex ×meserveae*

***Ilex* 'Bob Bruner'**. See *Ilex* 'Emily Bruner'

***Ilex* 'Brighter Shines'** (male). A hybrid between *I. cornuta* 'Burfordii' and *I. pernyi*, of neat, compact pyramidal habit. The dark glossy leaves are small, 4.5CM long by 2.5CM wide, spiny and essentially oblong in shape, as would be expected from their parentage. Hardy to Zone 7, 6b with protection.

***Ilex* 'Brilliant'** (female) (*aquifolium × ciliospinosa*). This old (1935) W. B. Clarke hybrid has a garden value similar to that of the excellent *I. ×aquipernyi* cultivars. It forms an upright, pyramidal tree 5–8M tall. The leaves are dark glossy green, 3.8–5CM long by a third as wide, narrowly ovate rather than angular, showing the ciliospinosa influence to a marked extent. Two seedlings from 'Brilliant' have been selected and introduced by Tom Dodd Jr., 'Dorothy Lawton' and 'Patricia Varner'. In keeping with its name, 'Brilliant' bears abundantly, with vivid red berries around 9MM wide. It is recorded as parthenocarpic, setting fruit without the need for a male pollinator (Flint 1997). Hardy to Zone 6b.

***Ilex* Bruner Hollies Group**. See *Ilex* 'Emily Bruner'

***Ilex* BUTTERCUP** = 'Hefcup' (female). A variegated sport of *I.* 'Nellie R. Stevens' of neat, upright pyramidal habit to around 6m tall, recommended by Galle as suitable for a screen, specimen or hedge. The colourful leaves are up to 8CM long by half as wide, bearing a few spines. The bold marginal variegation is bright and distinctive, maturing to a good bright yellow around an irregular green centre. Red-orange berries are also borne. Hardy to Zone 7.

***Ilex* CARDINAL.** See *Ilex* Red Holly Group

***Ilex* 'Carolina Cone'** (sex unknown). An intriguing hybrid made in 1982 by Gene Eisenbeiss at the US National Arboretum, between the distinctive and slightly tender species *I. dimorphophylla* and *I. cornuta*. A plant of narrow, upright growth, as would be expected from the *dimorphophylla* side of its parentage, with spiny, very angular small dark green leaves around 2.5CM long by 7MM wide. Hardiness is still being established, but Galle reports other seedlings of this cross as growing and fruiting in the Philadelphia area (Zone 6b).

The light-textured *Ilex cassine* lies behind the graceful habit of many *I.* ×*attenuata* cultivars.

Ilex cassine (dahoon holly) was described by Linnaeus in 1753. It grows in the southeastern USA, Cuba and Mexico, with its US range from southern Virginia through North Carolina and south to Florida, Louisiana and Texas, typically along the Coastal Plains. Its chosen habitats are characterised by the presence of water, and it is found along streamsides, in swamps and hammocks, usually growing in acid soils. As would be expected from its geographical range, it is fairly tender, and hardy between Zones 7 and 10.

Ilex cassine in the wild is variable in growth, typically shrubby with the potential to form a small tree of around 10M tall; the bark is typical of hollies, grey and smooth, with slightly pubescent young shoots. The leaves are spineless, quite

Ilex cassine fruits are borne in generous numbers, another characteristic passed on to the topal hollies.

glossy, and fairly narrow, 4–10CM long by 1–3.5CM wide. Small white flowers are followed on female plants by red (rarely yellow) fruits up to 7MM wide. A well-fruited plant is an attractive sight, although not necessarily to everyone: of this species and *I. myrtifolia*, Dirr (2002) writes, '*The species and two varieties grow in Athens, [Georgia,] and* none *inspire the average gardener*'.

The garden history of the dahoon began with its introduction to Britain in 1726, by Mark Catesby. In common with a number of North American hollies it did not take root across the Atlantic, and is very rarely found; Bean rather dismisses it with this comment: '*Nothing useful can be said about its hardiness or its garden value in Britain*'. In the USA, however, this species made a valuable and distinctive contribution, albeit principally as one of the parents (with *Ilex opaca*) of the natural hybrid *I.* ×*attenuata*. Where it is represented in gardens Galle reports it as mainly being the narrow-leaved form, *I. cassine* var. *angustifolia*, which is available in the trade. Its primary characteristic is the narrow leaves, around 7.5CM long by only 13MM wide. Red-fruited cultivars of this variety may be found, including 'Baldwin' and 'Wild Robert'. Yellow-berried forms may also be offered for sale, for example, 'Tyron Palace'.

Ilex **CHINA BOY** = 'Mesdob' (male). This Kathleen Meserve hybrid (*rugosa* × *cornuta*) was introduced by the Conard-Pyle Company in 1979. With such a parentage it is (as might be expected) a tough plant, compact and upright in habit forming a rounded shrub with semi-glossy leaves up to 6cm long by 3.5cm wide. Following their *cornuta* parentage the leaves are rectangular, with prominent spines. Flowers are borne in profusion, making for a good pollinator. Hardy in Zones 6a to 9.

***Ilex* CHINA GIRL** = 'Mesog' (female). Sister seedling of CHINA BOY, of the same raiser, parentage and introduction. Again, a compact upright rounded plant with similar *cornuta*-type foliage. Bright red fruits, around 8mm wide, are borne in profusion. Hardy in Zones 6 to 9.

Ilex ciliospinosa. The potential of hollies from the Far East (China and Japan) for our gardens has scarcely been scratched, although a small group of evergreen species, particularly *I. cornuta*, *I. pernyi*, *I. latifolia* and *I. rugosa*, have all made significant contributions to the wealth of plants from which we can now choose. *Ilex ciliospinosa* is another to add to that list of Far Eastern species with particular potential for success in breeding programmes.

Ilex ciliospinosa was described by Loesener in 1911, and is allied to *I. bioritsensis* and *I. dipyrena*. It is distributed in western China, from where it was another of E. H. Wilson's discoveries, in 1904 (in west Sichuan), introduced in 1908. It is upright-growing as a large shrub or small tree with an open structure to around 7m tall, with pubescent young shoots and leaves 3.5–7.5cm long by 1–2.5cm wide, dark green and with forward-pointing spines. The berries are red, around 10mm across.

Ilex ciliospinosa is a plant of good habit, Bean says, '*a neat, small-leaved holly, erect and slender when small*'. Dudley (1986a) admired this plant as a '*choice Chinese species with well-displayed often quite large red fruit; rapid grower and thrives in Northern climates*'; he also recognised its breeding potential, describing it as '*a parent species of some very fine new hybrid cultivars, such as 'September Gem' from the National Arboretum*'. Another fine cultivar is the aptly named 'Brilliant' (× *aquifolium*), which has itself been the source of two distinctive Tom Dodd Jr. selections, 'Dorothy Lawton' and 'Patricia Varner'.

Other first-generation hybrids involving *Ilex ciliospinosa* include 'Byam K. Stevens' and 'Dr. Hu' (× *pernyi*), while with ×*aquipernyi* the progeny include 'Coronet' and 'September Gem'. With *I. cornuta* it has produced a flurry of hybrids, including 'Edward Goucher', 'Harry Gunning', 'Howard Dorsett', 'Washington' and 'William Cowgill', although most are not well established in the trade.

Ilex 'Clusterberry' (female). This cultivar is of particular interest as the only hybrid generally available featuring the Japanese species *Ilex leucoclada*, which was crossed with *I.* 'Nellie R. Stevens' (*cornuta* × *aquifolium*) by William Kosar at the US National Arboretum in 1961. Their union has produced a fine, broadly pyramidal free-fruiting plant to 3M tall, with matt, essentially spineless olive-green leaves around 6CM long by 2.5CM wide. In its fruiting it lives completely up to its name: generous clusters of glossy vivid red berries in stem-circling clusters. Hardy to Zone 7.

Ilex colchica (Black Sea holly) is closely related to *I. aquifolium* and of relatively recent introduction (1966 in the USA, at the Arnold Arboretum). This species is distributed from Bulgaria and Turkey to the Caucasus. In the wild it grows as part of the understory in silver fir or beech forest. Dudley (1986a) thought it '*may extend [the] north and south cultivation range of* I. aquifolium-*like holly*', and indeed its eastern distribution gives hope for hardier 'English-style' hollies. This species forms a shrub 1–3M tall or a small tree to 6M tall. It is distinguished from the English holly by a number of characteristics. The leaves are typically narrower, variable in their undulation and their glossiness, with numerous forward-pointing spines. The red fruits are 8–10MM in diameter, and borne in clusters of two to five. Hardy to Zone 7, or possibly lower.

Ilex spinigera, a related species, is a large shrub or small tree introduced in 1972 by Roy Lancaster and Mrs Ala from the forests of northern Iran and mountains bordering the southern Caspian Sea. It has more undulate, spiny leaves and pubescent branches, and brings further promise of hardiness. Although nothing has yet appeared in cultivation, Dudley (1986a) reported hybrids of both these species and *I. aquifolium* as showing '*great promise and vigor*'. Doubtless more will be heard of these species in their own right and as parents in years to come.

Ilex cornuta (Chinese holly, horned holly) was introduced into Britain by Robert Fortune in 1846, having first been seen by him near Shanghai on his journeys in China on behalf of the Horticultural Society (now the Royal Horticultural Society). This characterful evergreen was rapidly brought to the attention of British gardeners, firstly in Paxton's Flower Garden in 1851 and then in *Curtis's Botanical Magazine* in 1858 (t. 5059). Even as a young, small plant it clearly impressed the journal's writer, who described it thus: '*This extremely handsome-leaved species … resembles our common European Holly; but the foliage is extremely different, and very peculiar*'; the small white flowers were, however, dismissed as '*quite destitute of beauty*'. At this time the fruit had yet to be seen in cultivation, and the ultimate dimensions of the plant were also unknown. A further Fortune introduction in 1853 (var. *fortunei*) was described in *The Gardeners' Chronicle* as having spineless leaves like a broad, entire-leaved European holly, but as with the species this is not a fixed characteristic, and variability in leaf shape is very much the norm.

Its subsequent history in cultivation in Britain makes the Chinese holly another species that demonstrates the divide between the experience and expectations of gardeners on either side of the Atlantic. In Britain and much of Europe it languishes in the second rank: Bean describes it as '*of neat compact habit … suitable for positions where other evergreens would soon become too large. Its distinct and handsome foliage also makes in interesting, but it bears fruit only shyly*'. *The Hillier Manual* is rather cooler: '*Leaves of a peculiar rectangular form, mainly 5-spined. The large red fruits are rarely abundant*'. Graham Stuart Thomas (1992), with an eye to its distinctiveness, is warmer in his appreciation, and describes it as '*a handsome evergreen [with] much to recommend it*'.

But take this species to the USA (where it was introduced in the 1890s)—and particularly to the parts that swelter under oppressive summer heat—and *Ilex cornuta* comes into its own as a landscape plant of the first rank. Dirr (2002) says unequivocally, '*For the hot, dry areas of the country, this evergreen large shrub/small tree would rank in the top five safe choices*'. Apart from a tough and durable constitution that can only be described as ironclad, it also brings to the party the crucial horticultural characteristics of the holly that mark it out as distinct from so many other evergreens: superb glossy foliage and a generous fruiting habit that in the right circumstances is positively spectacular. These sterling qualities are apparent throughout the large tribe of cultivars and hybrids developed from *Ilex cornuta* in the last half century.

The species is typically a rounded, spreading evergreen shrub, wider than high, although it will form a small tree up to 7.5M tall in its native habitat in central and eastern China. It also occurs in Korea, where it grows right by the sea, attesting to a tough constitution and tolerance of the most challenging types of exposure, including salt-laden winds. In Britain it slowly grows to 2.4–3M high, while in the USA it is capable of achieving 5M and over.

The Chinese holly has a very dense, bushy habit. The young shoots are smooth, pale green, and rather angular in their first year. They bear thick and leathery leaves, a lustrous dark green in colour with a high gloss finish, 3.7–10CM long and 2.5–7.5CM wide, typically distinctly rectangular in outline. A large, rigid and wickedly sharp spine is borne in each corner, and a further spine at the leaf apex is strongly curved downward. The Chinese and Korean common names of tiger spine and bony spine tree are very apt for this well-armed plant! As with other spiny hollies this character may vary between plants and even on a single plant: four smaller spines may occur along the leaf margins, giving a total of nine, or the spines may be reduced to a single one at the apex of the leaf (as in 'Burfordii'). Plants may also bear spiny leaves at the base and entire, spineless leaves at the top.

Creamy white, sweetly scented four-petalled flowers are borne in great quantities in the leaf axils of second-year growths in early spring, and are very popular with bees. Given a good season and absence of sharp frosts, they are followed on female plants by abundant glossy red fruits, 7–13MM across, which ripen in September and October and persist well into the winter. The habit of the plant will often show them off to perfection in generous trusses at the ends of the shoots as well as along them, a bravura performance to equal that of any other berrying evergreen.

Even by the standards of hollies *Ilex cornuta* is generally easy of culture, in full sun or light shade, tolerating heat and drought, and adaptable to a range of soils as long as they are well drained. In years when fruit production is particularly heavy the foliage may yellow in late summer as the plant's resources are redirected toward the berries. This has been observed frequently with 'Burfordii'; however, a summer application of fertiliser to make up the nitrogen deficit when the condition is first noted should correct it. Biennial fruiting can become a habit in plants that are not regularly fed, as they take a year off to recoup their strength after bumper fruiting years.

For situations where plants have to be kept within bounds, the Chinese hollies take pruning and shearing very well, and will rapidly regrow after even the most severe pruning. *Ilex cornuta* and its cultivars may be grown in Zones 7 to 9a, and in a sheltered site in Zone 6b.

'Anicet Delcambre' (female). Synonyms 'Needlepoint', 'Willowleaf'. A compact, rounded-conical plant of upright habit, more suited to today's smaller gardens, growing 4.5M tall by 3M wide. The dark green glossy leaves are comparatively narrow, up to 7.5CM long by 2.5CM wide, giving the plant a lighter texture than other *Ilex cornuta* cultivars. Vivid red 7MM-wide fruits are generously borne.

'Avery Island' (female). Of rather upright growth, this yellow-fruited cultivar has deep green leaves, variable in shape, from spiny and quadrangular to single-spined and rounded, up to 9CM long by 5CM wide. The 7MM-wide pale yellow berries are abundantly borne.

Ilex cornuta 'Bostic' fruits along the stems to the very end, a *cornuta* trait.

BERRIES JUBILEE = 'Greer' (female). A plant of compact, mounded growth slowly achieving 1.5M high by 2.1M wide, with glossy dark green leaves, around 7.5CM long by 4.5CM wide, bold and comparatively large for the size of plant. The berries are vivid red, large, up to 13MM wide, and abundantly borne. An ideal plant for low hedges or foundation planting, which may in time replace the stalwart 'Rotunda', a mound-former that does not berry so well as a young plant. Both of these cultivars are tremendous people-stoppers—few would try to cut through a planting of either. Those who would like the form of these spiky mounds in their gardens, but without their fighting qualities, might try the far less spiny 'Carissa'.

'Bostic' (female). A free-fruiting, compact mounded cultivar capable of over 4.5M in height and 3M in width. Named for its finder, Mrs L. Bostic, and registered in 1960, its dark olive-green leaves are around 6.3CM long by 3.8CM wide, distinctive in being rounded and spineless at their base while widening toward the apex with the typical *cornuta* spines on either side. The freely borne vivid red berries are around 10MM across.

'Burfordii' (female). A real holly classic, a large plant of compact spreading habit that will reach 5M. The leaves are dark green, very glossy, with only one terminal spine, 4.5–8CM long by 2.5–4.5CM wide, and the fruits are large, to 13MM wide, vivid red and abundantly borne. The Burford holly may be considered the great progenitor in the story of the Chinese holly in America. This invaluable landscape plant arose in the early 1900s, as a chance seedling of indeterminate origin planted in Atlanta's West View Cemetery. The sharp-eyed nurseryman W. L. Monroe spotted it and obtained cuttings with the permission of the cemetery's caretaker, Thomas Burford, for whom it was named. Since the mid 1930s its remarkable qualities have been ever more widely appreciated, and it has assumed great importance and popularity for landscapers and gardeners alike. The Burford holly is still important to the landscape industry, but is now considered rather large for today's smaller gardens, and perhaps too often used given the number of other hollies available. (Holly guru T. R. Dudley [1986a] has written of it as '*the overplanted 'Burfordii'*'!) However, it has been used as a parent in many well-known hybrids, e.g., 'Lydia Morris', 'John T. Morris', 'Brighter Shines' and others. The scaled-down version for restricted spaces, 'Dwarf Burford', is described below.

'Cajun Gold' (female). Variegation is not frequent among the Chinese hollies, but there are several distinctive coloured-leaved forms. This cultivar arose as a sport from 'Burfordii', and has entire leaves bearing bold irregular yellow bands and blotches.

'Carissa' (female). A sport from 'Rotunda', forming a wide-spreading low mound of superb lustrous glossy deep green leaves around 3.8CM long by 2.5CM wide, with one long apical spine. Many of the leaves are slightly cupped, bringing the pale olive-green leaf margins into view, giving a very distinctive effect. As yet this appears to be even more shy-fruiting than 'Rotunda'.

Opposite, top: Close-textured and free-fruiting, *Ilex cornuta* 'Dwarf Burford'.

Opposite: Distinctive in leaf, *Ilex cornuta* 'Ira S. Nelson' can fruit prolifically.

'D'Or' (female). A yellow-fruited cultivar, whose dark green leaves are usually spineless. It bears generous clusters of 13MM-wide vivid yellow berries, which colour late and hold well into spring.

'Dazzler' (female). A California introduction with prolifically borne clusters of particularly large red fruits over 13MM wide.

'Dwarf Burford' (female). Synonyms 'Burfordii Compacta', 'Burfordii Nana'. Arising as a sport in a tray of cuttings in 1947, this has all the good characteristics of its big sister 'Burfordii', at around only half the size, with leaves of up to 2.5CM long and freely borne 8MM-wide fruits. It has a dense, compact habit and will only slowly reach 1.8M.

'Fine Line' (female). An upright-growing selection, and slower-growing than 'Burfordii': it reaches 3.6M tall by around half as wide, making it a valuable selection for smaller gardens. The leaves are variable in shape and spininess, around 5CM long and half as wide, giving a rather less heavy-textured effect; its berries are red, typical in size, and freely borne.

'Ira S. Nelson' (female). A striking foliage plant, with leaves up to 10CM in length by 6CM wide, strongly rectangular in outline, of dark olive-green, embodying the quintessentially unique character of the Chinese holly. This selection bears perhaps the most dramatic foliage of any *Ilex cornuta* cultivar, and the bold leaves are accompanied by equally bold 13MM-wide vivid red berries, produced in large clusters on a large and vigorous shrub.

'Needlepoint'. See 'Anicet Delcambre'.

'O. Spring' (male). The most commonly grown variegated Chinese holly. A spreading plant to 2M or more, its leaves are very irregular, varying in shape

around the basic rectangular *cornuta* template, up to 10CM long by 3CM wide. The variegation is striking and distinctive. Within a broad irregular creamy yellow margin, the central part of the leaf is a medley of dark and pale green. Those who appreciate foliage plants of real character will find this intriguingly attractive. In common with many variegated plants the chlorophyll-free areas are less hardy than the normal green, and thus plants may be burned by frost that would leave other Chinese hollies untouched.

Opposite: The variable variegation and leaf shapes of *Ilex cornuta* 'O. Spring'.

'Rotunda' (female). A remarkable spiny mound of deep glossy green foliage, introduced during the mid 1930s. The leaves are elongated, up to 9cm long by 2.5CM wide. The two pairs of major spines along the sides are borne either side of a pronounced narrow waist, which with the typical apical spine gives a strongly architectural and densely spiky effect. Distinctive and characterful, it makes a valuable landscape plant, usually growing wider than high, with typical *cornuta* vivid red fruit.

'Sunrise' (female). Synonym 'Burford Yellowleaf'. Discovered at Tom Dodd Nurseries and introduced in 1990, this distinctive cultivar develops very irregular yellow flushing and blotching, stronger on those parts of the leaf that are exposed to full sun (similar to *Ilex aquifolium* 'Flavescens' and *I.* ×*attenuata* 'Sunny Foster'). The foliage is rounded, up to 5CM long by 2.5CM wide, with one small apical spine; it is slow-growing and of dense habit.

'Willowleaf' (female). See 'Anicet Delcambre'.

Ilex cornuta has a strong record as a parent of a range of valuable hybrids, dealt with in detail elsewhere in the Directory. A few highlights to demonstrate its quality include 'Nellie R. Stevens' (with *I. aquifolium*), which when crossed with *I. leucoclada* produced the distinctive 'Clusterberry'. With *I. latifolia* it gave rise to the Bruner Hollies Group (including 'Emily Bruner'), and with some assistance from *I. pernyi* the excellent 'Mary Nell'. There are numerous primary hybrids with *I. pernyi*, including 'Doctor Kassab', 'Hohman's Weeping', 'Indian Chief', 'Lydia Morris' and 'John T. Morris'. In the hands of Kathleen Meserve *I. cornuta* with *I. rugosa* gave rise to CHINA BOY and CHINA GIRL. Finally, there is one natural hybrid which, although variable, shows distinct horticultural potential, *I.* ×*wandoensis* (*cornuta* × *integra*), from Korea.

***Ilex* 'Coronet'** (female). An interesting cross between *I.* 'Nellie R. Stevens' and the Chinese species *I. ciliospinosa*, made by William Kosar. This cultivar forms a compact, broadly columnar tree, which in fifteen years can reach 3.7M tall by 2M wide. The softly spiny dark green leaves grow to around 6.5CM long by 3.8CM wide. 'Coronet' is also parthenocarpic, developing its good-sized bright red fruits, 12MM wide, without need of a pollinator. Hardy to Zone 7.

Ilex crenata (Japanese holly) is an unassuming but valuable and functional plant, which can be put to a great number of uses in the garden. It has a long history in cultivation, attesting to its usefulness and adaptability. *Ilex crenata* was named by Thunberg, who saw it during his travels in Japan in 1776–77, and wrote of it in his *Flora Japonica* (1784). It first came into cultivation in the West in 1864, introduced by Carl Maximowicz to the St. Petersburg Botanical Garden, from where it soon made its way to other European gardens. Charles Sargent (1894), who was responsible for introducing it to the USA via the Arnold Arboretum in 1898, came across it in his travels in Japan, calling it '*the most widely distributed and the most common of the Japanese Hollies with persistent leaves … abundant in Hokkaido, on the foothills of Mt. Hakkoda, and on the sandy barrens near Giffu, on the Tokaido… . I encountered it in nearly every part of the empire which I visited*'. Its natural distribution (including its varieties) is wider still; as well as occurring throughout Japan it also grows on Sakhalin Island, the Kurile Islands and in South Korea.

The Japanese holly's value as a garden plant for many situations follows naturally from the remarkably wide range of habitats in which it is found; they encompass deep forest shade, seaside exposure on sandy beaches, and wet swampy places. John Creech (2003) reports *Ilex crenata* growing '*from the coast to the highest mountains. This range of habitats accounts for a great deal of the variation found in the wild*'. He goes on: '*In the upland meadows of small volcanic cones, such as Seidagawa and Koshodake on Kyushu,* I. crenata *flourishes in large colonies … up to 2M tall and densely branched. At the rocky windswept crest of these cones and at similar sites at Kirishima, [it] becomes diminutive with tiny, rounded leaves*'. The remarkable plasticity of the species has enabled it to evolve and change in response to varied and sometimes harsh environments. It accounts in large part for its widespread distribution, its diverse morphology, and its success in cultivation.

Sargent (1894) also commented upon the remarkable range of Japanese

The characteristic black fruits of *Ilex crenata*.

holly forms that he saw, and speaking of *Ilex crenata* as a garden plant reported, '*This is the most popular of all the Hollies with the Japanese; and a plant usually cut into a fantastic shape is found in nearly every garden*'. Noting its previous lack of success in Western gardens he said, 'Ilex crenata *and several of its variegated varieties were introduced into western gardens many years ago and are occasionally cultivated, although the value of this plant as an under-shrub appears to be hardly known or appreciated outside of Japan*'. He went on to bestow high praise upon this modest plant (considering his experience as a botanist and plantsman). Notwithstanding the wealth of hollies and other evergreens he had seen in Japan, he said of the Japanese holly, '*Of the broad-leaved evergreens, I have the most hope of* Ilex crenata *in [the USA's] climate; and if it proves really hardy it will be a most useful addition to our shrubberies*': prescient words indeed.

The Arnold Arboretum promoted the Japanese holly in the 1930s, bringing it to the attention of nurserymen and gardeners, with a success that effectively fulfilled Sargent's prediction, as Galle (1997) reports: '*Nurseries and landscape architects found the species and its cultivars adaptable and useful in the landscape as foundation plants, in mass plantings and hedges, and for general use. Today Japanese holly is one of the most popular landscape plants in the United States*'. Not bad going for the sort of plant that cannot boast of any particular distinguishing feature that might draw it to the attention of the passing gardener—indeed, it even eschews the almost universal recognition points of the great majority of hollies of horticultural importance, by having small, relatively anonymous spineless leaves and black berries, which from a distance tend to merge into the foliage rather than brashly advertising themselves to passers-by.

These characteristics, however, are key elements of the garden value of many cultivars of *Ilex crenata*; and for those seeking more ornamental plants, there are a number of distinctive Japanese holly cultivars from which to choose. Sargent (1894) spoke of the Japanese taste for more showy selections ('*Varieties with variegated leaves are common, and apparently much esteemed*'); this estimation is now more widely shared.

Many *Ilex crenata* forms that originated in Japan are now in cultivation in Western gardens; decades of further selection, particularly in the USA, have resulted in there now being more than a hundred named cultivars of the Japanese holly available in the USA, and nearly forty are listed in the *RHS Plant Finder 2005–2006*. To those with a general gardener's interest many might appear to be very similar to one another; indeed, even as Dudley in the mid 1980s noted the superfluity of cultivars, he urged that superior selections be sought from the wild. Much work has been done toward raising and selecting plants for hardiness, as well as distinct habit or foliage. The plants described here have been chosen to provide a representative selection of plants for a range of garden purposes.

Ilex crenata and its cultivars are generally easy to grow, doing well in mainland Europe, Great Britain and Ireland, as well as much of the USA. Hardiness varies according to provenance, but it is generally accepted that it falls between Zone 5b (for a few cultivars) and Zone 9, with the majority certainly hardy to Zone 7. It is often recommended that in hotter climates (Zone 8 and upward) Japanese holly should be grown in partial shade. It can suffer from mite attack under stressful conditions, and its root system may require protection from excessive cold or heat.

Under good conditions, however, Japanese holly can naturalise freely;

I have seen thriving populations in open woodland at the Hemelrijk Arboretum in Belgium. *Ilex crenata* is also a good subject for container cultivation. The natural growth habit of many cultivars fits them superbly for all types of container gardening, including bonsai, and venerable containerised topiary specimens may be seen in Japanese gardens.

Having spent so much time highlighting its great variety it is only to be expected that *Ilex crenata* is a challenge to describe succinctly. Always evergreen, it varies from a dwarf shrub (sometimes spreading) to an upright small tree capable of reaching 6m tall and more, typically densely branched. Fine-textured in its foliage, it bears dark olive-green leaves 1–2.5CM long by 0.5–1.5CM wide, with up to ten small teeth along each side. White flowers around 4MM in size are followed on female plants by black fruits up to 7MM across. The fruits are rarely pale yellow, as in forma *watanabeana*. A number of cultivars are shy-flowering.

'Allen Seay' (male). Synonyms 'Nigra', 'Alan Seay'. An upright-growing tall selection from the same parentage that produced 'Compacta', with dark green leaves of around 1.8CM long by around half as wide. Recommended for good winter colour and hardiness to Zone 6b.

'Beehive' (male). A hardy cultivar derived from a cross of 'Convexa' and 'Stokes' by Elwin Orton. This should be a special plant: Fred Galle reports that it was selected from a batch of twenty-one thousand seedlings! It is slow-growing, with a dense, compact habit, the original plant having taken twenty-two years to grow to 1.05M tall by 1.5M wide. The leaves are small, dark green, around 1.8CM long by 0.7CM wide. Hardy to Zone 6 and tolerant of exposure, salt spray, and pollution.

'Bennett's Compact'. See 'Compacta'.

Bennett Hybrid Group. See 'Compacta'.

'Carolina Upright' (male). A relatively large-leaved cultivar, introduced in the 1970s, of erect pyramidal habit, with dark green leaves 1.8–2.5CM long and 0.8MM wide.

Opposite: *Ilex crenata* 'Convexed Gold' has intriguing pale yellow–flushed leaves that form an effective backdrop for the black fruits.

'Compacta' (male). Under this descriptive name there are a number of plants of similar habit, which can lead to confusion. They were derived from a mass crossing of 'Convexa' with 'Rotundifolia', made by E. L. Bennett at Greenbriar Farms, of Norfolk, Virginia, in 1945, in order to find plants of improved winter hardiness. After a vicious episode of 'survival of the fittest' over the winter of 1947–48 only 1% of the original 300,000 seedlings survived; those three thousand survivors were reduced by selection to a mere twenty named forms of varying habit. 'Compacta', as the name suggests, is low-growing, close-textured and globose to around 1.8M tall, with dark green leaves up to 2.5CM long by 1.3CM wide. The offspring of this cross are referred to as the Bennett Hybrid Group, and include 'Allen Seay', 'Bennett's Compact', 'Compacta' and 'Fastigiata'. Galle recommends 'Bennett's Compact' as a tough clone, hardy to Zone 6.

'Convexa' AGM (female). Synonym 'Bullata'. An old cultivar, introduced to the Arnold Arboretum in 1919 from a cultivated plant from Japan. This is a stalwart selection which has proved itself in the USA, Great Britain and Ireland, and in mainland Europe. It has also received the RHS Award of Garden Merit. Named for its distinctive convex, lustrous dark green leaves, typically 13–18MM long by around 6MM wide; they reflect the light from almost any angle, giving the plant a bright appearance. The habit is bushy and upright, to around 1.2M high by slightly wider. *The Hillier Manual* recommends it as '*a superb low hedge*', and its box-like habit equips it to be a substitute where true box *(Buxus sempervirens)* may not thrive due to climate or disease. It has been involved in the parentage of many fine cultivars. Hardy to Zone 6b.

'Convexed Gold' (female). A vigorous new cultivar of upright growth, which appears to have the potential to grow into a medium-large shrub. The foliage is Convexa-shaped, distinctively flushed with creamy yellow after the fashion of *Ilex aquifolium* 'Flavescens' and *I.* ×*attenuata* 'Sunny Foster'; like those cultivars the colour seems to be best in full sun, fading to green in shade. This selection is distinctive and potentially of considerable garden value, with black berries that stand out dramatically against their pale backdrop.

'Dwarf Cone' (male). One of a number of selections from the crossing of 'Convexa' and 'Microphylla', which has produced a race of diminutive, hardy cultivars. Broadly conical in habit, it has dark green leaves around 1.5CM long by 5MM wide. A good selection for dwarf hedges, but capable of over 1.5M high by 0.9M wide when left to grow.

'Dwarf Pagoda' (female). One of a number of very distinctive Japanese holly cultivars of very slow growth and great character, ideal for the rock garden, containers or troughs, or bonsai. An offspring from the old cultivar 'Mariesii', it shares that plant's distinctive upright growth and stiffly horizontal branching habit, growing less than 5CM per year. Close and densely textured, its leaves are tiny, dark green, stiff and rounded, around 8MM long by 6MM wide. Tiny black fruits are borne only sparsely. Hardy to Zone 6b.

Standing soldier straight against a wall, *Ilex crenata* 'Fastigiata'.

Right: The bolt-upright growths with black berries of 'Fastigiata'.

'Fastigiata' (female). Prior to the recent introduction of another fastigiate cultivar, 'Sky Pencil', this was the only upright cultivar generally available. Introduced by Greenbriar Farms of Norfolk, Virginia, 'Fastigiata' forms a narrow erect plant capable of around 1.8M in height, with convex dark green foliage and generously borne black fruit. The habit is dense, and it seems to be able to hold its shape well as it grows. It arose from the crossing of 'Convexa' with 'Rotundifolia', a pairing that has produced several good cultivars.

'Glory' (male). Another 'Convexa' offspring, this cultivar is considered one of the hardiest Japanese hollies, proven to –30C. A compact, mound-forming plant of relatively light texture, it can reach 1.5M tall by 2.4M wide in twelve years. The leaves are small, dark green and flat, 0.6CM–1.8CM long by around half as wide. Hardy to Zone 6.

Ilex crenata 'Golden Gem' AGM can grow quite freely into a medium-sized shrub.

'Golden Gem' AGM (female). This distinctive, bright yellow-leaved cultivar received its RHS Award of Garden Merit in 2002. The leaf colour is most strongly expressed at the tips of the purple shoots, brightest in high light, reverting steadily to green with age or in shade; the leaves are 13–18MM long by 7–13MM wide. Shy-fruiting and of low growth. Confusingly, there are similar plants in cultivation in mainland Europe that appear to be male. Reputedly hardy to Zone 6b.

'Golden Heller' (female). One of a number of plants similar to or derived from the highly successful 'Helleri'. Introduced in the early 1970s, it has a low hummocky habit very similar to its namesake, the distinguishing factor being the yellow flushing of its leaves.

'Green Dragon' (male). A tiny shrublet, the result of an Orton crossing of 'Mariesii' with 'John Nosal'. Effectively a shrunken 'Mariesii' with leaves just under 13mm long by around half as wide. Galle reports this essentially upright plant reaching 27.5cm high by 10cm wide in seven years, making it an excellent subject for bonsai treatment. It will put on a steady 2.5–3.7cm or so a year in the open garden, growing gradually beyond truly dwarf stature. Hardy to Zone 6b.

'Green Island' (male). A selection dating back to 1935, with a spreading, vigorous habit, forming a wide, low shrub. The dark green leaves are 1.3–2cm long by 6.5–13mm wide. A good choice for a low hedge. Hardy to Zone 6a.

Ilex crenata 'Helleri' forming a dense-textured informal flowing feature. Photograph courtesy of Susyn Andrews.

'Helleri' (female). Considered an important 'benchmark' cultivar, 'Helleri' is highly valued for making low hummocks of relatively fine foliage, with small, narrow leaves around 13mm long. Since its naming and introduction in the 1930s it has become a deservedly popular landscape plant, growing to around 1.2m high by up to twice as wide in twenty years or so. Fruit is only sporadically borne. Hardy to Zone 6a. Numerous plants have been named from seedlings of 'Helleri', many bearing the Heller name; among the most distinctive is 'Golden Heller'.

'Hetzii' (female). Possibly a hybrid of 'Convexa', and similar to it in leaf, although a larger-growing plant. Dark green convex leaves of around 2.5cm long by half as wide are borne on an upright spreading shrub. Hardy to Zone 6a.

'Highlander' (male). This is definitely a 'Convexa' seedling, upright in habit and fast-growing, forming a broad pyramid 3.3–6.3M in height, possibly more, making it one of the tallest-growing Japanese hollies. It has dark green foliage of medium size, up to 1.8CM long. Tidy in growth, it requires little trimming to keep it in shape. Recommended as hardy to Zone 5.

'Hoogendoorn' (male). A cultivar of compact upright growth forming a low rounded shrub. The dark green leaves are around 2.5CM long by 1.3CM wide. Very cold hardy.

'Ivory Hall' (female). A dwarf plant selected from seedlings of *Ilex crenata* f. *watanabeana*. A slow-growing cultivar: the original plant was reported by Galle as having reached 42.5CM high by 71CM wide after nine years. The fruits are small and greenish yellow, gradually turning to ivory.

'Ivory Tower' (female). Another seedling of the pale-fruited *Ilex crenata* f. *watanabeana*, introduced in the 1970s and now established as one of the most popular yellow-fruited cultivars. A vigorous, broadly upright grower, with foliage of pale green, a little over 13MM long. The greeny yellow fruits are very distinctive; 'Ivory Hall', from the same raising, is of similar fruit colour but more compact.

Ilex crenata 'Kifujin', a new and distinctively variegated cultivar from Japan.

'Jersey Pinnacle' (male). A seedling of 'Green Lustre' produced at Rutgers University by Elwin Orton. As its name would suggest, this is an upright-growing plant, of dense habit, with dark green leaves up to 1.8CM long by nearly half as wide. Pyramidal in growth, it slowly achieves 1.8M tall by 1.2M wide after nearly twenty years. Hardy to Zone 6b.

'Kifujin' (sex unknown). A brightly variegated cultivar currently grown in Japan. A plant of low, spreading habit, its distinctiveness lies in its bold, irregular creamy white variegation, typically in the form of a generous edge to the leaf but frequently taking up almost the entire leaf blade.

'Kingsville Dwarf' (female). Synonym 'Kingsville'. A chance seedling of 'Microphylla' dating back to 1912, introduced to cultivation in 1940. A very dwarf, compact, twiggy plant similar to 'Helleri', it makes a slightly less formal mound to 1.2–1.5M tall by up to one and a half times as wide.

'Mariesii' (female). Introduced into cultivation to Britain in 1879 by Charles Maries, who travelled in Japan collecting for the Veitch nursery. This is one of the least typical of the hollies, a stiffly erect-growing shrub of great character, even as a young plant. It will reach 2M tall and less than a third as wide in time. The dark green foliage is stiff, rounded, usually less than 12MM long and wide. The small black fruits are generously produced, adding to its eccentric winter appeal; it is the parent of a number of distinctive hybrids. 'Nakada' (male), introduced by John Creech from Japan in 1957, who found it in the Nakada nursery when seeking new ornamental plants in Japan, is very similar in habit to 'Mariesii', slightly more vigorous and larger in time, but with the same densely clustered foliage. Hardy to Zone 7.

'Microphylla' (female and male). This epithet was first applied as a varietal name to plants that had been in cultivation since the late 19th century, whose chief distinction was their small-leaved habit. A plant collected in Hokkaido, Japan, by Charles Sargent and sent to the Arnold Arboretum in 1892 as forma *microphylla*, proved itself a very hardy selection of low, spreading habit. This is considered to be the probable parent of a number of clones, male and female, now confusingly grown under this name. The true 'Microphylla' of cultivation (which is a valuable plant and well worth seeking out) is usually female, a low, wide-spreading shrub of relatively open habit, with small dark green leaves under 12MM long by half as wide, and very hardy.

Opposite, top: *Ilex crenata* 'Midas Touch', a spreading plant with gold-edged grey-green leaves.

Opposite: Forming a small bun over time, the dwarf slow-growing *Ilex crenata* 'Piccolo'.

'Midas Touch' (male). A distinctive variegated cultivar which arose as a sport among seedlings of *Ilex crenata* f. *watanabeana* × 'Microphylla', discovered by Elwin Orton. This attractive selection forms a low, spreading plant capable of reaching 0.9M high by 1.2M wide, with narrow leaves 1.3–1.8CM long by around 7MM wide. They are variably margined with creamy yellow, with further grey-green and olive mottling at their centres. Hardy to Zone 6b.

'Nakada'. See 'Mariesii'.

'Nigra'. See 'Allen Seay'.

'Piccolo' (female). This is a real bun-forming dwarf, excellent as a tiny specimen plant or for the smallest hedges. It arose from backcrosses of hybrids between the seemingly ubiquitous 'Convexa' and 'Microphylla'. This selection is a dwarf, dense mound of rounded dark green leaves around 1.3CM long by a little over half as wide. A very slow grower, taking seven years to get to 15CM tall by 22.5CM wide. While it can be trimmed to shape it may also be left to form an informal low hedge. For those seeking a more upright-growing dwarf plant, the cultivar 'Tee Dee', which arose as a sport of 'Helleri', is narrower in leaf, slow and dense in habit.

'Rotundifolia' (male). One of the larger-growing cultivars, important in the nursery trade but again rather confused in its background. It is possibly another Japanese selection renamed on introduction to the West, but one whose success has led, as Dudley and Eisenbeiss (1992) report, to the situation where '*a large number of obviously different clones of independent and often obscure origins are labeled as 'Rotundifolia' and extensively grown in U.S. nurseries*'. The true 'Rotundifolia' is a deservedly popular plant, broadly upright and dense in habit to around 3.6M tall. The dark green leaves are 1.8–3CM long by around 1.3CM wide.

'Sentinel' (female). A fine, upright-growing clone capable of growing to 2M tall by 0.8M wide in seven years. Its dark green leaves are quite glossy, around 2.5CM long by half as wide. It is reputedly very heavy-fruiting and very hardy, has good resistance to spider mite attack, and is recommended as a hedging plant.

'Shiro-fukurin' (female). Synonym 'Snowflake'. An old clone from Japan, introduced into the USA in the late 1950s and subsequently renamed by Dudley and Eisenbeiss. The original Japanese name is descriptive and simply means 'white margin'; in the USA it has been made a synonym of 'Snowflake', under which name it is most often sold, although in the UK the older name prevails. This is a very distinctive variegated cultivar, with light-textured grey-green foliage, and very stable. It is moderately vigorous in growth, upright in habit, and capable of over 3M in height. The leaves are quite long, up to 3CM by 1CM wide, with cool pale creamy white margins and mottled grey-green centres. It takes trimming well and can be used to make distinctive upright topiary. Hardy to Zone 7.

The cool grey leaves of *Ilex crenata* 'Shiro-fukurin'.

'Sky Pencil' (female). This narrowly erect cultivar was discovered in the wild in Japan and introduced to the USA in 1985; its distinct habit is attested to by Galle, who says it is typically at least ten times as tall as wide. The dark green leaves are around 2.5CM long by up to 1CM wide. Very similar in character to the long-established 'Fastigiata', it is understandably confused with it in the trade.

'Snowflake'. See 'Shiro-fukurin'.

'Stokes' (male). An old cultivar, dating back to 1925, introduced to cultivation in 1951. This plant ranks very highly among the many named

Japanese holly selections; Dudley and Eisenbeiss (1992) describe it succinctly and enthusiastically: '*extremely dwarf, compact, semi-formal; new lvs. golden green; exceptionally heavy root system; extremely hardy; adaptable to varied soil conditions*'. The mid-green leaves are around 1.3CM long by half as wide, of good lustrous green, paler when young. A noted hardy selection, it may well be hardier than 'Convexa', certainly worth trying in Zone 6a. All those encomiums lead to the conclusion that this is very much a cultivar to seek out for low hedges and a multitude of other landscape uses. The faster-growing 'Green Lustre' is similar, with slightly larger leaves.

'Variegata' (sex unknown). Synonyms 'Luteo-variegata', 'Aureovariegata'. This useful plant has a confused background. A variety of names on the 'variegata' theme have been applied to several Japanese selections over the years, and (to further confuse the issue) to chance sports and mutations subsequently. The original plant was introduced from Japan to Russia by Maximowicz in 1863. The chief distinguishing factor of this group is the variability of the bright yellow leaf markings, taking the form of spotting, flushing and splashing. The plant cultivated in Britain under this name is a moderately vigorous, upright spreading shrub, growing to 1.8M tall by 1.2M wide in under ten years. The variegation is brightest on young and fully exposed growths. A useful and showy plant for winter effect.

Ilex crenata 'Variegata', whose brightly coloured leaves develop best on young growths in good light.

f. *watanabeana*. This name was originally applied to a yellow-fruited form found in southern Japan (which in every other respect closely resembles the typical species). Introduced into the USA in 1956 by John Creech, it has been quite widely distributed and has been used to breed a number of yellow-fruited cultivars known as the Watanabeana Group.

Cultivars in the *Ilex crenata* Watanabeana Group typically have pale greeny yellow berries.

Watanabeana Group. Under this heading are included plants raised from the original plant of *Ilex crenata* f. *watanabeana*. Most are yellow- or pale-fruited; among these are 'Alba', 'Ivory Hall', 'Ivory Tower' and 'Xanthocarpa'.

'Weismoor Silber' (female). It is remarkable how often 'Convexa' shows up in the background of modern cultivars of the Japanese holly. This distinctive grey and white variegated form arose as a sport of its illustrious forebear, found by Martin Zimmer of Weismoor, Germany. It shares the distinctive convex leaf shape, up to 1.8CM long by half as wide. The variegation takes the form of a varied mottling and splashing of green, grey-green and creamy white. Plants are mounded in growth, forming a flat, compact bush. Slower-growing than 'Convexa', as might be expected, it is a valuable plant for low hedges and foliage effect.

Ilex dimorphophylla. An unusual and very distinctive species from the Ryukyu Islands of southern Japan. An upright-growing shrub related to *I. cornuta*, capable of reaching over 2.4M, its name attests to its bearing two distinctively different leaf shapes, which characteristic, while common to many hollies, it has developed to a high degree. The young foliage of *I. dimorphophylla* is very spiny and undulating in outline, around 3CM long by 13MM wide and typical of a holly. As the plant outgrows its juvenile state, it develops thick, more rounded leaves with but one apical spine. The fruits are small, around 4MM in diameter, deep orange-red in colour, and may be borne freely. The juvenile form can be used to make a dense, low hedge. The female cultivar 'Somerset Pixie' is offered in the UK; it combines small spiny leaves and red berries on a compact plant. *Ilex dimorphophylla* also lends itself to making characterful bonsai plants. As a mature plant it can be rather gaunt unless pruned, when it will respond and develop into a dense and compact shrub. It has been crossed with *I. cornuta* with promising results (see *I.* 'Carolina Cone'). Hardy in Zones 8 to 10.

Ilex dipyrena. The Himalayan holly (so called because it was first named from Nepal) is a widespread species occurring in southwest China, Upper Myanmar (Burma), Assam and the Himalaya. It grows into a medium-sized tree in cultivation, exceeding 13.5M tall in Britain. Its leaves are dark green, relatively matt-surfaced, oblong to narrowly oval, 5–12.5CM long by 1.5–3.7CM wide, spiny when young, and entire on older or upper branches. The flowers are numerous, in dense clusters in the leaf axils, and followed by oval red fruits around 8MM wide. A species related to *I. aquifolium* (with which it hybridised to create *I. ×beanii*), it is thought to have considerable potential for breeding; however, plants currently in cultivation in Europe and the Pacific Northwest may be from provenances that would lead to their being relatively tender over much of the northern and eastern USA. It has proved hardy at Kew for many years.

***Ilex* 'Doctor Kassab'** (female). A hardy hybrid (*cornuta* × *pernyi*), initially selected by Dr. Joseph Kassab, which has become very popular. A free-fruiting, upright and compact selection of pyramidal habit, whose dark glossy olive-green leaves are oblong and spiny, as would be expected from its parentage, up to around 4.5CM long by 2CM wide. The small brilliant red fruits, around 6mm wide, are borne abundantly. Hardy to Zone 6a.

***Ilex* 'Dorothy Lawton'** (female). A hybrid of compact, pyramidal habit with *I. ciliospinosa* in its parentage; it is a seedling of 'Brilliant', selected by Tom Dodd Jr. of Semmes, Alabama, in 1967. The glossy dark green leaves are slightly rounded, lightly spined and around 5CM long by 2.5CM wide. The fruits, borne in clusters of one to five, are a vivid red, around 7MM wide.

***Ilex* 'Drace'** (female). A distinctive hybrid of *I. cornuta* 'Burfordii' and *I. pernyi*, introduced by Hohman and with much of the dense, glossy small-

Opposite: The large, lustrous deep green leaves and abundant (if immature, here) berries of *Ilex* 'Emily Bruner'.

leaved character of its *pernyi* parent. This is an upright plant, forming a compact pyramidal mound of bright green stems bearing dark, oblong five-spined leaves, around 3.7CM long by 1.5CM wide, and vivid red berries, around 8MM wide. Hardy to Zone 6.

Ilex **DRAGON LADY**. See *Ilex ×aquipernyi* DRAGON LADY

Ilex **EBONY MAGIC** (female). Cultivar name unknown. A very hardy selection, discovered as a chance seedling in Ohio, possibly from a blue holly (*I. ×meserveae*) parent, distributed by Monrovia. This distinctive cultivar is pyramidal in growth, moderately vigorous, and achieves its dramatic effect through its combination of dark purple-black stems with glossy, undulate, purple-flushed deep olive-green spiny leaves up to 6CM long by 2.5CM wide. Deep red-orange berries up to 10MM wide are very freely borne. Hardy in Zones 5 to 9.

Ilex **'Edward Goucher'** (female). The rare crossing of *I. cornuta* with *I. ciliospinosa* gave rise to this slow-growing narrowly columnar cultivar, which can take sixteen years to achieve 2.9M by 1.2M. The flat, sparsely spined olive-green leaves grow to 9.5CM long by 2.5CM wide, and the berries are red. Hardy in Zones 7 to 9.

Ilex **'Elegance'** (female). This interesting hybrid, a sibling of 'Accent', arose from the crossing of *I. integra* with *I. pernyi* by William Kosar. A plant of upright, pyramidal habit, well named for its elegant small sparsely spined deep green leaves up to 3CM long by 2CM wide, against which the relatively large 8MM-wide red fruits stand out well.

Ilex **'Emily Bruner'** (female). This hybrid has steadily carved a niche for itself in southern landscapes and gardens over the past thirty years. Dirr (2002) describes it succinctly as '*a stately, dense, broad pyramid of leathery lustrous*

dark green leaves'. Initially discovered in 1960 in Knoxville, Tennessee, by the sharp-eyed gardener whose name it bears, it was developed commercially by Don Shadow (of Shadow Nursery, Tennessee). With its excellent parentage (*cornuta* 'Burfordii' × *latifolia*), it represents a fine example of the gardening serendipity of a few chance seedlings producing a high strike rate in the number of valuable plants resulting. The leaves are quite large, up to 11.3CM long and 5CM wide. In colour they show the *cornuta* influence, being dark glossy olive-green; they are also distinctly spiny. The vivid red berries are around 7MM in diameter, ripen in September and persist well (although in common with a number of other hybrids from species hailing from continental climates, they may not fully ripen in cooler maritime climates). A steady grower to 6M or more high by around half as much across, it is ideal for use as a specimen or screening plant, or in informal groups.

Other hybrids within the Bruner Hollies Group include 'James Swan' (male), from the same batch of seedlings and the recommended pollinator for 'Emily Bruner'; it is similar in leaf effect but with pendulous branches, creating a more rounded habit. 'Ginny Bruner' (female) is smaller in leaf and more delicate in texture, and fruits well on young plants; 'Arthur Bruner' (male) is an upright pyramidal plant and good pollinator, and another male, 'Bob Bruner', has handsome deep olive-green foliage. The Bruner hollies are hardy to Zone 7.

Ilex fargesii. This variable, attractive species comes from southwest China (Yunnan, Sichuan, Hubei and Xijang) and neighbouring regions of Burma. It was collected several times in the late 19th and early 20th centuries by such luminaries as Augustine Henry, Ernest Wilson and George Forrest, and originally described from the collections made by Paul Farges in east Sichuan in the mid 1890s. Susyn Andrews (1986) unravelled its somewhat confusing nomenclature; a rarely grown species, the plants in cultivation in Europe derive in great part from two introductions: Wilson's collection for the Veitch nursery in 1900 (the first plants in cultivation), which should bear the name *I. fargesii* subsp. *fargesii* var. *fargesii*, and Forrest's collection in Burma in 1924, which Andrews has classified as subspecies *melanotricha*. Both have been grown across much of the British Isles, with the tallest gradually achieving over 7.1M in height.

Ilex fargesii subsp. *fargesii* var. *brevifolia*, a fine variety of this variable species.

Ilex fargesii was figured in *Curtis's Botanical Magazine* (t. 9670). In his description, J. R. Sealy wrote of it thus: '*In its long and very narrow oblanceolate or oblong-lanceolate leaves which are sparsely toothed only in the apical third or quarter, the typical form of this species is unique in the genus*'. The accompanying illustration shows a very handsomely fruited narrow-leaved specimen, and it is no surprise that the species was given an Award of Merit by the RHS in 1926. Plants of subspecies *fargesii* var. *fargesii* are variable in leaf, spineless and typically finely toothed only in the upper half; leaves in the most desirable horticultural forms may be very long and narrow, over 12.5CM long by around 1CM wide, creating a very distinctive and elegant evergreen. Subspecies *fargesii* var. *brevifolia* is a relatively new designation (Andrews 1986); this fine form is distinguished from the true *fargesii* by its smaller, 6–7.3CM long leaves, which are more distinctly toothed (plants in cultivation in Europe under this name are derived from a Wilson collection in west Hubei). Subspecies *melanotricha* is again variable, but with broader leaves, typically 3–4CM, with finely toothed margins.

The difficulty in telling the subspecies apart in the garden is highlighted when one considers that the chief distinguishing factor between the two is the pubescence on the fruit pedicels! The bright red fruits on female plants add to the attractions of this distinctive species. With the wide geographical distribution of *Ilex fargesii* and its subspecies, and an altitudinal range between 900 and 3350M, variable hardiness is only to be expected. Plants of *fargesii* subsp. *fargesii* have been reported as hardy to Zone 5b; subsp. *melanotricha* has been killed in the most severe British winters. This species is very much a plant for lightly shaded acid woodland, where Andrews (1986) reports it as fruiting heavily.

***Ilex* FESTIVE**. See *Ilex* Red Holly Group

***Ilex* 'Ginny Bruner'**. See *Ilex* 'Emily Bruner'

Ilex glabra (inkberry) is another example of a holly of quiet demeanour proving itself to be an excellent plant, particularly across much of its native North America, where it is very much at home. Its sterling qualities make it potentially as valuable in the landscape as many more exotic holly species and cultivars (and in some cases even more so). Dirr (1997) comments upon this directly, noting that horticulturists '*spent so much time making selections of* Ilex crenata *that they forgot to assess the landscape worth of* I. glabra, *a most aesthetic native species*'. He goes on to pay the inkberry (so named for its ink-black fruit) the compliment of being '*one of the great plants for massing—trouble-free and beautiful. Certainly not used enough in modern landscaping, but many of the newer cultivars offer great promise*'. This gentle admonishment to remember always to look in one's own horticultural backyard is one that should ever be borne in mind.

But whatever its qualities may be for North America, the inkberry is another example of a plant that does not cross the Atlantic well. It has been in cultivation in Britain since 1759, but has never caught on. Bean describes it as '*a neat-habited evergreen, quite unarmed, but of no particular merit, and rather like a phillyrea*'. It remains something of a curiosity in cultivation in Britain, grown mainly in botanic gardens and holly collections. Once again with the hollies, the perceived merits of a plant depend to a considerable degree upon the challenges that local conditions (and planting styles) might place upon it.

Ilex glabra was first described by Linnaeus in 1753, as *Prinos glabra*, and reassigned to *Ilex* by Asa Gray in 1856. It is widely distributed, from Nova Scotia in Canada southward along the eastern seaboard of the USA to Florida, and west to Texas and Missouri. This distribution gives it the ability to be grown across a similarly wide range, Zones 4 to 9a (with one cultivar,

'Chamzin', reported hardy to Zone 3). It occurs principally along the coastal plains, and with this natural distribution it goes without saying that here we have another holly that can take exposure and salt spray. It also makes appearances as an understory plant; Galle (1997) reports that '*extremely variable shade-tolerant plants exist throughout its range*'. Thus at a stroke the demands of two of the most challenging garden habitats can be met by the humble inkberry.

Ilex glabra is mound-forming in habit; to quote Dirr (1997), '*In its wildest form, [it] is a spreading, suckering, colonizing broadleaf evergreen shrub of rather billowy constitution*', varying in height, 0.9–3M, typically broader than high. The upright young branches have a velvety pubescence and bear spineless glossy leaves, 2–5CM long by 1.5–2CM wide, varying in colour from light to dark olive-green, with some selections having attractive purple winter colour. The small white flowers, borne on two-year-old wood, are on female plants (as long as a male is within pollinating distance) followed by glossy black fruits (rarely white in forma *leucocarpa*), 6–10MM wide.

It is a plant of equable constitution, easily pleased as long as it is in soil that does not exceed neutral pH. It will thrive in full sun or shade, wet or dry, and is as unfazed by hot summers as it is by bitter winters that no other evergreen holly in cultivation will survive. The final piece of armour-plating upon this ironclad shrub is its tolerance of salt spray and exposure, as befits a plant from coastal habitats. It may also be put to use for low to mid-height hedges; further details are given in Chapter 2.

'Chamzin' = NORDIC (female). A remarkably hardy cultivar, selected from an entire field of seedlings being assessed for hardiness and leaf colour, and introduced by Ohio's Lake County Nursery. A relatively small-growing, rounded plant to 0.9M, with dark leaves up to 4CM long and black fruits. Hardy to Zone 3 at −33C.

'Compacta' (usually female). This name has been applied to a number of clones of dense, low growth; however, Dirr (1997) reports 'Compacta' growing as tall as 1.8–3M and tending to become leggy and bare at the base. Some nurseries also list 'improved' strains, so the nomenclatural situation is certainly somewhat confused. Suffice to say that as 'Compacta' is quite widely available in nurseries, one should seek out a good clone from a reputable supplier. Galle says that 'Princeton's Compacta' is considered by most to be the best compact

The white-fruited inkberry, *Ilex glabra* 'Ivory Queen'.

form of *Ilex glabra* and recommends it himself as being of '*rounded habit [and] a good, compact evergreen, dwarf plant for the Midwest and Northeast*'.

'Densa' (female). A selection dating back to 1938, upright and rounded in habit, reaching 1.2–1.8M in around ten years, eventually 2.4–3M. As its name suggests, the foliage is very dense, dark green, tinting purple in winter, with leaves up to 4CM long by 3CM wide; black fruit. Hardy to Zone 4.

'Ivory Queen' (female). This is a chance seedling discovered in the wild in New Jersey; it is of upright, rounded habit, to around 2.4M high and wide. Mid-green in leaf, its chief distinction is its freely produced ivory-white berries. Galle reports that plants of 'Ivory Queen' open up with age.

'Nigra' (female). Another cultivar name of questionable status. Plants listed in the trade are described as having relatively thick, lustrous dark green leaves, and reaching around 0.75M four years from planting.

'Princeton's Compact'. See 'Compacta'.

'Shamrock' (female). A popular, very hardy cultivar of upright, compact habit, denser in habit and slower in growth to around 1.5M or more. The leaves are smaller than the type, up to 3.5CM long by 10MM wide, dark green with bronze tints in winter.

***Ilex* 'Hohman'** (female). Often grouped with the Koehne hybrids, although its parentage is uncertain; Galle gives it as (*cornuta* × *pernyi*) × *latifolia*. Its origin too is unclear; possibly it hails from its namesake's nursery in Maryland. In leaf, fruit and in its narrowly pyramidal habit it resides easily with the

The handsome, large burnished green leaves of *Ilex* 'Hohman' show its *I. latifolia* parentage.

×*koehneana* hybrids. Its leaves are dark olive-green, very reminiscent of *I. latifolia*, to 10CM long by 4.5CM wide, with numerous small spines. Vivid red berries around 8MM across are freely borne. A fine hybrid with a good track record in cultivation and certainly hardy to Zone 7.

***Ilex* 'Indian Chief'** (female). A handsome hybrid, another example of the productive crossing by Hohman of *I. cornuta* 'Burfordii' and *I. pernyi* that resulted in twenty-eight named cultivars, although rather fewer have made their way into general cultivation. This is a plant of compact broadly pyramidal habit, with glossy dark green leaves of typical squarish shape, fairly small at around 3.75CM long by 2CM wide, bearing two sharp spines on each side. Vivid red fruits are borne in clusters of one to three. 'Indian Chief' grows and fruits well in maritime climates, showing the influence of its *pernyi* parentage. Hardy to Zone 5b.

The young foliage of *Ilex integra* 'Gold Leaf', a new Japanese cultivar, is among the brightest of all hollies.

Ilex integra. An interesting species distributed from Japan through the Ryukyu Islands and Okinawa to Korea and Taiwan. A plant of low-elevation woodlands, often found growing close to the sea. It has a long history in cultivation dating back to 1864, and has proved hardy in the British Isles, where it can reach over 6M. Charles Sargent described it as '*a beautiful and distinctly desirable ornamental tree, often cultivated in the temple gardens of Japan, where it frequently reaches a height of thirty or forty feet*', and Bean calls it '*a handsome evergreen*'. Its leaves are quite large, around 7.5CM long by 2.5CM wide, and distinctive in that they are completely spineless. The orange-red fruits, quite large at around 13MM, were described by Sargent as '*rather long-stalked, ... nearly half an inch in diameter, and very showy during the winter*'.

Ilex integra is reported by John Creech (2003) as being very popular in Japan '*up to the Tokyo area, where it is reliably hardy in gardens, ranking second to* I. crenata *because of its pyramidal habit*'. He remarks upon the fruit as being '*especially large and borne in heavy clusters*' and on there being white- and yellow-fruited ('Xanthocarpa') forms in Japanese nurseries. A form with yellow mottled and splashed leaves is also grown in Japan, where I have seen a distinctive new cultivar, 'Gold Leaf' (sex unknown), with brilliant yellow young leaves which fade to green as they age—a broader-leaved version of *I.* ×*attenuata* 'Sunny Foster'; apparently, this style of plant is called *akebono* ('daybreak'). The cultivar 'Green Shadow', with marginal cream variegation on grey-green leaves, is not yet in general cultivation. The species is hardy between Zones 6b and 9, but 'Gold Leaf' may require shelter in colder areas.

There is considerable potential for hybridising with this species, which is allied to *Ilex aquifolium*. A hint of this potential can be seen in *I.* ×*wandoensis*, the natural hybrid with *I. cornuta*, from Korea. Two interspecific hybrids with *I. pernyi*, 'Accent' (male) and 'Elegance' (female), are well established.

***Ilex* 'Jade'**. See *Ilex* ×*koehneana* 'Jade'

***Ilex* 'James Swan'**. See *Ilex* 'Emily Bruner'

***Ilex* 'Jermyns Dwarf'** (female). This dwarf evergreen shrub, which arose as a chance seedling, is thought to be a *pernyi* hybrid. It is slow-growing, with arching stems that slowly create a low, dense mound (Galle reports one plant as being no more than 32CM high by 1M wide after sixteen years). It may, however, form a leader in time and reach around 1.8M high. The leaves are burnished, strongly spiny, around 5CM long by 2.5CM wide. It bears bright red fruits but is grown more as a foliage plant, and makes an excellent subject for raised beds and rock gardens, or for bonsai or pot culture.

***Ilex* 'Joe McDaniel'** (male). A hybrid between *I.* ×*aquipernyi* and *I. cornuta*, made by McDaniel in 1964. This is a compact pyramidal shrub, reaching 2.1M tall by 75CM wide in ten years. As might be expected with both *I. pernyi* and *I. cornuta* in its background, it has quadrangular, spiny leaves with curved margins, dark glossy olive-green, around 3.5CM long by nearly as much wide, and held very close to the stems. Hardy to −26C.

***Ilex* 'John T. Morris'** (male). This distinctive hybrid between two Chinese species, *I. cornuta* 'Burfordii' and *I. pernyi*, was made in 1948 by H. Skinner, and introduced as the male companion to 'Lydia Morris'. It is a very fine plant in its own right, and forms a dense glossy cone up to 6.6M tall by 4.5M wide of handsome dark green quadrangular five-spined leaves (as its parentage would suggest) around 5CM long. Hardy to Zone 7.

Ilex kingiana. This is a very distinctive large-leaved species from the Himalaya (Sikkim, Darjeeling and Bhutan), and Yunnan in southwest China, allied to *I. dipyrena* and *I. latifolia*. It is a handsome plant whose synonyms show the respect that it inspired among botanists: the specific name *I. insignis* (given

Opposite: *Ilex ×koehneana* 'Chestnut Leaf' AGM, bold in leaf and generous in fruit.

by J. D. Hooker at Kew in 1875) means 'striking', certainly true in the case of this species (but unfortunately it had previously been given to a fossil species). Its other synonym, *I. nobilis*, was also illegitimate. *Ilex kingiana* (given by Cockerill in 1911), however, seems quite appropriate for what Dudley (1986a) describes as '*a truly noble, awesome red-fruited tree, rarely cultivated except occasionally in California and the Pacific Northwest*'. In the wild it is found at intermediate altitudes (2000–3000M), where it forms an upright small- to medium-sized tree. In cultivation in Britain it has achieved over 15M at Caerhays Castle in Cornwall. Its foliage is certainly striking, with mid-to dark green glossy leaves up to 20CM long by 8CM wide, very spiny when young, becoming less so as they age until they are simply spine-toothed; the red fruits are 5–10MM wide.

It is hardy only in the milder regions of the British Isles, western North America and possibly parts of the southeastern USA to Zone 7, but hardier populations may exist at higher altitudes in its natural range. *Ilex hookeri* is another rarely cultivated but stately species from the Himalaya, with a distribution including Myanmar (Burma) and Yunnan, China. It forms a tree up to 18M tall, with leaves up to 10CM long by 4.5CM wide and red fruits 6mm wide. *Ilex sikkimensis*, from Bhutan and Sikkim, also occurs at intermediate elevations (2000–3340M), where it forms a tree to 17M, with large leaves 12–20CM long by 3–6.5CM wide, and red fruits. Hardy in Zones 8b and 9.

Ilex ×koehneana (*aquifolium × latifolia*). The Koehne holly was described by Loesener in 1901, having spontaneously occurred in cultivation in Florence, Italy, in the 1890s or before. It is undoubtedly a valuable and distinctive introduction, with tremendous potential for the larger garden and wider landscape planting. Dudley (1986a) commented that '*this hybrid has extended the northern and southern range of* I. aquifolium*–like hollies*'. Its *latifolia* parentage undoubtedly brings a greater tolerance of high temperatures than the English holly, which its progeny appear to share. Not only has it extended the range of hollies of *aquifolium* character, but the Koehne holly has added another distinct subgroup to it, being larger-growing and bolder in leaf than many *I. aquifolium* and *Ilex ×altaclerensis* cultivars.

In one trial, Dirr compared the performance of *Ilex ×koehneana* as a landscape plant with the American holly, *I. opaca*; he reported that in ten years the Koehne holly '*has outgrown the* I. opaca *by 50 percent and is much more dense, well*

shaped and aesthetically pleasing: compact pyramid, densely branched, with bronze-purple new growth and lustrous dark green mature leaves' (Dirr 2002). These observations echo those of Charles Sargent a century before in his comparison of the Koehne holly's parent, *I. latifolia*, with American evergreen hollies (see *I. latifolia* in the Directory). Where they grow well, cultivars of *I. ×koehneana* will undoubtedly provide stiff competition to previously established large-growing hollies. They are robust, vigorous, medium to large plants to 12M, with some capable of 18M or more, typically conical to pyramidal in outline. The leaves are usually large, often glossy, varying from quite spiny to toothed; the berries are red, persistent, and freely borne. The hardiness of Koehne hollies ranges from Zone 6b (when carefully sited or against a wall) to Zone 9.

'Chestnut Leaf' AGM (female). The most commonly grown cultivar in Europe, 'Chestnut Leaf' is an old French selection with lightly spined olive-green leaves up to 15CM long by 5CM wide. It fruits very freely, and has a vigorous, open pyramidal habit with distinctly downward-sweeping branches, capable of growing to 10M or more. For its dependability and excellent qualities in British gardens, the RHS Award of Garden Merit was bestowed upon it in 2002. It is not cultivated in the USA but is reputedly among the hardiest Koehne hollies in continental Europe.

'Lassie' (female) arose as a volunteer seedling at McLean's Nursery, in Maryland. The plant habit is pyramidal, with horizontal branches. The dark olive-green leaves are on the small side for Koehne hybrids, up to 10CM long by 4CM wide. The abundant red berries are 8MM in diameter.

'Loch Raven' (male). Another introduction from McLean's Nursery, similar to 'Lassie' but with more definitely spined leaves. Recommended as a pollinator for 'Lassie'.

Opposite: *Ilex ×koehneana* 'Martha Berry' displays the conical habit of growth common to all Koehne hollies, with the added bonus of generous trusses of large berries (**below**).

'Martha Berry' (female). Raised from seed collected by Tom Dodd Jr. from a plant of *Ilex latifolia* in 1979. The growth of the original plant demonstrates the vigour of the cross, being dense and pyramidal, achieving a creditable 6M tall by 3.3M wide in only twelve years. The glossy dark green leaves have a real *aquifolium* character, distinctly spined and with the characteristic twist of many English hollies, up to nearly 12.5CM long by 5CM wide, borne upon dark stems. Persistent vivid red berries over 13MM wide are produced in abundance.

'Wirt L. Winn' (female). Named in the 1960s, this plant has the excellent qualities of vigour, pyramidal habit and superb small-spined deep glossy green leaves, up to 10CM long, which typify the Koehne hybrids. The abundant vivid red berries are around 10MM across. This cultivar has a proven track record in cultivation; Fred Galle, not given to bestowing praise in his plant descriptions, referred to this as '*a very good plant*'.

Several other Koehne hybrids are in cultivation and commercially available. The US National Arboretum selection 'Agena' (female) is proving itself vigorous, achieving 10M by 6M in twenty-one years, tolerant of poor soil and drainage, with generous trusses of large fruit. 'Ajax' (male), from the same source, is equally robust and a pollinator for 'Agena'. 'Kurly Koe' (female) is a cultivar of upright pyramidal habit whose chief distinguishing characteristic is the size of the leaves, 12–25CM long. 'Ruby' (female), raised by William Kosar, is compact, with smaller deep green leaves, handsome purple stems and red fruit that does not ripen until December; 'Jade' (male) was introduced by Kosar as its pollinator. 'San Jose' (female) is a cultivar dating back to the 1940s (which should not be confused with the *Ilex ×aquipernyi* cultivar of the same name); its spiny dark olive-green leaves, up to 12CM long by 5.5CM wide, should give the game away.

Ilex latifolia, from *Curtis's Botanical Magazine*.
Courtesy of the Lindley Library.

Ilex latifolia (lusterleaf holly, tarajo). This distinctive species is distributed in southern Japan and nearby coastal provinces of China. Although long cultivated, it has spent much of that time languishing in obscurity: not very widely grown, but highly respected by those who knew it. Now assuming a role in our gardens more fitting to its charms, it is both a plant of high quality and a parent of distinct groups of hybrids.

Ilex latifolia was introduced to Europe from Japan by Siebold in 1840. It did not take long to make its mark and was figured in *Curtis's Botanical Magazine* (t. 5597) in 1866. In the description, eminent botanist J. D. Hooker wrote of it thus: '*This noble Holly ... has long been cultivated in the Royal Gardens, where it has stood without protection, trained against a wall, for many years, and quite uninjured.... It is a beautiful shrub, of a paler green than the common holly, with similar berries, and the flowers are produced in round heads of a pale yellow-green colour*'.

Another great authority on woody plants, Charles Sargent, in his Forest Flora of Japan (1894), spoke of the qualities of Japanese holly species (in direct comparison with American hollies), saying, '*Some of the Japanese Hollies are much larger and far more beautiful than any of our species. The most beautiful of them all is certainly the southern* Ilex latifolia, *an evergreen tree now occasionally seen in the gardens of southern Europe*'. Sargent noted that it could make a tree of up to 18M high, with '*a straight tall trunk covered with the pale smooth bark which is found on the stems of most plants of this genus*'. His enthusiastic description cannot be bettered: '*The leaves are sometimes six inches long and three or four inches wide, and are very thick, dark green, and exceedingly lustrous. The large scarlet fruit of this tree, which does not ripen until the late autumn or early winter months, and which is produced in the greatest profusion in nearly sessile axillary clusters, remains on the branches until the beginning of the following summer*'. Sargent also observed it frequently in large gardens and temple grounds in Japan, concluding that 'Ilex latifolia *is probably the handsomest broad-leaved evergreen tree that grows in the forests of Japan, not only on account of its brilliant abundant fruit, but also on account of the size and character of its foliage*'.

In cultivation this handsome species does superbly in warmer regions, and is hardy in Zones 7 to 9. Dirr (2002) describes it as an '*extremely durable plant, tolerating full sun, moderate shade, drought, and heat [, which] can be effectively espaliered against a wall. Makes a noble specimen or accent, screening or grouping plant*'. It is also one of the most remarkable of hollies in flower, with the males bearing large axillary masses of pale yellow-green blossoms. The handsome, shiny dark green lightly toothed leaves may reach 17CM long by 7.5CM wide, and have led

Opposite: Male plants of *Ilex latifolia* bear particularly striking flowers.

to this species being proposed as a foliage plant substitute for *Magnolia grandiflora*, confirming its high esteem among knowledgeable plantsmen. Fruiting is prolific, especially in warmer areas, with small glossy berries around 7MM wide borne in profusion, usually persisting until February or March.

Selections of *Ilex latifolia* are few. At least one distinctive variegated cultivar, which I saw on a recent visit there, is grown in Japan: a very rare and valuable plant that was being grafted onto *I. latifolia* seedlings (it also figures in Hirose and Masato, *Variegated Plants in Color*, 1998). This cultivar has leaves with an irregular rich creamy yellow margin, the rest of the leaf being splashed with both deep and pale olive-green. Another marginal cream-variegated form, which may be the plant known as 'Variegata', has been reported. An intriguing cultivar of recent introduction is 'Purple Power', described by Bobby J. Ward in *The Plant Hunter's Garden* (2004) as having leaves 20CM long by 7.5CM wide. The leaves bear widely spaced teeth and have bright purple petioles. It produces orange-red fruits, and is said to be self-pollinating.

Ilex latifolia 'Variegata', a slow-growing plant whose leaves are distinctively mottled and blotched.

The lusterleaf holly is a desirable plant in its own right, but it is as a parent of two groups of fine hybrids that it is making a further distinctive and valuable contribution to the range of hollies in our gardens. With *Ilex aquifolium* it produced the *I.* ×*koehneana* hybrids, and with *I. cornuta* it has been successful both as a primary (first-generation) parent and also when crossed with *cornuta* hybrids.

Noted lusterleaf hybrid cultivars include 'Adonis' and 'Venus' (*Ilex latifolia* × 'Nellie R. Stevens', raised at the US National Arboretum). The famous Bruner clan arose from *I. cornuta* 'Burfordii' crossed with *I. latifolia*, and includes 'Emily Bruner', 'Ginny Bruner', 'Bob Bruner' and 'James Swan'. It is also a parent of the successful 'Mary Nell', *I. latifolia* × (*cornuta* 'Burfordii'× *pernyi*). This places *I. latifolia* in the background of the recently introduced Red Holly Group, derived from open-pollinated seedlings of 'Mary Nell'.

Ilex leucoclada. An interesting species from Japan, distributed mainly in the north of the country (Hokkaido and Honshu), particularly at high elevations. This distinctive low-growing shrub is very closely related to *I. integra*, and was for many years considered a variety of that species. John Creech (2003) reports it as growing with a group of other northern species (including *I. crenata* var. paludosa, *I. sugerokii* and *I. rugosa*) '*in bogs throughout the mountains where they are protected by deep snow cover in winter*'. It is a low, sprawling shrub, with spineless, comparatively long leaves, 7.5–15CM by 2–4CM wide, very similar to *I. integra*, as are its glossy red fruits of around 10MM. A natural hybrid with *I. rugosa*, *I.* ×*makinoi*, occurs on Mt. Hakoa in Honshu. Creech reports having made this under controlled conditions, and that the resulting hybrid population '*exceeded both parents in vigour, plant size and fruits*'. Currently there is one distinctive and successful leucoclada hybrid established in cultivation, *I.* 'Clusterberry'. Certainly the qualities of dwarfness and hardiness of this species must create further possibilities for breeding, especially for the smaller garden.

***Ilex* LITTLE RASCAL** = 'Mondo' (male). A very distinctive new dwarf cultivar, with upright stems forming a low mound 60CM tall by 90CM wide. The deeply toothed small leaves are leathery, mid-green, turning purple in winter. The small white flowers are comparatively showy against the small leaves. This is very much a plant for restricted space, ideal for the small garden, terrace, foundation planting or containers, which although said to require little trimming is also recommended as a low hedge. To top this off it is also very hardy (to Zone 5), and deer resistant.

***Ilex* LITTLE RED**. See *Ilex* Red Holly Group

***Ilex* 'Lydia Morris'** (female) (*cornuta* 'Burfordii' × *pernyi*). The sister to 'John T. Morris', and another fine upright-growing selection, although slightly smaller than her consort. The habit of growth is dense, with glossy, black-green, five-spined quadrangular leaves around 5CM long. The red fruits are around 10MM across, in clusters of up to five. Hardy to Zone 7.

***Ilex* 'Malcolm S. Whipple'** (male). A chance seedling, thought to be a hybrid between *I. aquifolium* and *I. cornuta.* A broadly conical shrub, slow-growing to around 1.8M tall by 1.1M wide, with distinctive dark glossy green leaves around 4.5CM long by 3.5CM wide. Hardy to Zone 7.

***Ilex* 'Mary Nell'** (female). This fine cultivar has proved highly successful since its introduction by Tom Dodd Nurseries in the 1980s. It is the result of a deliberate cross in 1962 by Joe McDaniel, between *I. latifolia* and a hybrid (*cornuta* 'Burfordii' × *pernyi*). The offspring of this union combines a good upright pyramidal habit, glossy dark green leaves and generous fruiting to excellent effect in the landscape. The distinctly spiny foliage is slimmer in outline than many of the latifolia hybrids, up to 8.5CM long by half as wide, on light green stems. Abundant vivid red fruits around 8MM in diameter are borne in generous trusses that can completely encircle the stems. 'Mary Nell' is one of the parents of a distinct group of modern cultivars, the Red Holly Group.

***Ilex* ×*meserveae*.** The Blue Holly Group was originally derived from the crossing of a female plant of the dwarf Far Eastern *I. rugosa* with a male English holly, *I. aquifolium.* The cross was initially made by Kathleen Meserve in the 1950s. Her aim was to harness the innate (Zone 5b) toughness of *I. rugosa*, derived from its ability to thrive in the harsh winter climate of its native habitats in northern Japan, the Kurile Islands and Sakhalin Island, to create a new race of hardy hollies with English holly characteristics for the eastern seaboard of the USA. In this she was very far-sighted and highly successful. Her legacy to gardeners is a distinctive group of cultivars, whose overall characteristics of glossy foliage and copiously borne red fruit are clearly derived from their *aquifolium* parentage. Their comparatively low habit of growth is evidence of the powerful dwarfing influence of *I. rugosa*, as, more crucially, is their Zone 5 or 6 winter hardiness. Their heat tolerance is more or less in line with *I. aquifolium* at Zone 9a, not unexpected given the provenance of both parents.

Close inspection of the various cultivars shows subtle hybrid foliage characteristics such as their more conspicuously veined leaf surfaces inherited from the rugose (i.e., wrinkled or rough) leaf surfaces of *Ilex rugosa*, sometimes leading to a more leathery texture than the high gloss of *I. aquifolium.* The edges of the leaves are also typically intermediate between the dentate leaf margins of *I. rugosa* and the definitely spiny *I. aquifolium*. Their other major characteristic, from which their name is derived, is the colour of the foliage, which while it can be distinctive in its blue-green cast, is by no means sufficiently blue to merit being described as glaucous; indeed, Graham Stuart Thomas (1992) remarks that '*'blue' is somewhat far-fetched*'. The stems are usually attractively purple-tinged, and some cultivars have distinctly purple-flushed young growths. Small white flowers are followed by generous bunches of glossy red fruits of true *aquifolium* character.

The blue hollies have certainly fulfilled their creator's hopes, and within a relatively brief period have established themselves firmly both with gardeners and the landscape industry in the USA (always an excellent indication of a plant's ability to perform under demanding conditions). They have not enjoyed similar success in Britain. It seems that in cooler maritime conditions they fulfil their potential best only after occasional hot summers, when they give a tantalizing glimpse of their qualities. Conditions more suitable to this group are found in mainland Europe.

All the plants described below were bred by Kathleen Meserve unless otherwise stated, and represent the 'true' blue hollies. This Group does not include the other Meserve hybrids between *Ilex cornuta* and *I. rugosa*, CHINA BOY and CHINA GIRL, or *I.* DRAGON LADY, which are all occasionally and mistakenly referred to as *I. ×meserveae* cultivars.

BLUE ANGEL = 'Conang' (female). A second-generation (*rugosa* × *aquifolium*) × *aquifolium* hybrid, introduced in 1975 through the Conard-Pyle Company (as were a number of other blue hollies in the 1970s). This is typically compact, with upright spreading growth to around 2M or more. The second infusion of English holly genes produced a plant with glossy, spiny leaves around 3.8CM long by 2CM wide. The abundant vivid red fruits are 8–9MM wide; Bean reports that this cultivar '*sets fruit without any need for pollination, the ovaries start to swell rapidly even before the petals have fallen*'. The input of English holly may also be responsible for this selection being slightly less tough, rated only to Zone 7.

'Blue Boy' (male). One of the original blue holly introductions in 1963, low-growing but achieving around 2M in time. The purplish stems bear dark green leaves with forward-pointing soft spines typical of the cross. Hardy to Zone 7.

'Blue Girl' (female). The other original 1963 introduction, with small olive-green leaves around 3CM long by 13MM wide, with forward-pointing spines. The fruits are vivid red, around 9MM wide. Hardy in Zones 6 to 9a.

BLUE MAID = 'Mesid' (female). A more recent introduction (1978), of mounded pyramidal growth to around 3.4M tall by 2.4M wide, with dark olive-green, glossy, lightly spined foliage and prolific vivid red berries. This cultivar takes the hardiness of the blue hollies to Zone 5b, 5a with protection.

BLUE PRINCE = 'Conablu' (male). One of the second-generation release of blue hollies introduced in 1972, this more vigorous selection is broadly upright in growth, to around 3M tall by 2.4M wide, and an effective pollinator for *Ilex ×meserveae* cultivars and other hollies. The glossy olive-green leaves borne on purple stems are distinctly oval in shape, around 3.8CM long by 2.5CM wide, with the small spines typical of the cross. Reputedly hardy to Zone 5b.

BLUE PRINCESS = 'Conapry' (female). Another of the second-generation 'blues', introduced in 1973. This selection (like her consort) is a taller, more pyramidal plant, with similar foliage.

Above: A fine plant of *Ilex ×meserveae* BLUE PRINCESS = 'Conapry'.

The brilliant glossy berries of BLUE PRINCESS stand out well against the deep olive-green foliage.

Abundant glossy red fruit is produced, 8MM wide. Hardy in Zones 5b to 9a.

BLUE STALLION = 'Mesan' (male). Introduced in 1979, this is a typical *Ilex ×meserveae* cultivar, with oval, lightly spined leaves of a medium olive-green on purple stems. This is possibly the most vigorous selection, growing to 4.5M tall and 3.6M wide, hardy, and a good pollinator.

GOLDEN GIRL = 'Mesgolg' (female). An exciting departure for the blue hollies, this is the first golden-fruited cultivar, introduced in 1989. A vigorous, compact plant of upright habit approaching the size of BLUE STALLION, with narrow dark green leaves around 5CM long by 1.9CM wide. The dark foliage provides a good foil for the generous quantities of brilliant yellow berries, of typical size at around 8MM wide. A hardy selection, reputedly Zones 5 to 9.

'Honey Jo' (female). Another distinctive departure, this variegated sport from 'Blue Girl', a chance discovery in 1979, was registered in 1996 and is now becoming more widely known. The young leaves, borne upon purple stems, are around 3.8CM long by 2.5 wide; generously splashed or suffused with bright yellow, they are sometimes entirely yellow. As might be expected in such a heavily variegated plant, it is relatively slow-growing. Galle reports the original plant to be scarcely 0.9M tall and wide after nearly twelve years. A useful bright dwarf evergreen for general garden use and containers.

'Pendleton Miller' (male). An interesting chance seedling discovered in the early 1980s and introduced in 1992, this plant has a genuinely prostrate habit of

Opposite, top: *Ilex ×meserveae* 'Honey Jo', with distinctive yellow-flushed young growths.

Opposite: The warm yellow leaves of 'Honey Jo' combine well with its purple stems.

Left: The small leaves and comparatively large fruits of 'Miniature' are derived from *Ilex pernyi*.

growth. The foliage is softly spiny and dark green, but the dimensions of the original plant, at only 45CM tall by 2.4M wide after around fifteen years, set this apart as a truly ground-covering selection.

***Ilex* 'Miniature'** (female). A hybrid between 'Nellie R. Stevens' and *I. pernyi*, made by William Kosar at the US National Arboretum in 1961. This hybrid shows the Perny holly's influence strongly in its habit and foliage; the original plant grew into a compact broad cone over 1.8M high by 2.4M wide in fourteen years. The small dark green glossy leaves are essentially oblong, with the typical *pernyi* strong apical spine, up to 4.5CM long by 1.25CM wide. Brilliant red berries are borne on short stems, nestling at the base of the leaves, again in *pernyi* style. Hardy to Zone 7.

Ilex 'Miniature', a small-growing conical hybrid.

Ilex myrtifolia (myrtleleaf holly) is very closely allied to *I. cassine* (dahoon holly), and shares much of its Coastal Plains habitat, particularly in swamps and wet places from North Carolina to Florida and Louisiana, but with a more coastal distribution. It forms a grey-barked large spreading shrub or small tree to 7M tall. The principal distinguishing factor of the myrtleleaf holly is its very narrow foliage, with almost linear spineless deep olive-green leaves 2–4CM long by only 8–10MM wide. Bright red fruits (rarely yellow) up to 8MM wide are freely borne. Gardeners can consider this species as a lighter-textured alternative to *I. cassine*, and Galle reports it as being used as a background plant in landscaping. Cultivars may be available in nurseries; 'Autumn Cascade' is described by Dirr as a heavy-fruiting semi-pendent selection. The myrtleleaf holly has contributed to one *I. ×attenuata* hybrid, 'Tanager'. Hardy in Zones 7 to 10.

***Ilex* 'Nellie R. Stevens'** (female). This remarkably successful hybrid is, as Dirr (2002) puts it so well, '*the grand dame of landscape hollies in the Southeast: common, overused, but functional to a pragmatic fault*'. Although its exact parentage is unknown, it is generally accepted to be *aquifolium × cornuta*. It arose from a collection of seed from a plant of *I. cornuta* at the US National Arboretum by the woman whose name it bears, around the turn of the 20th century. It was 'discovered' in 1952, named and introduced in 1954 by G. A. Van Lennep Jr., from whence it has gone on to become one of the most widely planted of hollies. Upright, dense and broadly pyramidal in habit, it will grow up to 7.5M high by around 5M wide. The lustrous, dark olive-green leaves have a distinct twist and are around 7.5CM long by 4.5CM wide, with a few marginal spines. Glossy brilliant red fruits 8–10MM wide are very freely borne, and ripen well in cooler maritime climates such as western Britain. Dirr goes on to remark that this benchmark plant is '*sun- and shade-tolerant, adaptable to any soils except wet. . . . Eminently prunable; great hedge or screen. From Washington, D.C., to Florida, the first choice*'. Hardy in Zones 6 to 9. Its male counterpart 'Edward J. Stevens' (so much in the shade of its sibling that it has languished under the synonym 'Male Nellie'!) is in most respects (barring fruiting) very similar.

Ilex **OAK LEAF**. See *Ilex* Red Holly Group

Ilex opaca (American holly). When the Pilgrims landed in Massachusetts in November 1620, the similarity between the prickly leaves and red berries of the American holly and the familiar *I. aquifolium* of their home shores must have been both striking and reassuring. The American holly was soon pressed into service by the colonists of the New World as a highly effective substitute for its European counterpart, taking its place in the wide range of practical, cultural and decorative purposes to which *I. aquifolium* was put in the Old World. Loudon, in his *Arboretum et Fruticetum Britannicum* (1838), says of the American holly, '*This species was formerly supposed to be only a variety of* I. aquifolium. *In America, it is applied to all the uses which the common holly is in Europe. It forms hedges; is an ornamental tree or shrub in gardens; is employed for making birdlime; and the wood is used in turnery and cabinet-making*'.

Ilex opaca has continued to play an important part in both the cultural and the horticultural life of North America, and is described by Fred Galle as '*the most commercially important holly native to North America and, more specifically, to the eastern United States*'. Yet of all the hollies in our gardens none so epitomises the difference between the plants grown and appreciated by holly growers on either side of the Atlantic as does *I. opaca*, which has largely failed to make the transition from west to east.

In the USA the American holly's sterling qualities have seen it used widely, especially in its native eastern coastal states. Its popularity over the years is reflected in the fact that more than a thousand cultivars have been named (if not formally registered), of which well over a hundred are available from nurseries (although rather fewer could be described as widely available). Compare that with the situation in Britain, where in the *RHS Plant Finder 2005–2006*, *Ilex opaca* is listed as being stocked by only one supplier, and that as the species, rather than as a cultivar: availability of the American holly is rather better in mainland Europe, where the climate may be expected to be more suitable, but even there only around ten cultivars are generally offered.

The American holly and its cultivars are, therefore, only rarely grown in the British Isles and Europe, although they may occasionally be found in botanic gardens and arboreta. The failure of *Ilex opaca* to capture the imagination of British and European gardeners, even after two and a half centuries in cultivation, can be put down mainly to its inability to thrive under the climatic conditions found across much of Western Europe. It seems that when abroad it hankers for the heat and humidity of the eastern USA; *The Hillier Manual* remarks of the American holly that it is '*best in a continental climate*', while Bean says that it '*sometimes bears fruit very freely in this country, but it is never so attractive as our common native species*'.

The comment from Bean highlights that there is a key difference to the lay gardener between *Ilex opaca* and its English counterpart, which can be summed up as that the American holly typically lacks the combination of glossy leaf and berry that gives *I. aquifolium* its characteristic sparkle. Although numerous selections have now been made for shiny leaves, the majority do not have the same immediate glossy appeal that makes the English holly such a cheerful element in the landscape. It is doubtful, however, whether many of the *I. opaca* cultivars which are closer to *I. aquifolium* in their habit and gloss have ever been tried under British and European conditions, and most modern European references still describe *I. opaca* as being typically matt-leaved.

Another factor to consider is that among the many American holly cultivars which have been named there are only two variegated selections available, 'Steward's Silver Crown' and 'Christmas Snow'. This contrasts starkly with the tremendous range of variegated and coloured-leaved cultivars which are such an important element of the English holly's popularity and garden value. This combination of factors, taken together with the American holly's pining for conditions more to its liking, does much to explain the relative lack of success of *Ilex opaca* among British and European gardeners.

The same does not hold true, of course, of *Ilex opaca* on its native turf, but even here this venerable garden plant is coming under pressure, a situation which has been remarked upon by specialist American holly grower Paul Hanslik of the Holly Ridge Nursery in Geneva, Ohio. Quoted in *Green Times* (1999), he discusses the difficulty of finding nurseries and garden centres that carry *I. opaca*, apart from a small number of eastern nurseries. Among the reasons he advances for this situation are that the limited commercial availability of 'super hardy' cultivars for Zone 5 gardens had reduced the area where plants could be grown (and thus the demand from gardeners).

More tellingly, perhaps, from the horticultural industry's point of view, he notes that a crop of American holly could take eight or more years to reach 'landscape size'. This is as much as twice as long as some other subjects, and has also been remarked upon by Michael Dirr. Another point made by Hanslik is that American holly is not an easy subject for the modern container growing systems that have replaced field cultivation for many plants. Both factors would militate against the American holly being grown by nurseries where productivity, throughput and relative ease of cultivation are important to commercial success. There are, however, specialist holly suppliers who continue to do good work in maintaining the availability of a representative selection of cultivars of this fine plant.

If one adds to these factors the competition from other novel holly groups (Hanslik singles out the blue hollies, *Ilex* ×*meserveae*, as one group that has usurped the role of *I. opaca* to a degree), and the requirements of today's smaller gardens, then it can be seen that from a situation where the American holly ruled the roost in the early and middle years of the 20th century, it now has to find its niche among an ever-increasing variety of hollies and other evergreens. This it is well equipped to do; for among the range of cultivars of *I. opaca* available there are many distinctive plants that combine high quality and garden merit with a robust constitution and proven track record.

Ilex opaca is distributed throughout the eastern USA, from eastern Massachusetts through to Pennsylvania and West Virginia, south to Florida, west to Texas and Missouri and north to Tennessee and Indiana. Its distribution takes in the coastal plain, Piedmont, and the Appalachians. The American holly is found in a wide variety of habitats, often as an understory plant in pine and hardwood forests, with some of the best specimens found on the deeper moist soils of low-lying areas of the coastal plain. Its association with swamps and bottom lands is in part due to its intolerance of fire. It also occurs as a coastal plant where it demonstrates a high tolerance of salt winds. At the northern extremes of its range almost pure stands of American holly can occur in coastal regions; one of the best examples is at Sandy Hook in New Jersey.

Ilex opaca will form a medium- to large-sized tree where conditions allow, particularly in moist habitats in the southeastern states. The National Champion, recorded in 1980 in the Congaree Swamp in South Carolina, had reached 30.2M tall, with a trunk diameter of 79CM and a 12.2M spread. Trees of over 30.3M have been recorded. A more typical height for the American holly is around 15M, and the natural habit is conical to pyramidal. The leaves are typically dark olive-green, 5–10CM long by 3–6CM wide. They usually bear from three to six spines on each side. White flowers are borne in mid to late spring followed on female plants by red (rarely yellow or orange) fruits 8–12MM wide, usually singly but rarely with up to three on a peduncle (fruiting stem).

Ilex opaca is a robust, adaptable species, capable of tolerating wide extremes of heat and cold. The natural hardiness range of *I. opaca* runs from Zone 6 to 10, but there are numerous selections which are guaranteed to survive in Zone 5. Survival in more marginal areas can be greatly assisted by the provision of shelter from the desiccating effects of cold winds. The American holly grows well in sun or partial shade, and will survive happily in quite deep shade, although for best fruiting good light is required. A male is required to ensure fruit set, but many gardeners over much of its range will find there are male plants close enough to provide pollen for lone specimen females. Otherwise there are male cultivars of high quality which are well worth a place in the garden ('Jersey Knight', for example).

The variety of soil types where *Ilex opaca* will grow is wide. This corresponds to the wide range of habitats in which it occurs, from salt-rich sands by the coast to thin mountain soils, dry gravels and the deep, moist organic soils characteristic of valley bottoms and swamps. Best growth of the American holly is obtained in moist, well-drained, slightly acid conditions.

Although growers had been selecting plants from around the 1920s onward, the heyday of selection and description of American holly cultivars, according to Galle, was the 1950s and 1960s—and the process of selection and naming continues.

'Arden' (female). An old cultivar dating back to the 1920s, with dark olive-green leaves which turn reddish brown in autumn, around 7.5CM long by 3CM wide. The 10mm-wide fruits are vivid red and borne singly. This cultivar is reported as being easy to propagate from cuttings, and is grown in European nurseries.

Opposite, top: Deep green foliage provides a backdrop for the yellow berries of *Ilex opaca* 'Boyce Thompson Xanthocarpa'.

Opposite: The black-tipped berries of 'Boyce Thompson Xanthocarpa'.

'Arlene Leach' (female). Introduced in 1960 by Orlando Pride, who was responsible for the selection of a number of hardy clones of the American holly, sometimes known as the Grace Hybrid Group, although no other species was involved. His selections were also made for vigour, habit and ease of culture, and a number of them are included in this directory. 'Arlene Leach' is a compact grower, narrowly pyramidal in habit, to around 12M high. The leaves are dark, spiny and large at around 7.5CM long by 5CM wide. Deep red-orange berries are borne heavily every year, and persist well. Hardy to Zone 5, and resistant to leaf spot.

'Arthur Pride' (male). Introduced in 1961, this is another typically hardy Pride selection. A fast-growing, broadly pyramidal tree to around 10m, with dark olive-green spiny leaves 5–7.5CM long by 3.8CM wide. Hardy to Zone 5, and such a good pollinator that it is recommended for orchard work.

'Betty Ann' (female). Selected by W. Wheeler before 1963, this cultivar has mid-green leaves up to 5CM long by around 2.5CM wide; the vivid red berries are around 10MM wide. Available from European nurseries.

'Big Red' (female). A very generous-bearing cultivar originating in southern New Jersey, growing to around 12M high, with dark green spiny leaves up to 7.5CM long by 4.3CM wide. The bright red, matt fruits are borne in clusters of two and three, to colourful effect. Hardy to Zone 5b.

'Bountiful' (female). A vigorous, symmetrical conical tree up to 15M high, with pendulous branches and dense foliage. The leaves are olive-green, with wavy spiny margins, 7.5CM long or more by up to 5CM wide. Vivid red berries are prolifically borne every year. Hardy to Zone 5.

'Boyce Thompson Xanthocarpa' (female). A shapely, pyramidal tree introduced in the 1920s, reportedly wild-collected in Virginia. It bears dark olive-green leaves up to 7CM long by half as wide. The 5MM-wide bright yellow berries bear a conspicuous terminal black spot.

Stately mature plants of *Ilex opaca* 'Canary' (left) and 'Hume's Choice' (right).

'Brilliance' (female). One of the more glossy opaca selections, which originated in the 1950s, it will grow to 12M high. The long, glossy, spiny dark olive-green leaves grow to 8.5CM long by 4CM wide; a heavy-fruiting variety with large bright red berries. Hardy to Zone 5.

'Canary' (female). A heavy-fruiting old yellow selection dating back to the early 1930s, growing to around 7.5M tall. The spiny leaves are around 7.5CM long by half as wide, deep olive-green, creating a fine backdrop for the abundantly borne vivid orange-yellow fruits. Hardy to Zone 6.

'Cardinal' (female). A smaller, compact, upright and slow-growing cultivar from Massachusetts eventually reaching around 9M high. The spiny, dark olive-green leaves are around 7.5CM long by half as wide. The berries are slightly lighter red than the type, generously borne from a young age. Hardy to Zone 5.

'Carnival' (female). A fast, strong-growing Pride selection from the 1960s, of broadly pyramidal habit, capable of 15M in height, with dense dark green spiny leaves up to 7CM long by 4CM wide. The abundant vivid red fruit persists well through the winter. Very hardy to Zone 5.

'Carolina' (female). Synonym 'Carolina Large Leaf'. Descriptively named, this cultivar was found growing in the grounds of a North Carolina hotel. It grows to around 10.5M tall, with slightly glossy leaves reaching up to 9.5CM long by 4.5CM wide. The vivid red berries are borne freely. Hardy to Zone 6.

'Cheerful' (female). A selection from Kingsville, Maryland, with small dark olive-green spiny leaves to 5.5CM long by around 3.5CM wide. The vivid red fruits are borne singly on stalks, in abundance. Hardy to Zone 6.

Ilex opaca 'Clarendon Spreading' has leaves that are among the largest of the cultivars.

'Chief Paduke' (female). A chance discovery in a cemetery in Paducah, Kentucky, introduced in 1963. The dark olive-green leaves bear few spines (one to three each side), and are relatively broad at around 8.5CM long by 4CM wide. The red-orange berries are prolifically borne. Hardy to Zone 6.

'Christmas Carol' (female). A narrow-growing form, particularly when young, from Massachusetts. Spiny, dark olive-green leaves grow up to 7CM long by 3CM wide. The dark red berries are frequently borne in clusters. Hardy to Zone 5.

'Clarendon Spreading' (female). Introduced from Clarendon Gardens, North Carolina, this is a selection of distinct dense, mounded and spreading habit, which can grow to 3.6M across or wider. The leaves are quite large, oval, spiny and olive-green, to 8CM long by 5CM wide. Orange-red fruits are sparsely borne. Hardy to Zone 6.

'Clarissa' (female). A strong-growing plant to 12M tall, again from the Pride stable, originating in Buckhannon, West Virginia. The leaves are among the largest in the Pride group, up to 8CM long by 4CM wide, olive-green and spiny, and the vivid red berries are also among the largest of the Pride cultivars. 'Clarissa' is grown in Europe. Very hardy to Zone 5. 'Cobalt' is a male selection from the same provenance, again very hardy, reputedly down to −32C.

'Corpening No. 3' (female). One of three yellow-fruited cultivars originally found growing in North Carolina. The leaves are olive-green, relatively broad and spiny, up to 6.5CM long by 4CM wide. The distinctive quality of No. 3 lies in its brilliant orange-yellow berries; 'Corpening No. 1' and 'Corpening No. 2' bear yellow fruits.

'Cumberland' (female). Originally selected in 1949, by C. R. Wolf, this is a truly distinctive American holly cultivar, with reputedly the glossiest foliage of the entire group. The burnished dark olive-green leaves are up to 6CM long by 4CM wide, rather delicately spined, and the fruits are comparatively large and a vivid matt red. Hardy to Zone 5.

'Dan Fenton' (female). A comparative rarity among the American hollies, a deliberately made cross, from Elwin Orton at Rutgers University in New Jersey and registered in 1987. This distinctive plant is broadly conical in growth, reaching 6M tall by 4M wide in only twenty years. The broad, spiny leaves are dark glossy green, up to 8CM long by 5.5CM wide. Small dark red berries are generously borne. Hardy to Zone 6b.

'David' (male). A handsome densely textured cultivar from near Millville, New Jersey. The dark olive-green leaves are small, spiny, up to 5.5CM long by 3CM wide.

'David G. Leach' (male). Synonym 'David Leach'. Another Pride cultivar, introduced in 1965. This is a fast-growing, broadly pyramidal tree to 7M tall, with spiny, olive-green slightly glossy leaves up to 7CM long by 4CM wide. A strong pollinator recommended for orchard work. Very hardy to Zone 5.

'Delia Bradley' (female). Originating in Maryland, and introduced by H. Hohman in around 1930, this cultivar grows to around 6M tall. The dark green leaves are around 7.5CM long by 3.5CM wide. Vivid red berries are abundantly borne, with up to three on each stalk. Hardy to Zone 6.

'Emily' (female). Vigorous and fast-growing, an early-bearing selection by W. Wheeler from West Barnstable, Massachusetts, in the 1940s (Galle reports others judged this cultivar to be the '*best and most spectacular*' of Wheeler's selections). This has wavy-margined dark olive-green leaves up to 7CM long by 4CM wide. The fruits are generously borne in clusters, and are a clear bright red. Hardy to Zone 6.

'Fallaw' (female). A vigorous, compact-growing yellow-fruited cultivar, discovered in 1939 near Batesburg, South Carolina, with lightly spined olive-green oval leaves up to 10CM long by half as wide. Vivid yellow berries are profusely borne. Hardy to Zone 6.

'Farage' (female). Selected from the wild in New Jersey, this cultivar is vigorous, broadly pyramidal and symmetrical in habit. It has good-sized dark olive-green leaves, around 8CM long by 4.5CM wide. The vivid red fruits, around 8MM wide, are persistent. '*Considered to be of superior quality*', writes Galle, and available in Europe.

'Felten's Selection' (female). Synonym 'Felton Special'. A plant of dense habit to 6M tall, with dark olive-green foliage, reportedly even darker green-black in shade. The leaves are broad, spiny, up to 7CM long by 4.5CM wide. The vivid red berries stand out well against the deep green foliage. Hardy to Zone 6.

'Galyean Gold' (female). A yellow-fruited cultivar from Dobson, North Carolina, registered in 1994. It bears oval, spiny olive-green leaves up to 7CM long by 3.5CM wide.

'Golden Knight' (male). This could be said to be the American holly's version of the well-established *Ilex aquifolium* moonlight hollies, or of *I.* ×*attenuata* 'Sunny Foster'. It certainly brings the possibility of enjoying yellow-flushed holly foliage to a wider range of climates. This intriguing cultivar was discovered by Ron Solt as a sport on 'Silica King' in the 1960s. The original plant is narrow and pyramidal in form, over 7.5M tall, with typical spiny opaca leaves whose strong yellow suffusion is best expressed in full sun.

'Goldie' (female). A popular yellow-fruited selection, which hails from Wilmington, Delaware, discovered by Mrs W. K. du Pont and introduced in 1940. It has mid-green leaves around 6CM long by half as wide. The good-sized berries are vivid yellow, 10MM wide, and abundantly borne.

Right: The dense habit of *Ilex opaca* 'Hedgeholly'.

'Hedgeholly' has comparatively small leaves and fruits well.

'Hedgeholly' (female). This well-named selection originating from West Virginia grows naturally into a broad mound up to 7.5M tall. The foliage effect is very dense, with closely spaced and overlapping spiny dark olive-green leaves, comparatively small and wide, up to 6CM long by 3.5CM wide. Brilliant red berries add to the garden value of this cultivar, which is also very hardy, to Zone 5.

Ilex opaca 'Hume's Choice' has excellent foliage and large berries.

'Hume's Choice' (female). Introduced and named by Bill Kuhl c.1976 for H. Harold Hume. A handsome cultivar, broadly conical with down-swept branches. Olive-green leaves are up to 6.5CM long by 3CM wide; vivid red fruits of a good size, around 10MM, are abundantly borne. Hardy to Zone 6.

'Janice Arlene' (female). This cultivar, which originated in New Jersey, was selected by L. Steward (Sr. and Jr.) for its excellent fruit production; it is also a fine performer in shade, and has some resistance to holly berry midge. The spiny leaves are olive-green, up to 7CM long by 3.8CM wide. Deep reddish orange berries 11MM wide are freely borne.

'Jersey Knight' (male). One of a number of excellent hollies introduced through Rutgers University, collected from the wild in 1945 and registered in 1965 by Elwin Orton. It will grow to 10.5M tall, and bears handsome slightly glossy dark green leaves around 6.5CM long by 3.5CM wide. This selection has proved itself as a valuable pollinator and parent, capable of passing on its best qualities to a high proportion of its progeny (see 'Jersey Princess'). Hardy to Zone 6.

'Jersey Princess' (female). Another product of Rutgers University, this time the result of a deliberate cross using 'Jersey Knight'. This is a very special cultivar, growing to around 9M tall and, as Galle puts it, '*noted for glossy foliage, which is the darkest foliage of any* I. opaca'. The spiny dark green leaves are oval in shape, up to 6.5CM long by 4CM wide, and the berries are a dramatic bright red, shown off superbly against the dark background. Hardy to Zone 6.

'Ling' (female). A fast-growing selection from the Pride group (introduced in 1964) with a pyramidal habit to 10.5M tall. The leaves are mid-green, wavy margined, spiny and grow up to 7.5CM long by 3CM wide; the berries are reddish orange. Hardy to Zone 5.

'Mamie Eisenhower' (female). A selection from New Jersey, introduced in 1952, growing to 10.5M, and a prolific fruiter. The leaves are dark olive-green, lightly spined (two or three each side), around 7.5CM long by 4.5CM wide. The good-sized fruit is deep reddish orange in colour. Hardy to Zone 6.

'Mary Holman' (female). Another Pride selection, growing to 9m, with spiny olive-green leaves, up to 7CM long by 4CM wide. Dependable for fruit, bearing good quantities of deep reddish orange berries. Hardy to Zone 5.

'Maryland Dwarf' (female). A low, spreading plant, eventually forming a broad mound up to 0.9M tall by 3.6M wide of small, lightly spined dark olive-green leaves up to 5CM long by 3CM wide. The red berries are only sparsely produced. Hardy to Zone 6b.

'Menantico' (female). A handsome selection from Salem County, New Jersey, introduced in 1949, growing to around 10.5M tall. The dark green leaves are wavy-edged and sharply spiny, up to 5.5CM long by 3CM wide; the berries are vivid red. This cultivar has a reputation of being resistant to holly leaf miner.

'Merry Christmas' (female). Originally discovered in the Catskill Mountains of New York, this is a vigorous hardy cultivar growing to 12M tall, making a good specimen with slightly glossy foliage of a good deep green. The leaves grow up to 6.5CM long by 3.5CM wide; brilliant red fruits of good size persist well.

'Miss Helen' (female). A reliable and adaptable plant, selected in 1936 from south of Baltimore, Maryland, by S. McLean, and of proven quality in the north and south. Steady in growth, eventually making a broad pyramid 12M in height, with olive-green leaves around 6.3CM long by 3CM wide, bearing short spines. The glossy dark red berries are prolifically produced. Hardy to Zone 6 and available in Europe.

'Mrs Santa' (female). A compact selection dating back to 1924, with a closely pyramidal branching habit, ideal for a tall hedge or screen. It bears dark green leaves around 5.5CM long by 2.5CM wide. Smallish vivid red fruits are abundantly borne, with up to three berries on a stem.

'Morgan Gold' (female). An old, tried and tested yellow-berried selection first discovered in North Carolina in 1902, and introduced into cultivation in 1959. The leaves are relatively broad, olive-green, up to 8CM long by half as wide; vivid yellow berries are of good size, up to 10MM in diameter. Hardy to Zone 5b and available in Europe.

The berries of *Ilex opaca* 'Miss Helen', a venerable, hardy selection, are particularly dark.

'Nelson West' (male). A very distinctive and attractive cultivar, originally discovered in New Jersey. It is very delicate in habit by comparison with the typical American holly, relatively dwarf and slender in growth, with narrow olive-green spiny leaves up to 5CM long by 1.5CM wide. Hardy to Zone 5.

'North Wind' (male). A relatively recent cultivar, which originated as a chance seedling in Kit Richardson's garden in Baltimore, Maryland. This is an elegant narrow, compact and conical tree; in around ten years the original grew to 3.6M high by 1.2M wide, with spiny dark green leaves up to 6.5CM long by 3.2CM wide. Hardy to Zone 6 and an early and prolific flowerer.

'Old Heavy Berry' (female). A cultivar of proven merit and performance, originating in Burlington, New Jersey, and popular for many years: it has set

the standard against which other fruiting cultivars are judged. It is a relatively slow-growing plant, forming a rounded cone to 9M tall, with dark green leaves up to 10CM long by 5CM wide. Good-sized vivid red berries are borne prolifically. A very tough selection, hardy to Zone 5b.

Opposite: *Ilex opaca* 'Old Heavy Berry', a popular, hardy cultivar of the American holly.

'Princeton Gold' (female). Selected from nursery-grown seedlings by the Princeton Nursery in the late 1940s and introduced in the 1980s, this is a vigorous, pyramidal tree grown for its effective dark green winter foliage and persistent yellow fruits. The leaves are dark olive in colour, lightly spined, up to 6.5CM long by 3CM wide. Vivid yellow berries around 7MM wide are prolifically borne, persist well and do not seem to interest birds.

Ilex opaca 'Satyr Hill', the Holly Society of America's 'Holly of the Year' in 2004.

'St. Mary' (female). Synonym 'Saint Mary'. This cultivar originated in West Barnstable, Massachusetts. A compact, large-berried, early-fruiting selection, this has been used for the Christmas pot plant trade. It has dark olive-green leaves up to 6.5CM long by 3.5CM wide, and deep reddish orange fruit.

'Santa Claus' (male). A prolifically flowering selection, with a reputation of being a very effective pollinator. Growing to around 10M tall, this recently rediscovered cultivar has smallish, spiny olive-green leaves up to 6CM long by 3CM wide. Hardy to Zone 5.

'Satyr Hill' (female). A chance seedling discovered by S. McLean in Maryland, this very popular cultivar is fast becoming the 'industry standard' American holly, which status was previously enjoyed by 'Old Heavy Berry'. Its quality was recognised in its nomination as the HSA's 'Holly of the Year' in 2004. This is a vigorous selection, making a pyramidal tree of 10M or more, with handsome, spiny dark olive-green leaves up to 6CM long by 5CM wide. Good-sized vivid red berries around 10MM wide are generously borne. Hardy to Zone 5.

Ilex opaca 'Steward's Silver Crown', a rare example of a variegated cultivar of the American holly.

'Steward's Silver Crown' (female). The American holly has proved nothing like as prolific in the production of variegated cultivars as its English cousin; indeed, for decades, this was the only variegated selection that had been nurtured to the point where it could make it into the trade. First discovered as a single-leaf mutation in 1956 by L. Steward Jr., this distinctive, colourful cultivar is slow-growing, with spiny leaves around 6.5CM long by 4CM wide, whose dark green centres are mottled and marbled with grey-green, within irregularly margined creamy white edges. The dark red fruits persist well. Hardy to −18C. 'Christmas Snow' (syn. 'Silver Crown Improved'), a second variegated sport developed and introduced by Steward in 1983, forms an upright pyramidal plant with dark red berries and a more distinctly yellow margin to its leaves; it is hardy to Zone 5. Both of these selections are attractive plants.

'Vera' (female). A wild-selected plant from Cape Cod, Massachusetts. This cultivar has a very compact upright habit and curly leaves, which are distinctively clustered with the fruits toward the end of the branches. The leaves are quite small, up to 4CM long by 2.5CM wide, distinctly twisted and bearing only one or two spines; the orange-red berries are around 8MM wide. Recommended for wreaths.

'Villanova' (female). A chance yellow seedling from Villanova, Pennsylvania, selected by Polly Hill and registered in 1984. This is a tall-growing pyramidal cultivar, with glossy olive-green leaves up to 8.8CM long by 5CM wide. Bright yellow berries of good size, 10MM wide, are borne in good numbers. This plant has been grown at RHS Garden Rosemoor in southwest England for a

The small leaves and clusters of orange-red berries of *Ilex opaca* 'Vera'.

Below, left: 'Vera' has a distinctive habit of growth.

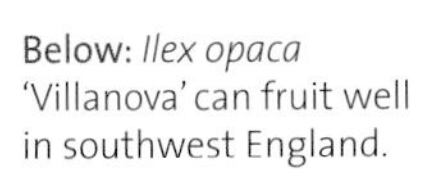

Below: *Ilex opaca* 'Villanova' can fruit well in southwest England.

number of years and regularly sets fruit in the absence of other male American holly pollinators.

'William Hawkins' (male). A very distinctive narrow-leaved cultivar originally discovered by its namesake as a witches' broom on a plant in the wild in Alabama, developed and introduced by Tom Dodd Jr. The plant has a compact habit, with leaves of dark olive-green, remarkably linear in shape, up to 5.5CM long by only 1CM wide, bearing several spines on each side and a long tapering tip. A characterful plant for a container, and ideal for use in bonsai.

'Winn Nursery' (female). One of the very few orange-fruited American holly cultivars, selected by the Winn Nursery, it grows to around 10M tall. The mid-green leaves grow up to 5.5CM long by 3CM wide, and the berries are vivid orange. Hardy to Zone 6.

'Wyetta' (female). A wild-collected seedling from New Jersey, registered in 1964. This is a fast-growing, compact, densely branched pyramidal plant with dark green, glossy leaves up to 5CM long by 3CM wide and deep reddish orange berries. Hardy to Zone 6.

'Xanthocarpa' (female). A name often applied to yellow-fruited cultivars, which may be of varied origin. A number of distinct golden cultivars are described above, e.g., 'Boyce Thompson Xanthocarpa', 'Goldie', 'Morgan Gold'.

***Ilex* 'Patricia Varner'** (female). A cultivar with *Ilex ciliospinosa* in its parentage, and the second seedling of 'Brilliant' to have been selected and introduced by Tom Dodd Jr. of Alabama, dating back to 1967. Like its sibling 'Dorothy Lawton', this is a compact pyramidal selection, bearing small dark green, glossy, lightly spined leaves up to 3.8CM long by around half as wide. Good-sized vivid red berries up to 10MM wide are abundantly produced in clusters of up to six.

***Ilex* PATRIOT**. See *Ilex* Red Holly Group

Ilex pedunculosa (longstalk holly) is a widespread Far Eastern species occurring in Japan (Honshu and Kyushu), and in eastern and central parts of China. It was first introduced from Japan by Charles Sargent to the Arnold Arboretum in 1893. In his *Forest Flora of Japan* (1894), he describes it enthusiastically: '*A very distinct evergreen species,* Ilex pedunculosa … *is sometimes a shrub two to three feet in height, and is sometimes twenty or thirty feet in height, when it is a well-formed tree, with a narrow round-topped head. The leaves are lustrous, two to three inches long [and] the stems of the flower clusters, from which is derived its specific name and which are longer than the leaves, hold the bright red fruit, which is solitary, or arranged in clusters of three or four, well outside the leaves, giving to the plants a peculiar and beautiful appearance in the autumn*'.

Another longstalk holly admirer, Dirr (1997) describes *Ilex pedunculosa* as '*an evergreen holly that looks like Mountain-laurel (Kalmia), with long-stalked, bright red fruit and excellent cold hardiness*'. Dudley (1986a) also rates this species highly, calling it '*one of the most select single- or few-trunked Asiatic hollies*'. Not everybody is as enamoured of this plant, however: John Creech (2003) opines that '*the red fruits borne singly on long stalks, coupled with the dull leaves, make this species of little garden value*'. Each to their own, of course, but having seen this plant doing well both in the USA and at the Bokrijk Arboretum in Belgium, I am happy to join those who would praise this most un-hollylike of hollies, which in its habit of growth and long-stalked fruits is strikingly reminiscent of *Photinia davidiana*.

As has already been noted, this species is variable in the wild. It can grow up to 10M tall, with a graceful habit. The leaves can reach over 7.5CM long by 3.5CM wide, bear no spines, and are variable in glossiness, but often of a good lustrous mid-green. The fruits are held on long pedicels, again variable in length, from around 4CM in typical forms, to around 7.5CM in plants I have seen, bearing out Sargent's description of pedicels longer than the leaves. Their nodding habit adds another graceful note to this attractive plant. This graceful habit belies a tough constitution: the longstalk holly is very cold tolerant, reportedly ranging from Zone 6 to 9, with some authorities recommending as low as Zone 5; it also tolerates exposure well. Dudley reports some susceptibility to disease, but this may have been related to the relatively narrow range of plants he could study. Other authorities state that it is less prone to some common holly pests than the American holly (Cook 1993).

A selection made from the New York Botanical Garden is in cultivation (under the name 'NYBG') in the USA; it has more rounded leaves of a deeper

green. Yellow-fruited and variegated forms ('Aurantiaca' and 'Variegata', respectively) are grown in Japan. It may well be that further selection is necessary to develop finer forms for our gardens; Dudley says that plants raised from seed may be variable. Pollination is usually by a male *Ilex pedunculosa*.

This desirable and distinctive plant is not easy to propagate vegetatively but is available in the USA and Europe. At Bokrijk Arboretum in Belgium I have seen superb seed-raised selections whose long peduncles create a very delicate and elegant effect.

Opposite, top: The fruits of *Ilex pedunculosa* are held on long stems over the foliage.

Opposite: A distinctive form of *Ilex pedunculosa*, with a cloud of berries held on extra-long stems.

Ilex perado. This distinctive species hails from the North Atlantic Islands of Madeira, the Canaries and the Azores, and from the far southwest of Europe. It has a long history in cultivation, dating back to 1760. Over the intervening years it became confused in its nomenclature (Bean speaks of it as being '*confounded with* I. aquifolium *and has hybridised with it in gardens*'), but the situation has been clarified by Susyn Andrews, who recognises four subspecies: subsp. *perado*, from Madeira; subsp. *platyphylla*, from the Canary Islands; subsp. *azorica*, from the Azores; and subsp. *iberica*, from the Iberian Peninsula (Andrews 1984b). An account of her fieldwork with hollies in the North Atlantic Islands, carried out in support of her work with the *I. aquifolium/ perado* complex, gives many interesting insights into how this species grows in its native habitats (Andrews 1983–84).

Aside from its qualities as a garden plant *Ilex perado* is, of course, of considerable importance as a parent of the valuable *Ilex ×altaclerensis* cultivar group. For our purposes the most important subspecies are those that were most probably involved in the hybrid: *perado* subsp. *perado* (the original 1760 introduction), and *perado* subsp. *platyphylla* var. *platyphylla*, introduced in 1842. *Ilex perado* subsp. *perado* was illustrated in Loddiges's *The Botanical Cabinet* in 1821. The text says that it '*is said to have been introduced in 1760 from Madeira, of which island it is a native. It is a strong evergreen shrub, or small tree, almost hardy enough to endure our winters. Its flowers are pretty, they come out in May and are sometimes succeeded by berries*'. The flowering shoot figured certainly showed quite large flowers. Paxton (*Paxton's Flower Garden*, 1850–53) illustrates the species in fruit and describes *I. perado* as '*an old inhabitant of our greenhouses, but to all appearances perfectly hardy near London*'. He speaks of it as a plant of '*the dense forest of Agua Garcia in the Canaries, where it forms a pyramidal tree twenty feet high … strictly a Canary plant,*

N° 549.

Ilex perado.

G.C. Fec.t

Opposite: An early painting of *Ilex perado*, from *The Botanical Cabinet* (1821).
Courtesy of the Lindley Library.

Ilex perado subsp. *platyphylla*, whose large almost spineless leaves impart their distinctive character to many *I.* ×*altaclerensis* cultivars.

and not to be known in Madeira… . The flowers are white, numerous, much larger than in I. aquifolium, *and are succeeded by bright red spherical berries. It is a truly noble evergreen*'.

Ilex perado subsp. *platyphylla* (and its variety *platyphylla*) is a plant of great merit, capable of growing to 15M in the wild, and has achieved nearly this height at Caerhays Castle in Cornwall, southwest England. Susyn Andrews reports that in the wild it occurs on deep soils in shade. It has handsome, broad, mainly spineless or sparsely spined leaves, 12.5–17.5CM long by around 7.5CM wide. The red berries are around 10MM wide, slightly larger than *I. aquifolium*. Subspecies *perado* differs in being a much smaller plant, typically up to 5M. It occurs in more open habitats, and has much smaller foliage, markedly spoon-shaped in cultivation, with leaves of around 7CM long by 5CM wide, almost spineless or with a few very small spines. Both subspecies are worth trying in Zone 8.

Ilex pernyi (Perny holly). China is home to a wealth of hollies, of which this is one of the few to have made their way into Western gardens. While *I. cornuta* is without doubt the most horticulturally important of these, particularly in North America, *I. pernyi* can claim to be the second most influential Chinese holly. Much of this influence is expressed through its offspring, as it has proved itself a productive parent over the years.

Ilex pernyi, an important parent of a number of modern holly hybrids bred for the smaller garden.

Ilex pernyi was initially discovered by Monsignor Paul Perny, who is described by Bean as '*a courageous French missionary who worked in the province of Kweichow between 1848 and 1862[,] the first naturalist [in] that province, which he is said to have entered in the guise of a Chinese beggar*'. Named and described by Franchet in 1883, *I. pernyi* was first introduced into cultivation in Britain by Ernest Wilson in 1900, collecting on behalf of the Veitch nursery. It was subsequently introduced to the Arnold Arboretum in the USA in 1908, and again in 1917.

Writing of a later visit to China in 1908, Wilson (1913) gives us an idea of the wealth of plants growing in the Sino-Tibetan border between 1220 and 1830M: '*The trees of this region, though not numerous or of any great size, include such remarkable subjects as* Davidia, Pterostyrax, Tapiscia, Tetracentron, *Beech and Horse Chestnut. Occasional trees of* Cornus kousa *occur, and were a wealth of white flower-heads enlivening the countryside… . In the grassy valley the beautiful* Ilex pernyi *occurs with* Rodgersia aesculifolia *and* Lilium giganteum' (the last is now *Cardiocrinum giganteum*).

It is noteworthy how even in such exalted botanical company Wilson acknowledged the quality of *Ilex pernyi*, a plant he must have met frequently in his journeys through its natural range of central and western China. It certainly made a splash in British horticulture, and was awarded the Royal Horticultural Society's prestigious First Class Certificate in 1908. Given its slow rate of growth, the eight-year-old awarded plant must scarcely have been of a size to be adequately assessed. William Dallimore (1908) thought highly of it, speaking of *I. pernyi* as '*without doubt one of the most interesting of the hardy evergreen species*'. Bean also took a shine to the Perny holly, describing it thus: '*Its habit, when young at least, is slenderly pyramidal and very shapely, and altogether it is a charming addition to dwarf, slow-growing evergreens*'. The other great authority on woody plants in the British Isles, *The Hillier Manual of Trees and*

Opposite: The combination of small leaves and comparatively large fruits is a distinguishing character of the Perny holly and many of its hybrids.

Shrubs, describes it as '*a distinguished large shrub or small tree*'. These comments also reflect the fact that *I. pernyi* is a dependable plant for British conditions.

Ilex pernyi is quite widespread in China, growing as a shrub or a small tree 6–9M tall. A plant of very distinctive, almost unique appearance: the stiff branches (pubescent initially) are densely crowded with small, hard, glossy leaves on very short stalks, arranged along the stem in a single plane which presents them most effectively to the light, in a manner very reminiscent of a fern frond. The leaves may persist for four or five years; they vary between 13MM and 2.5CM long, around half as wide, and are altogether very angular. They bear two spines at their squarish base, and a further, more substantial pair of spines roughly halfway along the blade, which is crowned by a very pronounced apical spine. While they bear a passing resemblance to *I. cornuta*, they are distinguished by the apical spine, which effectively sticks straight out, rather than being depressed (or downward pointing). There is something about the character of the Perny holly, in particular in the way that its branches carry themselves as they age, becoming lax and semi-pendent, that seems quintessentially oriental. It is certainly among the most 'architectural' of hollies in every aspect of its growth.

The final distinctive note struck by the Perny holly is its fruits. These follow the small pale yellow flowers in the leaf axils of two-year-old growths, tucked so snugly at the base of the leaves that they seem almost stemless. They are well described by Dudley (1986a) as '*flamboyant red, often enormous quadrangular fruits hiding [the] upper part of [the] stems*'. While not large in themselves, 7MM-wide vivid red berries cannot help but stand out against leaves under 2.5CM long and scarcely half as wide.

The plant known for many years as *Ilex pernyi* var. *veitchii*, which for a gardener's purposes is chiefly distinguished by larger leaves and a looser habit of growth, occurs throughout much of the range of *I. pernyi* (extending into Taiwan) and is now considered to be a separate species, *I. bioritsensis*. *Ilex pernyi* is not difficult to please, it grows well in sun or light shade (fruiting better in high light), and is hardy in Zones 5b to 9. It is well worth trying in neutral to slightly alkaline soils. Some light pruning may be required to keep older specimens tidy.

The breeding potential of *Ilex pernyi* has expressed itself in a number of ways both as a first- and a second-generation parent. A number of these hybrids have been very successful and have made their way into cultivation (several are also described in their appropriate places in the Directory).

The Perny holly has been crossed with *Ilex aquifolium* to produce a successful group of hybrids called *I.* ×*aquipernyi*, including such valuable plants as DRAGON LADY and 'San Jose'. With the Chinese holly (*I. cornuta*), *I. pernyi* has produced numerous cultivars, including 'Brighter Shines', 'Doctor Kassab', 'Good Taste', 'Lydia Morris' and 'John T. Morris'. When this hybrid cross was mated with the lusterleaf holly, *I. latifolia* × (*cornuta* × *pernyi*), it produced the popular landscape plant 'Mary Nell'. Two first-generation hybrids have been produced by crossing *I. pernyi* with the Japanese *I. integra*: 'Accent' (male) and its sister seedling, 'Elegance'.

Alongside its success as a primary hybrid, *Ilex* ×*aquipernyi* has also been involved in several second-generation hybrids in a number of interesting combinations. 'September Gem' (female) combines *I.* ×*aquipernyi* with *I. ciliospinosa*; and *I.* ×*aquipernyi* is also a parent of 'Joe McDaniel' (male), this time with *I. cornuta*. Other complex Perny holly hybrids include the distinctive cultivars 'Coronet' and 'Miniature', derived from *I. pernyi* crossed with 'Nellie R. Stevens' (*aquifolium* × *cornuta*). In keeping with the miniature theme *I. pernyi* was also involved in the dwarf hybrids 'Rock Garden' (*I. pernyi* crossed with *aquifolium* × *integra*), and the British cultivar 'Jermyns Dwarf' is an *I. pernyi* seedling or hybrid. A recent introduction from Elwin Orton at Rutgers University, RED BEAUTY, also has *I. pernyi* in its background.

This select group of Perny holly progeny includes numerous plants of high garden quality, with a high proportion particularly suited to small gardens, an ever more important section of the market. These plants provide the evidence for the importance of the contribution of *Ilex pernyi* to our gardens, a contribution which is likely to develop over the years.

Ilex purpurea. Synonym *I. chinensis* misapplied. This is a very handsome species of widespread Far Eastern distribution from China, Vietnam and Japan. Galle reports of its being '*long in cultivation [and] extensively used as an ornamental tree [, with] fruiting branches used in decorations from December to February, which includes the Chinese New Year*'. In China it is commonly known as 'winter green' or 'everlasting red'. It is described by Dudley (1986a) as '*a broad-spreading 1–4 trunked tree spectacular with large, ellipsoid very glossy fruit pendulous on long peduncles.... For many years perfectly reliable in Washington, D.C.*'. First introduced to England in 1810, it remains extremely rare in cultivation. It is a large-growing plant, to

15M tall, with dark grey bark and handsome, spineless, elliptical leaves up to 11CM long by 4CM wide. Purple-pink or red flowers (from which its name is derived) are followed by small bunches of large glossy red fruit 10–12MM wide. This very distinct evergreen deserves to be more widely grown; however, it is reputedly difficult to propagate from cuttings. Hardy in Zones 8b to 10.

***Ilex* RED BEAUTY** = 'Rutzan' (female). A new Elwin Orton hybrid, this is reputed to be a cross between *I.* ×*meserveae* and *I. pernyi*. It forms a dense, compact pyramid reaching around 2.1M tall by 1.2M wide after seven years. Its new growth has a purple-blue tinge, turning to dark glossy olive-green, and the relatively large red berries persist all winter. A hardy selection for Zones 5 to 9.

***Ilex* Red Holly Group**. This interesting group of open-pollinated seedlings from *I.* 'Mary Nell' was selected by Mitch Magee, in Poplarville, Mississippi, in the 1980s. While the male parent or parents are unknown, from the female side we have *I. cornuta*, *I. pernyi* and *I. latifolia*. All the cultivars described here are marketed under their trade names, and all are female. Among the factors they have in common are their compact, broadly pyramidal habit, good glossy foliage (which may be red as it emerges), and red fruits. They are relatively new in cultivation, and Dirr (2002) remarks of them: '*Certainly they offer new foliage textures but will be hard-pressed to supersede 'Nellie R. Stevens*'; however, as more compact growers they provide new opportunities to grow distinctive hollies for those with smaller gardens. All are rated as hardy between Zones 6 and 9.

CARDINAL = 'Conal' (female). Upright and pyramidal in growth to 4.2M tall by 2.4M wide, with distinctive spiny foliage, reddish when new, and red berries. Not to be confused with *Ilex opaca* 'Cardinal'.

FESTIVE = 'Conive' (female). Compact and upright, this selection rapidly forms a broad pyramid, 3M tall by 2.4M wide. Glossy, spiny leaves emerge green and remain mid-olive in colour. Recommended for hedges and screens.

LITTLE RED = 'Coned' (female). A smaller, less vigorous upright selection growing to 3M tall by 1.8M wide, with deep red new foliage. This cultivar is recommended for hedges or for trimming to create specimens in the landscape.

OAK LEAF = 'Conaf' (female). Named for the shape of its leaves, which emerge bright green, this is a vigorous upright plant to 4.2M tall by 2.4M wide.

PATRIOT = 'Conot' (female). Slow-growing to 3.6M tall by 2.4M wide, this selection forms a dense pyramid that holds its shape well. It is recommended as a specimen plant for a formal situation or for topiary work, and bears heavy crops of red berries.

ROBIN = 'Conin' (female). A larger- and faster-growing form, upright and pyramidal to 6M tall by 4.5M wide. The new foliage is deep red, and good numbers of red berries are borne. A potential choice for a taller screen or specimen plant.

***Ilex* RIVER QUEEN** = 'Wyeriv' (female). This arose from the putative open pollination of 'Nellie R. Stevens' (*aquifolium* × *cornuta*) by *I. cornuta* at the Wye Nursery in Maryland. The cross produced a very hardy, close-textured,

The influence of *Ilex cornuta* can be seen in foliage and fruits of *I.* RIVER QUEEN = 'Wyeriv'.

Generously produced, the red berries at the end of the shoots of RIVER QUEEN are characteristic of *cornuta* parentage.

upright-growing plant with distinct *cornuta* characteristics in its growth, foliage and fruits. It is very compact, reaching 3M tall by 2.4M wide after fifteen years. The dark green glossy leaves are around 6.8CM long by 2.5–5CM wide, with a few small spines and a distinct curve. Good-sized bright red berries, over 10MM wide, are generously borne in distinct clusters; they are early to ripen and persist well. RIVER QUEEN is recommended for hedges, screens and foundation planting, and as an added bonus is hardier than many *cornuta* cultivars, being guaranteed to Zone 6.

Ilex **ROBIN**. See *Ilex* Red Holly Group

Ilex **'Rock Garden'** (female). A very distinctive dwarf cultivar which arose from an Orton crossing of *I.* ×*aquipernyi* and I. 'Accent' (*integra* × *pernyi*), made in 1971. The product of this complex union is a compact, dense-growing shrublet with real holly character (i.e., spiny, glossy leaves and showy red berries). It is certainly slow: the original plant took fourteen years to reach 36CM tall by 55CM wide. Its leaves are spiny, a good glossy olive-green, and large for so small a plant at around 3.5CM long by 1.5CM wide; and the fruits are vivid red, up to 8MM wide. As its name suggests, this is a good subject for the rock garden, terrace, containers and bonsai. Hardy to Zone 6.

Ilex rotunda. This is a handsome large-growing species with a widespread distribution in the Far East, encompassing the southern provinces of China, southern Japan, Taiwan, Korea and Vietnam. Galle reports it as being much cultivated in Asian gardens, and American-born naturalist Carl Ferris Miller reports four- to five-hundred-year-old plants growing on Cheju Island, Korea. *Ilex rotunda* was first introduced to Britain in 1848 (as var. *microcarpa*) from a Robert Fortune collection. In the wild it grows up to 20M tall, with spineless and toothless dark green elliptic leaves 4–9CM long by 2–4CM wide, which, as Dirr (2002) puts it, '*provide no clue as to holly affinity*'. The glossy vivid red fruits, around 0.6MM wide, are borne in small bunches, with such freedom that (to quote Dirr again) '*in full fruit, the effect resembles a fireworks display*'. Like *I. purpurea* it is difficult to propagate, uncommon but very desirable. John Creech reports dwarf and weeping forms as being grown in Japanese nurseries. Bean states, '*It should be hardy if introduced from the northern end of its range in Japan, where it is much cultivated for ornament*'. Reliably hardy in Zones 8b to 10.

Ilex 'Rock Garden', a dwarf hybrid.

Ilex rugosa. This uniquely distinctive species is distributed in northern Japan, the Kurile Islands and Sakhalin Island. John Creech (2003) describes its habitat, which it shares with other northern Japanese species such as *I. leucoclada*, *I. sugerokii*, and *I. crenata* var. *paludosa*, as '*bogs throughout the mountains where they are protected by deep snow cover in winter*'. It is also recorded as an understory plant in coniferous forests. First introduced into cultivation in 1895, it remains rare; this is unsurprising as it is by no means among the more decorative of the hollies. It is low-growing, with a spreading, almost prostrate habit of arching branches that may grow to a metre long. The small, narrow, toothed leaves are around 2.5CM long by 10MM wide, of medium gloss and remarkable in their rugose (wrinkled) surface, from which the plant gets its name. Small white flowers are followed by small sparsely produced red fruits around 6MM across. It is remarkable that this anonymous little plant should be playing the important role it has as a parent

Ilex rugosa, a low-growing, hardy species from East Asia, in flower.

of the *I.* ×*meserveae* cultivar group (crossed with *aquifolium*), and of more recent hybrids with *I. cornuta*. Cold hardy to Zone 5b, but with its northern provenance it is not a heat-tolerant plant.

***Ilex* 'September Gem'** (female). A William Kosar hybrid of *I. ciliospinosa* and *I.* ×*aquipernyi*, which as its name suggests is of note for the early ripening of its fruit, a characteristic which is equally notable on both sides of the Atlantic. This cultivar is ideal for smaller gardens, growing into a compact upright pyramid of around 3M high by 1.8M wide, with narrow spiny leaves of a glossy deep green, around 4.5CM long by 1.5CM wide, and showy, freely borne brilliant red berries, which appear quite large among the small leaves, up to 10MM wide. Hardy to Zone 7.

***Ilex spinigera*.** See *Ilex colchica*

Opposite: *Ilex* 'September Gem' is welcome for its compact growth and early berries.

***Ilex sugerokii*.** A compact-growing red-fruited species from Japan and Taiwan, originally introduced by Ernest Wilson to the Arnold Arboretum in 1914. Although it is not yet firmly established in cultivation, its potential has

been noted by several plantsmen. John Creech (2003), who reintroduced *I. sugerokii* to cultivation in 1961, says of it, '*Of all Japanese hollies* I. sugerokii *has the best ornamental potential with a compact upright habit and deep green, lustrous leaves*'. He describes it as another of the 'northern' group of Japanese species, speaking of its variety *brevipedunculata*, which Galle describes as being '*locally abundant in high mountains of Hokkaido and Honshu, Japan, and southern and central Taiwan*'. This variety has spineless toothed leaves around 3CM long by 2CM wide, and quite large fruits around 8MM wide; its provenance should make it hardy to Zone 6.

***Ilex* 'Tanager'**. See *Ilex ×attenuata* 'Tanager'

***Ilex* 'Venus'** (female). This 'Nellie R. Stevens' × *latifolia* cultivar, from William Kosar at the US National Arboretum, is an excellent example of a hybrid representing a distinct development from its parents. Typically broadly pyramidal in habit, it is vigorous but slightly slower in growth than its sibling and pollinator 'Adonis'. The original plant reached 6M tall by 5.4M wide after nearly thirty years. Its foliage character leans toward the 'Nellie R. Stevens' parental influence, with quite large leaves, up to 13CM long by 6.5CM wide, spiny, dark olive-green in colour, although without such a high gloss. The abundance and persistence of its fruit are what really set it apart. Its berries are grouped in clustered masses of ten or more that combine to completely encircle the stems; they are vivid glossy red, 9MM wide, and persist until the following season. Hardy to Zone 7.

Ilex vomitoria (yaupon holly), native to the southeastern USA, is an invaluable, durable and adaptable plant for southern gardens. Dirr (2002) refers to it as '*the quintessential southern holly—native, used with impunity, prospering everywhere, multifunctional, and attractive*'. In inimitable style he goes on to describe it as a '*choice no-brainer selection for green meatballs, gobs-of-green, and innocuous spinach*'. Dudley (1986a) describes the yaupon as '*endlessly versatile for landscape purposes with enormous variation to growth habit, rate of growth, leaf size, shape and color, fruit size and color demonstrated by many cultivars*'.

Ilex vomitoria is a light-textured plant with generously produced small berries.

The all-round toughness of this species is derived in great part from its chosen habitat: it occurs mainly in coastal areas from southeastern Virginia to Florida and west to Texas and Arizona, with subsp. *chiapensis* found in the state of Chiapas in Mexico. The preference for a seaside habitat indicates (and demands) a resilient constitution; this is amply borne out by the yaupon's ability to grow in a wide range of soil conditions, from wet to dry, from acid to alkaline, and to recover rapidly from most setbacks. It is generally hardy in Zones 7 to 10, with some cultivars able to tough it out in Zone 6.

The yaupon was introduced to Britain prior to 1700 and grown initially in London; yet despite this long history in cultivation it has not succeeded in the hands of British gardeners: Bean, speaking of the British Isles, says that it is '*incapable of withstanding our hardest winters*'. It is considered tender even in the maritime regions of northwest Europe, where winter temperatures are generally mild.

Although it may be due in part to the yaupon's innate lack of cold hardiness, this perceived tenderness is almost certainly exacerbated by the yaupon's inability to ripen its growth in cool, moist summers. This can lead to winter die-back and that general failure to thrive and perform to their potential that is characteristic of a number of trees and shrubs from continental climates under British conditions. Once again the determining factor would seem to be the need for sustained high temperatures characteristic of continental summers. Unless (or with global warming, until) there are significant changes to the climate of northwest Europe, *Ilex vomitoria* may be consigned to that significant group of hollies currently restricted to gardeners who can provide adequate summer heat. Given its adaptability it may be persuaded to thrive if used as a wall plant on a southerly aspect, and treated to a good summer baking. Southern European gardens, however, could well be able to provide the requisite sunshine for this choice and accommodating plant.

Ilex vomitoria is a variable species in the wild, growing as everything from a 2M shrub to a tree of up to 9M, usually multi-stemmed, with the characteristic light grey bark found in so many hollies. The National Champion tree in the USA has grown to an impressive 13.5M tall by 12M wide. Yaupon foliage is relatively light-textured for a holly, up to 4.5CM long by 1–2CM wide. The leaves, which often have a purple cast on emergence, mature to a lustrous dark green, with serrated edges rather than spines. Some cultivars have been selected for distinctive winter foliage effects. Female plants bear fruit in prodigious quantities, sufficient to bend their branches, up to 8MM wide, glossy and semi-translucent. Their translucence is distinctive among hollies in general cultivation, and they have excellent persistence and the ability to last throughout the entire winter.

The yaupon is among the most adaptable of hollies, with a number of compact cultivars capable of being trimmed into a great variety of shapes; Patricia Joseph (1995) speaks of their being able to '*take just about any kind of pruning at any time*'. It can also be trained against buildings and trellises to fine effect, and the weeping forms make excellent specimen plants. The use of yaupon for hedges, screens and topiary is covered in Chapter 2. There is some confusion in the cultivar names of two of the most distinctive groups of yaupon, the weeping and dwarf forms, and care should be taken when purchasing either to ensure that the plant you buy will give you the results required. Specialist nurseries should be able to advise further.

Ilex vomitoria, in its place, and particularly in southern states, is as useful and adaptable as any other holly. Yet this characterful evergreen stands alone among its peers. Botanically speaking, in the classification of the genus *Ilex* it is a representative of hollies of more tropical distribution, unrelated to other North American species, and not capable of hybridizing with them.

BORDEAUX = 'Condeaux' (male). One of several dwarf cultivars, this arose as a branch sport of 'Stokes Dwarf' in 1988, and was selected for both its compact habit and the purple-red colour of its young shoots. The leaves are small and narrow, up to 2.5CM long by 13MM wide. Its natural habit is dense and compact, up to 1.5M tall by 1.8M wide—a very distinctive introduction.

'Dare County' (female). A unique selection, this orange-berried form was discovered as a wild plant by Barton Bauers Sr. in Dare County, North Carolina, in 1978. A moderately vigorous, upright plant, achieving 2.4M in height in fifteen years, with leaves larger than the type, up to 6.3CM long. The glossy orange berries, around 7MM in diameter, are prolifically borne.

'Dwarf' (female). Synonym 'Nana'. 'Dwarf' dates back to the mid 1930s, when it was collected as a seedling in Louisiana by S. Stokes and Tom Dodd Jr. A compact, slow-growing plant, this is the largest of the dwarf forms in cultivation; after thirty years it will reach over 1.8M high and somewhat wider. It is dense in growth, with olive-green leaves around 3CM long by nearly half as wide. It was grown for many years as a male until it was noticed that old plants had begun to bear typical glossy red yaupon fruit. Tremendously trimmable into a variety of forms, 'Dwarf' can be used to create close-textured hedges, buns, domes or other fancy shapes.

'Folsom's Weeping'. Female and male forms of this cultivar are sold, derived from the weeping *Ilex vomitoria* f. *pendula*, and synonymous with it. They may also be sold as 'Pendula' (female); to further confuse the situation there are also male forma *pendula* plants offered as 'Pendula'! While the nomenclatural rules stipulate that cultivars should be propagated clonally, and therefore with hollies can be of only one sex, it is perfectly possible for the botanical forma *pendula* to be offered as either male or female. What cannot be denied or questioned is the landscape value of this distinctive plant, a vigorous large shrub or small tree of upright stem habit with weeping branches. The leaves of this form are smaller than the type, up to 2.5CM long by a third as wide, and the

Ilex vomitoria f. *pendula* has given rise to a number of cultivars sharing its upright habit and weeping branches.

Right: A female plant of *Ilex vomitoria* f. *pendula*, generously sprinkled with small red berries.

females produce vivid red glossy fruits of typical size in great abundance. A very adaptable plant, with the correct formative pruning the weeping yaupon can be accommodated in very narrow spaces, or trained against walls and supports.

'Gray's Little Leaf' (male). A distinctive cultivar, of typical upright spreading habit but more finely textured in appearance due to the narrow dark green foliage. The leaves are 7MM to 2CM long by only 3MM wide.

'Hoskin Shadow' (female). Synonyms 'Round Leaf', 'Shadow'. A very hardy clone (to Zone 6), also selected for its distinctive lustrous dark green leaves, up to 3.8CM long by 13MM wide. The red fruits are of typical size, abundantly borne, and the habit of growth is compact and spreading. Another hardy female clone (to Zone 6) is 'Nanyehi', with slightly smaller dark green leaves and red berries.

'Nana'. See 'Dwarf'.

'Pride of Houston' (female). A fine cultivar, superior in growth, foliage and fruiting. Upright and vigorous, it has dark green leaves over 2.5CM long, and vivid red glossy fruits of typical size borne in great abundance.

'Saratoga Gold' (female). A vigorous upright spreading shrub, with small dark green leaves up to 1.8CM long by half as wide. The brilliant yellow berries are produced prolifically. Galle recommends this cultivar for either specimen or group plantings.

'Stokes Dwarf' (male). Synonym 'Schilling's Dwarf'. The other major dwarf cultivar, this is one of a number of plants which arose at the Stokes Nursery. As with other compact forms of the yaupon, this is excellent for clipping into dense, low hedges, or other architectural and topiary forms, and an effective

Ilex vomitoria 'Stokes Dwarf', a selection whose natural habit lends itself to clipping into hedges and topiary.

The close-textured foliage of *Ilex vomitoria* 'Stokes Dwarf'.

substitute for dwarf box in parterres and other formal hedging. This selection is capable of slowly reaching around 0.9M tall and 1.2M wide; its olive-green leaves are correspondingly small, scarcely a third of the size of the species at around 1.3CM long by half as wide. The young growths are distinctively flushed pinky purple.

'Tricolor' (male). A distinctive variegated form of vigorous, upright habit. The small mid-green leaves bear irregular yellow blotches, sometimes covering the entire leaf. In the winter the third colour referred to in its name becomes apparent, as the margins become purple; the best leaf colour is produced with good exposure.

'Will Fleming' (male). Introduced in the mid 1970s, this is a very narrowly fastigiate selection, with dark green leaves around 13MM long and half as wide. In common with a number of strictly upright selections of woody plants, it may lose its tightness of form as it ages, and unless the branches are subtly bound together is likely to fall apart: as Dirr (2002) puts it neatly, '*splays to the point of no redemption with time*'.

'Yawkey' (female). Synonym *Ilex vomitoria* var. *yawkeyi*. A chance discovery from South Carolina, this yellow-fruited cultivar is an upright spreading shrub, with dark green leaves, around 2.5CM long by up to half as wide, that provide an excellent foil for the abundant orange-yellow berries.

Ilex* ×*wandoensis. A natural hybrid (*cornuta* × *integra*), first found by chance by Carl Ferris Miller in 1982 as a wild-dug potted plant in the village of Wando, South Korea, whose name it bears. Subsequently it has been found on two small offshore islands. *Ilex* ×*wandoensis* shows some variation, but typically forms dense shrubs or small trees up to 5M tall, with oval, variably spiny (usually only two or three on each side), shiny leaves 3.5–5CM long by 2.5–3.5CM wide. Brilliant red fruits around 10MM wide may be freely borne on female plants. There are some handsome plants of this variable hybrid in cultivation, some made artificially prior to its discovery in the wild.

***Ilex* 'Washington'** (female). A distinctive hybrid between *I. cornuta* and *I. ciliospinosa*, made at the Glendale US Plant Introduction Station in Maryland in 1952 and then sent to Holland, where it was named. It has subsequently proved quite successful in Europe, including in softer maritime conditions, but remains almost unknown in the USA. It forms a glossy, neat pyramid of dense texture growing to around 5M tall by half as wide, with spiny deep olive-green leaves, around 5CM long by half as wide, and bright red berries around 8MM wide.

Left: An excellent hybrid (*cornuta* × *ciliospinosa*) for maritime climates, *Ilex* 'Washington' forms a compact broad pyramidal specimen.

'Washington' derives some of its close-textured habit from *Ilex ciliospinosa*.

***Ilex* 'William Cowgill'** (female) is another product of the marriage of *I. cornuta* and *I. ciliospinosa* at the US Plant Introduction Station in Maryland. In habit and foliage it resembles its sister plant 'Washington', being broadly conical but slower-growing, reported as reaching only 1.8M by 1.3M after sixteen years. A free-fruiting selection, suitable for small gardens.

Opposite: Another hybrid between *Ilex cornuta* and *I. ciliospinosa*, the fine *I.* 'William Cowgill' is a free-fruiting plant for the smaller garden.

Ilex yunnanensis (Yunnan holly). An attractive small shrubby tree of open habit to around 5M tall, from western China (Sichuan, Hubei and Yunnan) and Upper Myanmar (Burma). Allied to *I. sugerokii*, it was first introduced by Ernest Wilson through the Veitch nursery in Britain in 1901, and through the Arnold Arboretum in 1911; he describes it as having '*small, neat leaves, clusters of purplish flowers and hairy shoots*' (Wilson 1913). Bean takes up the description, calling the Yunnan holly '*a neat, cheerful-looking evergreen, allied to* I. crenata, *but the leaves are more leathery [,] the branches more downy and the fruits red*'. Bean also notes that the leaves may be '*a beautiful brownish red when young, becoming glossy with age*'; they are small, 2–3.5CM long by 1–2CM wide, with serrated edges. The flowers may be white (or in some populations pink to red), and the red fruits are small, around 6MM wide. *Ilex yunnanensis* occurs at quite high elevations, and is hardy to Zone 5. Dudley (1986a) shares the general good opinion of this species, saying that it is '*one of the most attractive red-fruited, tall or short, multiple-stemmed shrubs or small trees*'. In common with a number of other hollies the leaves of *I. yunnanensis* are used by local people as a tea, and its Chinese name along the Sino-Tibetan border is *shu cha tze*, which translates as 'water tea' (i.e., tea growing by the water).

Appendix

Where to Buy Hollies

Hollies are widely available in the trade, with many nurseries and garden centres holding a respectable selection of the more popular species and cultivars. Those seeking suppliers of a wide range of hollies in Britain and Europe should avail themselves of the excellent *RHS Plant Finder*, published by the Royal Horticultural Society, or the *PPP Index: The Europlant Finder*, published by Moorland Publishing Company, Derbyshire, England.

Similar plant databases are available in North America. Readers in North America are also referred to the Holly Society of America's *Sources for Unusual Hollies*, which is updated regularly and comprehensive in the range of plants listed; it covers nurseries across the USA and in Canada.

The nurseries listed here are principally retail outlets. The wholesale nurseries listed will be able to provide details of retail suppliers of their plants. Nurseries that specialise in hollies are well worth seeking out for advice upon plants for local conditions. Not all nurseries provide a mail order service.

Great Britain and Europe

Firma C. Esveld: Rijneveld 72, 2771 XS Boskoop, Holland
Highfield Hollies: Highfield Farm, Liss, Hampshire GU33 7NH, United Kingdom

North America

Fairweather Gardens: P.O. Box 330, Greenwich, NJ 08323
Forestfarm: 990 Tetherow Rd., Williams, OR 97544-9599

Gossler Farms Nursery: 1200 Weaver Rd., Springfield, OR 97487
Holly from Holley, Oregon: P.O. Box 264, Sweet Home, OR 97386-0264
Holly Haven Hybrids: 136 Sanwood Rd., Knoxville, TN 37923
Holly Ridge Nursery: 5125 South Ridge Rd., Geneva, OH 44041
McLean Nurseries: 9000 Satyr Hill Rd., Baltimore, MD 21234
Monrovia Nursery Company: P.O. Box Q, Azusa, CA 91702
Patuxent Valley Nurseries: 11018 Berrypick Lane, Columbia, MD 21044
Roslyn Nursery: 211 Burrs Lane, Dix Hills, NY 11746
Simpson Nursery Company: 1504 Wheatland Rd., P.O. Box 20, Vincennes, IN 47951
Solt Gardens Nursery: 85 Greenhouse Lane, Barto, PA 19504-9026
TNZ Nursery: 1800 Wickham Way, Louisville, KY 40223-1057
Wavecrest Nursery: 2509 Lakeshore Drive, Fennville, MI 49408

Where to See Hollies

Hollies are well represented in gardens generally. The gardens and arboreta listed below have particularly good collections that are well labelled and documented. Those marked with an asterisk * are designated as Official Holly Arboreta and Experimental Test Centres by the Holly Society of America; their collections are managed according to HSA guidelines, their plants are labelled and recorded, and they report upon their collections annually in the *Holly Society Journal*. In Britain a number of holly collections have been accorded the status of National Collection by the National Council for the Conservation of Plants and Gardens; again these collections are wide-ranging in their scope. In Holland a number of collections of woody plants are being set up under the auspices of the Royal Boskoop Horticultural Society, including a collection of hollies; these are currently being developed in commercial nurseries, but are available to visit.

Great Britain and Ireland

National Botanic Garden, Glasnevin: Glasnevin, Dublin, Ireland
Royal Botanic Garden Edinburgh: Inverleith Row, Edinburgh, Scotland
Royal Botanic Gardens, Kew: Kew, Richmond, Surrey, England

RHS Garden Rosemoor (NCCPG National Collection): Torrington, Devon, England
RHS Garden Wisley: Wisley, Woking, Surrey, England
The Savill and Valley Garden (NCCPG National Collection): Wick Lane, Englefield Green, Surrey, England
Sir Harold Hillier Gardens: Jermyns Lane, Ampfield, Romsey, Hampshire, England
Westonbirt Arboretum: Westonbirt, Tetbury, Gloucestershire, England

Europe

* Arboretum des Pres des Cutlands Conservatoire National d'Ilex; 14 Rue Jean-Baptiste Colbert, 45100 Orleans, France
Arboretum Trompenburg: Honingerdijk 86, 3062 NX Rotterdam, Holland
* Arboretum Bokrijk: Houthalen, Belgium
Nederlandse Dendrologische Vereniging (Dutch Plant Collections): Eindhovensedijk 34B, 5688 GN Oirschot, Holland

North America

* Bernheim Arboretum and Research Forest: State Highway 245, Clermont, Kentucky
* Blue Ridge Community College: Flat Rock, North Carolina
* Callaway Gardens: Pine Mountain, Georgia
* Chicago Botanic Garden: 100 Lake Cook Rd., Glencoe, Illinois
* Clarke-Landsbaum Deming Park Holly Arboretum: 500 Fruitridge Ave., Terre Haute, Indiana
* The Dawes Arboretum: 7770 Jacksontown Rd. SE, Newark, Ohio
* Denver Botanic Gardens: 909 York Street, Denver, Colorado
* Ebersole Holly Garden: Sandhills Community College, 2200 Airport Rd., Pinehurst, North Carolina
* Highland Park Arboretum: 108 Reservoir Ave., Rochester, New York
The Holden Arboretum: 9500 Sperry Rd., Mentor, Ohio
Holly Haven Hybrids: 136 Sanwood Rd., Knoxville, Tennessee
* Missouri Botanical Garden: 2345 Tower Grove Ave., St. Louis, Missouri
* Morris Arboretum of the University of Pennsylvania: 9414 Meadowbrook Ave., Philadelphia, Pennsylvania

* Planting Fields Arboretum: Oyster Bay, New York
* Scott Arboretum of Swarthmore College: 500 College Ave., Swarthmore, Pennsylvania

Secrest Arboretum: Ohio State University, Wooster, Ohio

* South Carolina Botanical Garden of Clemson University: 102 Garden Trail, Clemson, South Carolina
* John J. Tyler Arboretum: 515 Painter Road, Media, Pennsylvania

University of Alabama Arboretum: 338 Thomas St., Tuscaloosa, Alabama

University of British Columbia Botanical Garden, 6501 NW Marine Dr., Vancouver, British Columbia, Canada

* University of Tennessee Arboretum: 901 South Illinois Ave., Oak Ridge, Tennessee
* United States National Arboretum: 3501 New York Ave. NE, Washington, D.C.

VanDusen Botanical Garden: 5251 Oak Street, Vancouver, British Columbia, Canada

* Washington Park Arboretum: 2300 Arboretum Dr. E, Seattle, Washington

South Korea

* Chollipo Arboretum: Uihang-Ni San 185, Sowon-Myon, Taean-Gun, Chungchong Namdo 357-930

Hardiness Zone Maps

Centigrade		Fahrenheit
−45.6° and below	Zone 1	below −50°
−45.5° to −40.0°	Zone 2	−50° to −40°
−40.0° to −34.5°	Zone 3	−40° to −30°
−34.4° to −28.9°	Zone 4	−30° to −20°
−28.8° to −23.4°	Zone 5	−20° to −10°
−23.3° to −17.8°	Zone 6	−10° to 0°
−17.7° to −12.3°	Zone 7	0° to 10°
−12.2° to −6.7°	Zone 8	10° to 20°
−6.6° to −1.2°	Zone 9	20° to 30°
−1.1° to 4.4°	Zone 10	30° to 40°
4.5° and above	Zone 11	40° and above

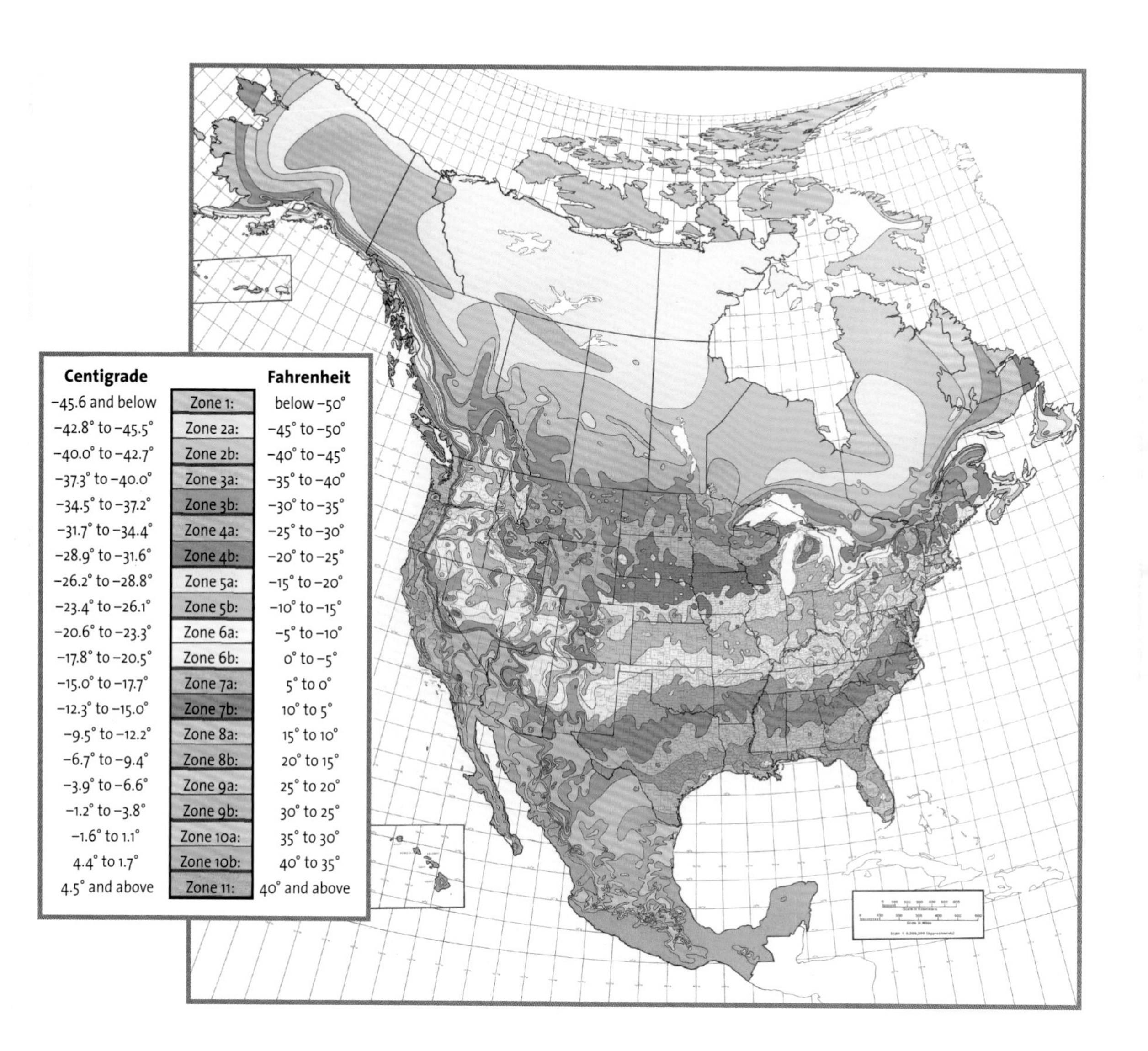
Centigrade
Fahrenheit
−45.6 and below Zone 1: below −50°
−42.8° to −45.5° Zone 2a: −45° to −50°
−40.0° to −42.7° Zone 2b: −40° to −45°
−37.3° to −40.0° Zone 3a: −35° to −40°
−34.5° to −37.2° Zone 3b: −30° to −35°
−31.7° to −34.4° Zone 4a: −25° to −30°
−28.9° to −31.6° Zone 4b: −20° to −25°
−26.2° to −28.8° Zone 5a: −15° to −20°
−23.4° to −26.1° Zone 5b: −10° to −15°
−20.6° to −23.3° Zone 6a: −5° to −10°
−17.8° to −20.5° Zone 6b: 0° to −5°
−15.0° to −17.7° Zone 7a: 5° to 0°
−12.3° to −15.0° Zone 7b: 10° to 5°
−9.5° to −12.2° Zone 8a: 15° to 10°
−6.7° to −9.4° Zone 8b: 20° to 15°
−3.9° to −6.6° Zone 9a: 25° to 20°
−1.2° to −3.8° Zone 9b: 30° to 25°
−1.6° to 1.1° Zone 10a: 35° to 30°
4.4° to 1.7° Zone 10b: 40° to 35°
4.5° and above Zone 11: 40° and above

Useful Conversions

inches	cm
1/10	0.3
1/6	0.4
1/4	0.6
1/3	0.8
1/2	1.3
3/4	1.9
1	2.5
2	5.1
3	7.6
4	10
5	13
6	15
7	18
8	20
9	23
10	25
20	51
30	76
40	100
50	130
60	150
70	180
80	200
90	230
100	250

feet	m
1	0.3
2	0.6
3	0.9
4	1.2
5	1.5
6	1.8
7	2.1
8	2.4
9	2.7
10	3
20	6
30	9
40	12
50	15
60	18
70	21
80	24
90	27
100	30
200	60
300	90
400	120
500	150
600	180
700	210
800	240
900	270
1,000	300
2,000	610
3,000	910
4,000	1,200
5,000	1,500
6,000	1,800
7,000	2,100
8,000	2,400
9,000	2,700
10,000	3,000
15,000	4,600

miles	km
1/4	0.4
1/2	0.8
1	1.6
2	3.2
3	4.8
4	6.4
5	8.0
6	9.7
7	11
8	13
9	14
10	16
20	32
30	48
40	64
50	80
60	97
70	110
80	130
90	140
100	160
200	320
300	480
400	640
500	800
600	960
700	1,100
800	1,300
900	1,400
1,000	1,600
1,500	2,400
2,000	3,200
2,500	4,000

square miles	square km
100	260
200	520
300	780
400	1,000
500	1,300
600	1,600
700	1,800
800	2,100
900	2,300
1,000	2,600
2,000	5,200
3,000	7,800
4,000	10,400
5,000	13,000
6,000	16,000
7,000	18,000
8,000	21,000
9,000	23,000
10,000	26,000
20,000	52,000
30,000	78,000
40,000	100,000
50,000	130,000
60,000	160,000
70,000	180,000
80,000	210,000
90,000	230,000
100,000	260,000
200,000	520,000
300,000	780,000
400,000	1,000,000
500,000	1,300,000

cubic miles	cubic km
1/10	0.4
1/4	1.0
1/2	2.1
3/4	3.1
1	4
2	8
3	13
4	17
5	21
6	25
7	29
8	33
9	38
10	42
20	83
30	120
40	170
50	210
60	250
70	290
80	330
90	380
100	420
200	830
300	1,200
400	1,700
500	2,100
600	2,500
700	2,900
800	3,300
900	3,800
1,000	4,200
1,100	4,600
1,200	5,000
1,300	5,400
1,400	5,800
1,500	6,300

pounds	tons	kg
100		45
200		91
300		140
400		180
500		230
600		270
700		320
800		360
900		400
1,000		460
2,000	1	910
	1 1/2	1,400
	2	1,800
	2 1/2	2,300
	3	2,700
	3 1/2	3,200
	4	3,600
	4 1/5	4,100
	5	4,500
	7 1/5	6,800
	10	9,100
	100	91,000
	1,000	910,000
	10,000	9,100,000

Conversion Tables for Length, Area, and Temperature

To convert length:	Multiply by:
Miles to kilometers	1.6
Miles to meters	1609.3
Yards to meters	0.9
Inches to centimeters	2.54
Inches to millimeters	25.4
Feet to centimeters	30.5
Kilometers to miles	0.62
Meters to yards	1.09
Meters to inches	39.4
Centimeters to inches	0.39
Millimeters to inches	0.04

To convert area:	Multiply by:
Square inches to square centimeters	6.45
Square feet to square meters	0.093
Square yards to square meters	0.836
Acres to hectares	0.4
Square miles to square kilometers	2.6
Square centimeters to square inches	0.155
Square meters to square feet	10.8
Square meters to square yards	1.2
Hectare to acres	2.5
Square kilometers to square miles	0.386

Temperatures

$°C = 5/9 \times (°F - 32)$

$°F = (9/5 \times °C) + 32$

Glossary

Acicular: Needle-shaped

Acuminate: Tapering at the end; long-pointed

Acute: Sharp pointed

AGM: Acronym for Award of Garden Merit

Alternate: Not opposite (as in leaves or other parts)

Anther: The pollen-bearing part of the stamen

Apex: The tip or distal end

Axil: The angle formed by a leaf or lateral branch with the stem

Axillary: Produced or situated in the axil

Bacco-drupe: Berry-like drupe or multi-seeded drupe

Berry: A pulpy, normally several-seeded indehiscent fruit

Bisexual: Both male and female organs in the same flower

Blade: The expanded part of a leaf

Bole: The trunk of a tree

Calcareous: Containing limestone or carbonate of lime, chalky or limy

Calcifuge: Avoiding calcareous soils

Callus: Undifferentiated tissue growing over the base of a cutting or a wound

Calyx: The outer part of the flower, the sepals

Clone: a group of plants derived from a single individual, propagated by vegetative means and genetically identical

Columnar: Cylindrical or tapering, like a column

Conical: Cone-shaped

Convex: Curved outwards on the upper surface

Coriaceous: Leathery textured

Corolla: The inner part of a flower; the petals

Crenate: Toothed with shallow, rounded teeth

Cultivar: A named horticultural or cultivated variety which when reproduced sexually or vegetatively retains its distinguishing characteristics. Cultivar names have capital initials and are enclosed in single quotation marks.

Cyme: A convex or flat-topped flower cluster with the central flowers opening first.

Cymose: Arranged in cymes, or cyme-like

Deciduous: Seasonally falling, not persistent

Dentate: Toothed, with teeth directed outward

Dimorphic: Having two foliage types, juvenile and adult

Dioecious: Male and female plants on different plants

Dorsal: The back or outer surface of a plant part

Downy: Covered in short hairs

Drupe: A fleshy indehiscent fruit with seed enclosed within a stony endocarp (a pyrene)

Elliptic: Widest at the middle, narrowing equally toward both ends

Elongate: Lengthened

Endemic: Native or confined to a particular area or region

Entire: Undivided, without teeth (as in a margin)

Evergreen: Remaining green for a full year or longer due to the persistence of leaves

Fascicle: A dense cluster of flowers

Fastigiate: With branches erect and close together, tapering to a point

Fertile: Stamens producing good pollen or fruit containing viable seeds

Floriferous: Bearing profuse flowers

Glabrous: Hairless

Glaucous: Bluish white or grey bloom which can be rubbed off

Group: A Group has no botanical status but may include plants of a species or hybrid which share similar features, or plants of the same parentage or origin. Examples include *Ilex* ×*altaclerensis* Camelliifolia Group and *Ilex* Blue Holly Group. When used for this purpose it always has a capital G.

Hastate: Triangular in shape like an arrowhead

Hermaphrodite: Bisexual, bearing both male and female organs in the same flower

Hybrid: Resulting from a cross between two plants of different species

Impressed: Sunken (as in the veins of a leaf)

Incised: Sharply and deeply or irregularly cut

Indehiscent: Fruits which do not burst open

Indumentum: Hairy or pubescent covering

Inflorescence: The flowering part of the plant

Internode: The portion of a stem between two nodes

Interspecific: Between species (as in hybrid)

Lanceolate: Lance-shaped, widening above the base and tapering to the apex

Lateral: On or at the side

Linear: Long and narrow with nearly parallel margins

Lobe: Any protruding part of an organ (leaf, corolla or calyx)

Misapplied: With reference to a name used in the wrong way or for the wrong purpose, e.g., *Ilex chinensis* misapplied

Monotypic: A genus of a single species

Mucronate: Terminated abruptly by a spiny tip

Nectary: A nectar-secreting gland

Node: The place on the stem where the leaves are attached, the 'join'

Nut: A nonsplitting, one-seeded hard and bony fruit

Oblanceolate: Inversely lanceolate, broadest toward the upper third of the apex

Oblique: Unequal sided

Oblong: Longer than broad, with nearly parallel sides

Obovate: Inversely ovate

Obtuse: Blunt (as in apex of a leaf)

Orbicular: Almost circular in outline

Oval: Broadest at the middle and rounded at both ends

Ovate: Egg-shaped, with the broadest end below the middle

Ovary: The basal part of the pistil, containing the ovules

Ovate: Broadest below the middle

Ovule: The body which after fertilization becomes the seed

Parthenocarpic: Developing ripe fruit without fertilization

Pedicel: The stalk of an individual flower on an inflorescence

Peduncle: The lower stalk of a flower cluster or of an individual flower

Pendent: Hanging or weeping

Pendulous: Hanging or weeping

Perianth: The calyx and corolla together

Persistent: Remaining attached

Petal: One of the separate segments of a corolla

Petiole: The leaf-stalk

Pistil: The female organ of a flower, comprising the ovary, style and stigma

Pollen: Spores or grains contained in the anther; the male element

Polymorphic: Variable in form

Procumbent: Lying or creeping

Prostrate: Lying flat on the ground; low, spreading habit

Puberulent: Minutely pubescent

Pubescent: Covered with short, soft hairs

Pyramidal: Pyramid-shaped (broad at the base and tapering to a point)

Pyrene: The nutlet in a drupe, comprising a seed within an endocarp

Recurved: Curved downward or backward

Reflexed: Abruptly turned downward

Reticulate: Like a network (as in leaf veins)

RHS: Abbreviation for The Royal Horticultural Society

Rib: A prominent vein on a leaf

Rugose: Wrinkled or rough

Sagittate: Shaped like an arrow-head

Scion: The shoot portion of a grafted plant

Selling Name: Cultivar names that are technically superfluous but which are used to market a plant. In some cases a plant may be better known under its selling name, or trade designation, which may or may not be a trademark. The selling name is given in small capital letters, and the cultivar name for the plant is usually given after the selling name, for example *Ilex* CARDINAL = 'Conal' (Red Holly Group).

Semi-evergreen: Normally evergreen but losing some or all of its leaves in cold weather

Sepal: One of the parts of a calyx

Serrate: Saw-toothed (teeth pointing forward)

Serrulate: Minutely serrate

Sessile: Not stalked

Shrub: A woody plant that branches from the base with no obvious trunk

Sinuate: Strongly waved (as in leaf margins)

Spine: A sharp, pointed end of a branch or leaf

Spinose: Having spines

Spinulose: Having small spines

Spur: A short, small branch

Stamen: The male element of the flower comprised of the filament and anther

Stigma: The summit of the pistil which receives the pollen

Stock: The root or lower portion of a grafted plant

Stolon: A shoot at or below the surface of the ground which produces a new plant

Style: The middle part of the pistil between the ovary and the stigma

Suckering: Producing underground shoots; also shoots arising from the stock of a grafted plant

Synonym: Old or invalid names of plants

Taxon (plural taxa): Applied to a taxonomic group at any rank such as species, genus or family

Tree: A woody plant that produces normally a single trunk and an elevated head of branches

Type: Botanically the original (type) specimen of a plant

Undulate: With wavy margins

Unisexual: Of one sex

Venation: The arrangement of veins

Bibliography

Acton, P. 2000. Winterberries. *Horticulture* 58 (Nov/Dec).

Anon. 2003. *Ilex opaca* 'Golden Knight'. *Holly Society Journal* 21(3):19.

Alford, D. V. 1995. *A Colour Atlas of Pests of Ornamental Trees, Shrubs and Flowers*. 448pp. Manson, London.

Andrews, S. 1983–84. Report on the *Ilex perado* complex of the North Atlantic islands, parts 1 and 2. *International Dendrological Society Yearbook* 1982:69–72, 1983:111–118.

———. 1983a. *Ilex* ×*altaclerensis* not *altaclarensis* (Aquifoliaceae) *Taxon* 32(4):625–626.

———. 1983b. Notes on some *Ilex* ×*altaclerensis* clones. *The Plantsman* 5(2):65–81.

———. 1984a. More notes on clones of *Ilex* ×*altaclerensis*. *The Plantsman* 6(3):157–166.

———. 1984b. A reappraisal of *Ilex aquifolium* and *I. perado* (Aquifoliaceae). *Kew Bulletin* 39(1):141–155.

———. 1985. Holly berries of a varied hue. *The Garden* 110(2):518–522.

———. 1986. The *Ilex fargesii* complex. *The Kew Magazine* 3(3):127–135.

———. 1999. The renaming of the *Ilex verticillata* males to 'Jim Dandy' and 'Southern Gentleman'. *The New Plantsman* 6(4):206–207.

Bauers, B. M. Sr. 1993. *A Guide to Identification of Cultivated Ilex*. 334pp. Holly Society of America.

Bean, W. J. (1970–80). *Trees and Shrubs Hardy in the British Isles*. 8th ed. by D. L. Clarke. 4 vols. London, John Murray.

———. 1988. *Trees and Shrubs Hardy in the British Isles*. Supplement. London, John Murray.

Blomfield, R. 1892. *The Formal Garden in England*.

Boardman, P. D. S. 1998. Excerpts from the second volume of *The Gardener's Dictionary* 1739. *Holly Society Journal* 16(4):2–8.

Boulger, G. S. 1906–07. *Familiar Trees*. Cassell and Co., London.

Brickell, C., ed. 1996a. *The American Horticultural Society Pruning and Training*. 336pp. Dorling Kindersley, New York.

———, ed. 1996b. *The Royal Horticultural Society A–Z Encyclopedia of Garden Plants*. 2 vols. Dorling Kindersley, London.

Brown, G. E. 1972. *The Pruning of Trees, Shrubs and Conifers*. 2nd ed., revised and enlarged by T. Kirkham, 2004. 338pp. Timber Press, Portland, Ore.

Buchmann, H-G. 1995. Holly in Germany: then and now. *Holly Society Journal* 13(4):2–14.

Bunting, A. Evergreen hollies. *Fine Gardening* 79:56–59.

Cook, A. D., ed. 1993. *Hollies: A Gardener's Guide*. Brooklyn Botanic Garden Inc. in cooperation with the Holly Society of America, Plants and Gardens vol. 49. 96pp.

Creech, J. 2003. Japanese hollies. *The New Plantsman* 2(4):202–206.

Culpeper, N. 1653. *Herbal and English Physician*. London.

Dallimore, W. 1908. *Holly, Yew and Box*. 284pp. London, John Lane Co.

Dengler, H. W., ed. 1957. Handbook of hollies. *The National Horticulture Magazine* 36:1–139.

Dickinson, C. L. *Sources for Unusual Hollies*. Holly Society of America.

Dirr, M. A. 1988. To know them is to love them: fruited, deciduous hollies can extend color, charm and profits. *American Nurseryman* 168(3). Reprinted 1999, *Holly Society Journal* 17(3):2–17.

———. 1990. *Manual of Woody Landscape Plants: Their Identification, Ornamental Characteristics, Culture, Propagation and Uses*. 4th ed. 1007pp. Stipes Publishing Co., Illinois.

———. 1997. *Dirr's Hardy Trees and Shrubs*. Timber Press, Portland, Ore.

———. 2002. *Dirr's Trees and Shrubs for Warm Climates*. Timber Press, Portland, Ore.

Dudley, T. R. 1980. A glimpse of the Colchic (*Ilex colchica*), Caspian (*I. spinigera*) and English (*I. aquifolium*) hollies. *Holly Letter* 67:2–5.

———. 1986a. *Hollies in the Landscape*. 11pp. Holly Society of America.

———. 1986b. The story of hollies, part 1: diversity and history. *Holly Society Journal* 4(3):1–5.

Dudley, T. R., and G. K. Eisenbeiss. 1973. *International Checklist of Cultivated Ilex, part 1, Ilex opaca*, US National Arboretum Contribution no. 3. 85pp. Washington, D.C., Government Printing Office.

———. 1977. *The Coin-Leaved Japanese Hollies*. Holly Society of America. *Bulletin* 16, 19pp.

———. 1992. *International Checklist of Cultivated Ilex, part 2, Ilex crenata.* US National Arboretum Contribution no. 6. 91pp. Washington, D.C., Government Printing Office.

Ecker, M., and R. A. Larson. 1996. Hollies for the Midwest. *Holly Society Journal* 14(3):4–15.

Eisenbeiss, G. K. 1996. *Holly Society Journal* 14(2):3–4.

Eisenbeiss, G. K., and T. R. Dudley. 1995. *Ilex Cultivar Registration List, 1958–1993. Holly Society Journal* 13(3):i–iv, 1–37.

Elmore, H. L. 1983. The Bruner hollies. *Holly Society Journal* 1(1):1–3.

———. 2002. The Bruner hollies revisited: 1982–2002. *Holly Society Journal* 20(4):11–12.

Elwes, H. J., and A. Henry. 1906–13. *Trees of Great Britain and Ireland.* 7 vols. Edinburgh.

Evelyn, J. 1664. *Sylva, or a Discourse on Forest Trees.* London.

Flint, H. L. 1997. *Landscape Plants for Eastern North America.* 2nd ed. 842pp. John Wiley, New York.

Fralish, J., and S. Franklin. 2002. *Taxonomy and Ecology of Woody Plants in North American Forests.* 612pp. John Wiley, New York.

Galle, F. C. 1997. *Hollies: The Genus Ilex.* 573 pp. Timber Press, Portland, Ore.

Gerard, J. 1597. *The Herball or Generall Historie of Plantes.* 1392pp. John Norton, London.

Gibbs, V. 1908. Rare shrubs in the open air. *Journal of the Royal Horticultural Society* (33):356.

Glenn, J. 2000. A plant for all seasons. *The Garden* 125(12):890–895.

Grelen, H. G. American holly—*Ilex opaca.* Trees of Western North Carolina. USDA Forest Service, St. Paul Field Office, wildwnc.org.

Hadfield, M. 1969. *A History of British Gardening.* 509pp. John Murray.

———. 1971. *Topiary and Ornamental Hedges: Their History and Cultivation.* 100pp. A & C Black, London.

Hanslik, P. 1999. Examining the elusive American holly. *Green Times* 4(1), Secrest Arboretum, Ohio.

Harada, J. 1928. *The Gardens of Japan.* G. Holme, ed. 180pp. The Studio Ltd., London.

Hartmann, H. T., D. E. Kester, F. T. Davies and R. L. Geneve. 1997. *Plant Propagation: Principles and Practices.* 6th ed. 770pp. Prentice-Hall.

Heywood, V. H., consultant ed. 1978. *Flowering Plants of the World*. 335pp. Oxford University Press, Oxford.

Hillier, J., and A. Coombes, eds. 2002. *The Hillier Manual of Trees and Shrubs*. 7th ed. 512pp. David & Charles, Newton Abbot.

Hirose, Y., and Y. Masato. 1998. *Variegated Plants in Color*. 296pp. Varie Nine Ltd., Japan.

Hooker, J. D. 1866. *Ilex latifolia. Curtis's Bot. Mag.* 92, tab. 5597.

Hooker, W. J. 1858. *Ilex cornuta. Curtis's Bot. Mag.* 84, tab. 5059.

Houtman, R. 2004. *Variegated Trees and Shrubs: The Illustrated Encyclopedia*. 338pp. Timber Press, Portland, Ore.

Howkins, C. 2001. *Holly: A Tree for All Seasons*. 80pp. Published by author, Addlestone, Surrey.

Hu, S.-Y. 1949–50. The genus *Ilex* in China. *Journal of the Arnold Arboretum* 30 (1949):233–387; 31 (1950):39–80, 214–240, 241–263.

Hume, H. H. 1953. *Hollies*. 242pp. Macmillan, New York.

Huxley, A., ed. 1992. *The New RHS Dictionary of Gardening*. 4 vols. Macmillan, London.

Johnson, H. 1973. *The International Book of Trees*. 288pp. Mitchell Beazley, London.

Johnson, O. 2004. *Collins Tree Guide*. 464pp. HarperCollins, London.

Joseph, P. 1995. *Ilex vomitoria*, yaupon hollies. *Holly Society Journal* 13(1): 19-22.

Kelly, J., ed. 2004. *The Gardener's Guide to Trees and Shrubs*. 640pp. David & Charles, Newton Abbot.

Krüssmann, G. 1983–86. *Manual of Cultivated Broad-leaved Trees and Shrubs*. 3 vols. Timber Press, Portland, Ore.

Lancaster, R. 1993. *Travels in China: A Plantsman's Paradise*. 516pp. Antique Collector's Club, Woodbridge, Suffolk.

———. 2001. Roy Lancaster's native plants—holly. *BBC Gardeners' World Magazine* (December):100–101.

Larson, R. A. 2000. Holly: rediscovering a jewel. *Holly Society Journal* 18(4):3–22.

Lindley, J., and J. Paxton. 1850–53. *Paxton's Flower Garden* 3:13, 55, 73.

Loddiges, J. 1821. *Ilex perado. The Botanical Cabinet* 4, t. 549.

Lord, T., ed. 2005. *RHS Plant Finder* 2005–2006. Dorling Kindersley, London.

Loudon, J. C. 1838. *Arboretum et Fruticetum Britannicum* (*The Trees and Shrubs of Britain*). 125pp. Longmans, London.

Mabberley, D. J. 1997. *The Plant Book*. 2nd ed. 858pp. Cambridge University Press.

Mabey, R. 1996. *Flora Britannica*. Sinclair Stevenson.

McCartney, R. 1991. Hollies native to the southeastern United States. *Holly Society Journal* 9(1):6–10.

Meyer, F. G., P. M. Mazzeo and D. H. Voss. 1994. A *Catalog of Cultivated Woody Plants of the Southeastern United States*. USDA Agricultural Research Service, United States National Arboretum Contribution no. 7.

Miller, P. 1739. *The Gardener's Dictionary*. 2 vols. London.

Moore, T. 1874–76. The common holly and its varieties. *The Gardeners' Chronicle*, published in 14 parts.

Morell, V. 1991. The smaller hollies. *Holly Society Journal* 9(2):2–6.

———. 1993. Hollies: versatile beauty for the landscape. 8pp. *Holly Society of America Bulletin* 26.

Ohwi, J. 1965. *Flora of Japan*. 1067pp. Smithsonian Institution, Washington, D.C.

Paul, W. 1863. Notes on the varieties of English Holly. *Journal of the Royal Horticultural Society* 3:110–117.

Poor, J. M., and N. P. Brewster, eds. 1996. *Plants That Merit Attention: Shrubs*. Garden Clubs of America/Timber Press, Portland, Ore.

Powell, M., V. Savolainen, P. Cuenoud, J.-F. Manen and S. Andrews. 2000. The mountain holly (*Nemopanthus mucronatus*: Aquifoliaceae) revisited with molecular data. *Kew Bulletin* 55(2):341–347.

Randall, J. M., and J. Marinelli. 1996. *Invasive Plants: Weeds of the Global Garden*. Brooklyn Botanic Garden, Brooklyn.

Rehder, A. 1974. *Manual of Cultivated Trees and Shrubs Hardy in North America*. 2nd ed, revised and enlarged. 996pp. Macmillan, New York.

Robinson, W. 1900. *The English Flower Garden*. 8th ed. 892pp. John Murray, London.

Royal Horticultural Society, The. 2004. *Holly Blight*. Plant Pathology Advisory Leaflet. 2pp. Wisley, Woking, Surrey.

Ruter, J. 2000. Some hollies like it hot! *Holly Society Journal* 18(1):2–9.

Salvesen, P. H. 1996. *Ilex aquifolium* in Norway. *Holly Society Journal* 14(4):2–8.

Sargent, C. S. 1894. *Forest Flora of Japan*. Houghton, Mifflin and Co., New York.

Sealy, J. R. 1946. *Ilex fargesii*. *Curtis's Bot. Mag.* 164, tab. 9670.

Simpson, R. C. 1991. Deciduous hollies: berried treasures waiting to be discovered. *Holly Society Journal* 9(2):7–14.

Smith, G., and H. Clay. 1986. Hollies for Georgia homeowners. *Horticulture* 1, Bulletin 664. 20pp. Cooperative Extension Service, University of Georgia, Athens.

Strouts, T. S., and T. G. Winter. 2000. *Diagnosis of Ill-health in Trees*. 2nd ed. 332pp. HMSO, Norwich, England.

Taylor, B. 1997. Using hollies effectively in the landscape. *Holly Society Journal* 15(3):2–7.

Thomas, G. S. 1984. *The Art of Planting*. 323pp. J. M. Dent & Sons Ltd., London.

———. 1992. *Ornamental Shrubs, Climbers and Bamboos*. 585pp. John Murray, London.

———. 1994. *Colour in the Winter Garden*. 210pp. Orion, London.

Tilt, K., D. Williams, W. Witte and M. K. Gaylor. 1995. *Hollies for the Landscape in the Southeast*. Circular ANR-837. 39pp. Alabama Cooperative Extension Service, Auburn University.

Verey, R. 1988. *The Garden in Winter*. 168pp. Frances Lincoln, London.

Ward, B. J. 2004. *The Plant Hunter's Garden: The New Explorers and Their Discoveries*. 340pp. Timber Press, Portland, Ore.

Watson, P. W. 1825. *Dendrologia Britannica*. 2 vols. Printed for the author, John and Arthur Church, Cornhill, London.

Williams, D. E. 1989. Prevention and control of wildlife damage in ornamental planting. *Holly Society Journal* 7(1):6.

Wilson, E. H. 1913. *A Naturalist in Western China*. 2 vols. Methuen, London. Reprint by Theophrastus Publishers, Rhode Island, 1977.

Wyman, D. 1960. *Ilex crenata*. *Arnoldia* 20:41–46.

Yinger, B. 1991. *Ilex* in Japan and Korea. *Holly Society Journal* 9(1):4–5.

Index

Illustrations are given in **bold type**.